THE THERAPIST IN MOURNING

Georgia O'Keefe, *The Faraway Nearby.* © The Metropolitan Museum of Art/
Artists Rights Society (ARS), New York.

ANNE J. ADELMAN
AND **KERRY L. MALAWISTA**

THE **THERAPIST**

IN MOURNING

From the Faraway Nearby

COLUMBIA UNIVERSITY PRESS / NEW YORK

Columbia University Press
Publishers Since 1893
New York   Chichester, West Sussex
cup.columbia.edu
Copyright © 2013 Columbia University Press

Library of Congress Cataloging-in-Publication Data
The therapist in mourning : from the faraway nearby/ [edited by] Anne J. Adelman and
Kerry L. Malawista.
    pages ; cm
    Includes bibliographical references and index.
    ISBN 978-0-231-15698-1 (cloth; alk. paper) — ISBN 978-0-231-15699-8 (pbk. : alk.
paper) — ISBN 978-0-231-53460-4 (e-book)
    1. Psychoanalysts—psychology.   2. Psychotherapist and patient.   3. Bereavement—
Psychological aspects.   4. Grief—Psychological aspects.   I. Adelman, Anne J.   II. Ma-
lawista, Kerry L.

    RC480.5.T5192 2012
    616.89'17—dc23

                                                        2012034121

Columbia University Press books are printed on permanent and durable
acid-free paper.
This book is printed on paper with recycled content.
Printed in the United States of America

Cover design: Julia Kushnirsky
Cover illustration: Gracia Lam
Book design: Lisa Hamm

For my mother, Mary

In memory of my father, Stanley

—AJA

For my parents, Robert and Barbara, and my daughter Anna

In memory of my mother, Helen, and Sarah

—KLM

CONTENTS

PART III. **AT THE CROSSROADS OF THE THERAPIST'S PERSONAL AND PROFESSIONAL WORLDS**

PART IV. **WHEN DISASTER STRIKES A COMMUNITY**

ACKNOWLEDGMENTS

WE ARE most grateful to all those who contributed their time and effort, with open minds and honest discourse, to this volume. It is their dedication to psychoanalysis and their creativity, skill, and persistence that make this book possible.

We would like to thank our editors at Columbia University Press, in particular Lauren Dockett, who deftly guided and supported this project from its inception, and Jennifer Perillo, who saw it to its fruition. We are truly grateful to all of the staff at Columbia, who lent this project their full enthusiasm and commitment.

This project would not have been realized without the support and encouragement of the faculty and participants of the New Directions Program and Winter Retreat. Their generosity and spirit have inspired us over the years.

We are deeply appreciative to Robert Winer for his wise and amazing editorial skills. He is a writer of uncommon erudition who can read a piece and find exactly what works and what doesn't. Linda Kanefield lent her unflagging support, always ready to read our drafts and offer valuable insights and edits. Julie Eill and Elizabeth Thomas were generous with their feedback and input. Sara Taber offered her unfaltering encouragement to keep writing. Paula Atkeson has been a consistent source of emotional sustenance.

We could not have completed this project without our husbands and children. They fed us, encouraged us, proofread drafts, and supported this endeavor.

Finally, we would each like to thank our coeditor. It is truly a miracle in life to find a writing partner and kindred spirit with whom anything is possible—who can finish the other's sentences, find the words when we are lost, laugh throughout the process, and, when needed, help find the perfect dress.

CONTRIBUTORS

ANNE J. ADELMAN, PH.D., is a clinical psychologist and psychoanalyst with the Contemporary Freudian Society. She is coauthor of *Wearing My Tutu to Analysis and Other Stories: Learning Psychotherapy from Life*. She is a faculty member of the New Directions Writing Program and maintains a private practice in Chevy Chase, Maryland.

CATHERINE L. ANDERSON, PH.D., is a psychoanalyst in private practice in Bethesda, Maryland, and a member of the Contemporary Freudian Society. She has worked in community mental health with a specialty in forensics and PTSD. She has taught and supervised interns and students and has written in the areas of sexual abuse and attachment theory. She is coauthor of *Wearing My Tutu to Analysis and Other Stories: Learning Psychotherapy from Life* and co-chair of the New Directions Writing Program.

JODY BOLZ is the author of, most recently, *A Lesson in Narrative Time*. Her poems have appeared widely in anthologies and literary journals (including *The American Scholar, Indiana Review, North American Review, Ploughshares*, and *Poetry East*). She taught for more than twenty years at George Washington University. Her honors include a Rona Jaffe Foundation writer's award. She is the editor of *Poet Lore*.

SANDRA BUECHLER, PH.D., is a training and supervising analyst at the William Alanson White Institute and a supervisor at the Institute for Contemporary

Psychotherapy. She is the author of two books: *Clinical Values: Emotions that Guide Psychoanalytic Treatment* and *Making a Difference in Patients' Lives: Emotional Experience in the Therapeutic Setting.*

RUSSELL CARR, M.D., is an active-duty U.S. Navy psychiatrist and currently serves as the chief of the Adult Behavioral Health Clinic at the Walter Reed National Military Medical Center at Bethesda. He is also a candidate in psychoanalysis at the Institute of Contemporary Psychotherapy and Psychoanalysis in Washington, D.C.

ROBERT GALATZER-LEVY, M.D., is a supervising, training, and child and adolescent supervising analyst who serves on the faculties of the Chicago Institute for Psychoanalysis and the University of Chicago. In addition to clinical psychoanalysis, he has a particular interest in life-course development and nonlinear dynamics.

SYBIL HOULDING, M.S.W., is a psychoanalyst in private practice in New Haven, Connecticut. She is a member of the faculty of the Western New England Institute for Psychoanalysis and is an assistant clinical professor in the department of psychiatry at the Yale School of Medicine.

LINDA KANEFIELD, PH.D., is a psychologist in Chevy Chase, Maryland, and a member of the Institute for Contemporary Psychotherapy and Psychoanalysis. She has published on reconciling feminism and psychoanalysis, the development of femininity, and the reparative motive in surrogate mothers. She teaches and supervises and consults in assisted reproduction, fertility, and loss.

KERRY L. MALAWISTA, PH.D., is a training/supervising analyst with the Contemporary Freudian Society. She is coauthor of *Wearing My Tutu to Analysis and Other Stories: Learning Psychotherapy from Life.* Her essays have appeared in the *Washington Post, Voices, Washingtonian Magazine*, and *Zone 3*, alongside many professional articles. She is co-chair of the New Directions Writing Program and is in private practice in Potomac, Maryland, and McLean, Virginia.

JENIFER NIELDS, M.D., is an assistant clinical professor of psychiatry at Yale University School of Medicine and a supervisor in the Yale long-term psychotherapy program. She has published articles on psychotherapy, psychoanalysis, and religion, as well as on the neuropsychiatric aspects of Lyme disease. She is in private practice in Fairfield, Connecticut.

BILLIE A. PIVNICK is a clinical psychologist in private practice in New York City and is on the faculties of the William Alanson White Institute's child and adolescent psychotherapy training program and the Institute for Contemporary Psychotherapy. She serves as a consulting psychologist to Thinc Design, which is partnered with the National September 11 Memorial and Museum.

LINDA PASTAN is a well-known American poet. She has received the Dylan Thomas award, a Pushcart Prize, the Bess Hokin Prize for Poetry, the Alice Fay di Castagnola Award, and the Ruth Lily Poetry Prize. Pastan served as poet laureate of Maryland from 1991 to 1995. She is the author of more than sixteen books of poetry and essays; two were finalists for the National Book Award.

ARLENE KRAMER RICHARDS, ED.D., is a training and supervising analyst at the Contemporary Freudian Society, a fellow of IPTAR, and an IPA training and supervising analyst. She is in private practice in New York City. She has written on female sexuality, perversions, and psychoanalytic technique.

SYLVIA J. SCHNELLER, M.D., is a retired training analyst at the New Orleans/ Birmingham Center for Psychoanalysis. She is the author of nonfiction narratives in *Voices Rising: Stories from the Katrina Narrative Project* and is presently working on her first novel, *Creoles.*

BARBARA STIMMEL, PH.D., is an assistant clinical professor at the department of psychiatry, Mt. Sinai School of Medicine; the director of seminar series at the Richardson Institute of History of Psychiatry, Weill Cornell Medical Center; and a member of the Contemporary Freudian Society. She is a member of the American Psychoanalytic Association and the International Psychoanalytic Association.

JUDITH VIORST, a graduate of the Washington Psychoanalytic Institute, is the author of many books for children and adults, including *Necessary Losses* and *Alexander and the Terrible, Horrible, No Good, Very Bad Day.*

RICHARD M. WAUGAMAN, M.D., is a training and supervising analyst emeritus at the Washington Psychoanalytic Institute; a clinical professor of psychiatry at Georgetown University; and the author of more than one hundred publications, thirty-five of which are on Shakespeare. His website is www .oxfreudian.com.

ROBERT WINER, M.D., is the author of *Close Encounters: A Relational View of the Therapeutic Process*; the cofounder of New Directions, the psychoanalytic writing program of the Washington Center for Psychoanalysis; and a teaching analyst at the Washington Psychoanalytic Institute.

ANOTHER KIND OF SORROW

When they called to tell me you were dead,
I dropped to my knees, pressed my head to the floor.

How many years had I dreaded that moment?
How many times had I panicked after calling you for hours—

then raced across town to find you at the door,
key in hand, with groceries or a laundry bag?

When they called to say you'd died, I knew
without thinking: This is it. And it was.

Then three years passed and I started to recover,
which feels to me like another kind of sorrow.

The day you died, I knew what I was losing.
But now—well—now, it's lost.

—Jody Bolz

PREFACE

WHEN A patient of mine died suddenly a few years ago, I was stunned. Her death was unexpected and shocking. We had worked together for several years in a lively and productive treatment that had steadily deepened, and the troubles that plagued her had gradually begun to resolve. Right before she died, she had begun to feel hopeful for her future. I was not ready for the abrupt end of her life and of our relationship. I grieved for her. I attended the funeral; I exchanged condolences with members of her family and made myself available to them for support and help as they moved through their grief. But I could not reconcile my own feelings of loss and sadness about her death, and it seemed I had few avenues in which to express them. I could not grieve among those who mourned her openly. I worried, perhaps overly so, about confiding in colleagues or friends how deeply affected I was. I began to feel eerily unsettled, as if haunted by a phantom whose contours I couldn't fully make out. One day, a vivid image of her as a ghostly presence came into my mind, and I began to write, grasping to put words to the complex set of emotions I was experiencing.

In searching the literature, I discovered that there is little written about the subject of the bereaved therapist. The idea of this book emerged as I gradually realized that a therapist's mourning process follows a singular and solitary trajectory. I knew firsthand that, for therapists, experiencing loss is complicated, whether losing a patient out of the blue or grieving over a personal loss, so what could account for the relative absence of literature about this topic? This question led me to consider both the special nature of the therapist's bereavement and the particular obstacles that stand in the way of exploring it. This book is the result of my efforts, along with those of my coeditor Kerry Malawista, to respond to the need in our field for a forum within which these questions can be addressed.

We invited a number of our colleagues to consider whether they might want to contribute to our project. We selected from a broad range of psychiatrists, psychologists, and social workers—psychoanalysts and psychotherapists alike—whose work we knew well and admired. Hoping to capture the breadth and complexity of the therapist's experience of loss, we sought out colleagues with diverse experiences in the mental health field, from those with expertise in trauma to those trained in child therapy to those who work with chronically mentally ill patients. Mostly, though, we asked each contributor to write from within his or her personal experience—we were seeking to open a dialogue that would be frank, open, and reflective.

We found the responses to be overwhelmingly positive and often very poignant. Many of our authors expressed the feeling that our invitation had tapped into a reservoir of unacknowledged and unarticulated aspects of their experience as therapists and analysts. All of them related an aspect of their professional life or practice that they had not written about before but that they found haunting and important. It was as though the invitation to contribute a chapter had opened up a wellspring of unexamined clinical insights and experiences. All of the chapters included in the book, with the exception of Judith Viorst's, were submitted as original work. Viorst's chapter, "The Analyst's Experience of Termination," was included because it provides a useful overview of the therapist's experience at the end of a treatment. All of our authors carefully considered the issue of confidentiality. Where it was appropriate, permission was secured to discuss confidential clinical material. In other cases, clinical material was disguised to preserve the confidentiality of all involved.

We begin our book with a section entitled "The Therapist's Experience of Loss: Traversing the Middle-Distance." In this section, we offer a window into how therapists' attachment to their patients and to their work, alongside their private lives and personal relationships, affects their experience of loss and grief. We introduce the notion of the "middle-distance" as a way to conceptualize the complex journey of grief and mourning.

The following sections of the book examine three major realms of the therapist's experience. The section entitled "When a Patient Dies" explores how a therapist experiences the unexpected death of a patient. Many of the authors in this section explored the feelings of isolation and loneliness that accompany the experience of losing a patient to unexpected death, whether illness, suicide, or unforeseeable catastrophic events. This section also examines the themes of helplessness and the resultant sense of therapeutic failure.

Similarly, therapists who experience a personal loss can feel isolated and alone. These experiences are examined in the next section of the book, "At the Crossroads of the Therapist's Personal and Professional Worlds." In general, therapists are trained to separate their personal experience from their work, to protect their patients from the intrusion of their own lives. Yet in the face of a profound personal loss, our attention necessarily turns inward, and our empathy for a patient's pain reverberates with our inner pain and loss. When the therapist lives and practices in a relatively small and close community, there is the additional layer of coping with the varied responses of others, who are suddenly left with what can be a frightening window into the therapist's personal life.

In our final section, "When Disaster Strikes a Community," we examine therapists' experiences of surviving situations that are globally catastrophic or massively traumatic alongside our patients. Throughout many of the narratives in this book, a common thread has to do with the therapist's sense of guilt at not having been able to control or prevent the inevitable impact of abrupt and cataclysmic events, such as Hurricane Katrina or 9/11. As therapists, we are susceptible to feeling that because we are there to help, there must have been something we overlooked—could we have done our job any better? Yet in the end, we see that each of us is ultimately enriched and made wiser by our struggles to prevail in the face of human tragedy. In some way, perhaps each of us is drawn to our profession through our personal knowledge of trauma and survival. We cannot hope to be helpful to our patients if we have not known, from the inside, the processes of loss and grief.

It is my hope that, in pulling together the work of our colleagues who have struggled with integrating their experiences of loss, a dialogue can begin that will help us understand and find the words to acknowledge the complex and often compelling facets of a therapist's experience of bereavement and grief.

—Anne J. Adelman

THE THERAPIST IN MOURNING

INTRODUCTION

IN THE following pages, we reflect on the experience of sadness and grief at various moments throughout the life of a therapist. We specifically address some of the factors that make it difficult for therapists to acknowledge and speak about the strong emotions they encounter over the course of their professional lives. We review some of the ways previous writers have conceptualized the process of grief, and, finally, we introduce the notion of the "middle-distance" as a framework for considering the experience of grief and mourning.

What are some of the challenges that make it difficult for therapists to address directly the feelings generated by the multitude of losses we experience? In particular, feelings of attachment, loss, and sorrow can be elusive and complex. As therapists, we often encounter a paradox: although we spend our working hours largely in the company of others—that is, with our patients—we are in many ways alone with our thoughts, our feelings, and our reflections about the work. We have, of course, ample opportunity to work alongside our colleagues, consult with them, and learn from them, but in the consulting room, we are on our own. We decide when to intervene, when to wait, what to say, and how to say it. At the same time, we try to pay attention to our own shifting emotional states. Such a sense of aloneness can be particularly palpable, even unbearable, at times of extreme grief or emotional pain. As Abraham Verghese (1998, 341) writes:

Despite all our grand societies, memberships, fellowships each with its annual dues and certificates and ceremonials, we are horribly alone. The doctor's world is one where our own feelings—particularly those of pain and hurt—are not easily expressed, even though patients are encouraged to express them to us. We trust our colleagues, we show propriety and reciprocity, we have the scientific knowledge, we learn empathy, but we rarely expose our own emotions.

So, too, therapists rarely expose their own feelings. In the consulting room, we, too, encounter what Verghese calls the "silent but terrible collusion to cover up pain."

WHEN THERAPISTS' PERSONAL AND PROFESSIONAL WORLDS COLLIDE

As therapists, we believe that finding meaning, creating a cohesive narrative, and giving voice to sorrow, pain, and confusion all promote healing and freedom from inhibitions. This gives rise to new, more adaptive constructs, more intimate and fulfilling relationships, and a more positive view of life. Yet there are times when each of us struggles to maintain some distance, to keep our therapeutic stance. These moments often come when we feel unhelpful or helpless in the face of a therapeutic process that has become chaotic, unworkable, confusing, or out of control. When we no longer feel we have anything therapeutic to offer our patients, we feel lost. Similarly, when we lose a patient, we cannot help but wonder what went wrong. Many who contributed to this volume found themselves wondering, "What more could I have done?" While rationally knowing that we did the best we could, we are nonetheless left with our own musings and unanswerable questions. The unexpected loss or death of a patient, or a personal loss, is an experience that can engender such feelings of helplessness. So, too, can personal changes that affect our ability to function, such as illness, aging, or physical incapacity.

When we work with our patients, they take up residence in our internal world in a particular way that is unique to our self-as-therapist. Our working selves develop around the internal meanings that our patients have for us. They become, in a sense, a significant facet of our own inner landscape. Every time a patient leaves and, perhaps especially, when the departure is sudden or one-sided—whether the patient no longer wants the therapy, decides to move, loses interest in the work, or no longer likes the therapist—it resonates in a particular way for the therapist, as a certain regret or hollowness, if only momentarily. We continue on, other patients come and go, but we've lost an integral part of who we are: not only the actual patient but what the patient has come to represent for us.

Over the course of our professional lives, we immerse ourselves in the work in ways that are not taught to us but that develop and deepen over time as we experience and learn more with and about our patients. Thus, as therapists, we carry every loss with us into the consulting room—whether the death of a patient, a personal loss we are mourning, or a catastrophic event that has global impact. We grieve for the person, the place, and the world we once knew that is now gone, but we also grieve for that aspect of our working self that had existed in relation to—or as a function of—that particular person or place.

How the therapist works through such experiences may be, in some ways, unique to our profession and somewhat apart from the common rites we observe in our culture. In the day-to-day world, familiar rituals such as funerals serve to mark the loss and to acknowledge the sorrow that accompanies death. We tell stories to remember and to pay tribute. A light-hearted joke, a warm memory, an outpouring of affection all soften the edges of our grief and make it more bearable. For example, at the funeral of the father of one of the coeditors, an old and dear friend spoke eloquently about her long friendship with him, which spanned two continents, a catastrophic war, two New York City boroughs, marriages, families, and countless meals of a Polish concoction known only as "*galareta*," a great favorite. Only later was it discovered that all those years, she'd been serving calf's foot jelly! When the friend stepped down from the podium, she tripped on the bottom step. Steadying herself against the casket, she smiled. Tears sparkled in her eyes as she said, "There you are, old friend, always catching me when I fall." The room of mourners erupted into warm laughter, remembering his strength and presence of mind. It was as if her remark had resurrected him then and there. The force of the collective memory had conjured him up.

In this way, when someone we love dies, such rituals—the funeral, the wake, family visits, mourners' prayers—serve as scaffolding for our grief. Amid the circle of grievers, these funeral rituals provide a way to contain and temper overwhelming feelings of loss and grief, to reconstitute a sense of stability and cohesion in the face of sudden changes, and to help the mourner feel held, supported, and able to put words to powerful and destabilizing emotions. Such rituals, perhaps like any rite of passage, sustain the bereaved. When we are free to mourn in public and our expressions of grief, rage, and despair are understood and accepted, the process of grieving and coming to terms with loss can begin its long, gradual unfurling.

For therapists grieving a loss, these familiar rites of grief and mourning are often not available. Because of the intricacies of our working selves and the complex nature of our ties to our patients, we process our grief on multiple levels. Our mourning is complicated by the idiosyncrasies of our work. For example, a therapist may attend the funeral of a patient, and he or she will likely experience a blend of emotions there. It is often as if we are invisible among the mourners, who are absorbed in their grief, the service, and the privacy of their loss. Most of them do not know us. We sit among them but cannot share our own recollections, remembrances of, and relationship to the deceased. We may wonder whether our patient's family is able to take solace and comfort from our presence. Do we belong there, among the mourners, seeking to soothe their pain and grief as well as, perhaps, our own?

As therapists, we are taught to be wary lest our internal states intrude into the analytic space and interfere with the integrity of our work. We try to maintain the precarious balance between being aware enough of our blind spots without allowing that awareness to sidetrack or mislead us. If we are lucky, then we can use what we know of our shifting internal states to shed light on the therapeutic work. If we are careless, then we can be led astray by the intensity of our own unconscious responses to a patient or a piece of the process.

In our writing and in what we share with our colleagues in a public forum, we are taught to seek discretion, to not reveal too much of ourselves either in the consulting room or outside of it. However, there is a cost to maintaining too singular a focus on avoiding self-exposure. A disapproving or condemnatory stance among colleagues could significantly interfere with our ability to share our ordinary professional losses and to learn from one another about how we bear therapeutic loss. As Sandra Buechler (2000, 84) writes, "We would be unlikely, if a colleague, or friend, or relative died or permanently left, to expect ourselves to 'move on' without grieving. But because, in some fundamental sense, our role encourages the denial of the personal impact of our relationships with patients, we also deny the personal meaning of their death or departure."

This sense of isolation and loneliness ultimately erodes our capacity to bear grief and to go on being helpful. As Sybil Houlding writes in her chapter, "This was the third time a patient had died in five years, and I wondered if I had the psychic energy to do the work of mourning. But what choice did I have? I felt tired and on some level resentful that this had happened again. . . . I also knew about the toll and trajectory of mourning a patient one has lost to death." Going through the process of mourning can deplete us psychically and physically. However, bearing it alone, with the vague sense that we are feeling more than we ought to be or feeling things we cannot openly discuss with our colleagues, runs the risk of overtaxing our ability to do our work well. The process of grieving and working through loss is complex.

GRIEF AND BEREAVEMENT: AN OVERVIEW

Over the last fifty years, the literature on grief and bereavement has proliferated. Practitioners have examined the nature of bereavement across a broad spectrum of human experience, from losing a loved one to working in end-of-life care. Indeed, the field of bereavement has developed into its own area of specialty, with hundreds of articles and books addressing every aspect of death and dying. While we cannot hope to cover the breadth and range of this topic, we offer here a brief overview of the historical context and current thinking about loss and grief.[1]

Mourning is the process of grieving the rupture of any meaningful attachment, whether the death of a significant person or the loss of a place or even one's sense of self.[2] Profound grief is a normal and complex experience that manifests as devastating sadness. Its course is determined by a number of factors, including the timing of the death, the significance of the person lost, the developmental timeframe, previous losses, the mourner's ego functioning, the cultural context in which the death occurred, the presence of a supportive community, the personal meaning of the loss, and other factors.

The early stage of deep loss is chaotic and overwhelming. It is a biologically raw state that can include shock, numbness, and disorganization. Rapidly shifting experiences of intense emotion may immerse the individual in unpredictable and intense bursts of inconsolability or feelings of deadness and dissociation. Weeping, longing, searching, irritability, anger, and anxiety may all be present. Often there is sleeplessness, fatigue, physical pain, and loss of appetite. Samuel Johnson describes it as a state of wandering, lost and disconnected from the world: "I have ever since seemed to myself broken off from mankind; a kind of solitary wanderer in the wild of life, without any direction, or fixed point of view: a gloomy gazer on the world to which I have little relation" (Boswell 1791, 264).

The irrevocability of death makes the pain of loss feel unbearable, as if one might not survive. Thus, for one's psychological protection, death is only gradually accepted and slowly integrated into consciousness. It is like a wound that requires time and attention to heal. Yet, as Freud wrote, at some point the reality of death sets in: "Death will no longer be denied; we are forced to believe it. People really die" (1915, 291). Such awareness is psychically overwhelming and thus only transiently available. As a result, it is necessary for the mourner to find a way to titrate the awareness of a significant loss; otherwise, the shock and grief would be overwhelming. This helps us understand how the bereaved can attend to all the public and social symbols of death, sign documents, plan a memorial service, and even make decisions on burial, all while still not truly knowing or fully acknowledging the death.

There can be times, nonetheless, when the focus on the loss is unremitting. Then grief remains unresolved and may never heal. Many researchers (Klass 1996, Archer 1999, Walter 2003) show that extensive periods of rumination during mourning can lead to a deep and entrenched depression, one characterized by a continual revisiting of the death. This type of depression prevents painful emotions from transforming or being repaired. Instead, the bereaved remains frozen at the threshold of loss, unable to work through the death. Joan Didion (2006) uses the term "the vortex effect" to describe how, for the bereaved, some event or interaction triggers a thought about the person who died, which leads to another thought and then another, until one is eventually awash in remembering.

Freud's classic paper "Mourning and Melancholia" (1917, 243) opens with the idea that "mourning is regularly the reaction to the loss of a loved person, or to the loss of some abstraction which has taken the place of one, such as one's country, liberty, an ideal and so on." Elsewhere, he writes: "Mourning has a quite specific psychical task to perform: its function is to detach the survivor's memories and hopes from the dead" (1913, 65). In this view, the bereaved can only recover from the loss when detachment from the internal object is complete. The goal of mourning is thus to separate oneself from the person one has lost. Freud's idea is that the work of mourning is internal rather than focused on the actual death and the loss of the relationship.

In "Mourning and Melancholia," Freud differentiates between normal grief and mourning, on the one hand, and the more pathological, depressive state of melancholia, on the other—the state of unremitting grief we refer to above. He describes how the grieving process is compromised when there is unresolved anger at the loved one, which compounds loss with disappointment, resulting in feelings of guilt, self-reproach, and a loss of self-esteem. In Freud's theory, we understand the mourner's self-deprecation as displaced anger and ambivalence. Instead of withdrawing the attachment from the loved one, the anger and ambivalence are redirected from the lost, "disappointing" loved one and turned against the self. According to Freud, when the mourner is able to acknowledge such guilt and self-reproach, he is better able to redirect his affection elsewhere.

However, Freud's theoretical stance—that loss requires detachment from the loved one and the substitution of a new love object—is in stark contrast to his personal experience of mourning the untimely death of his daughter Sophie. In a 1929 letter consoling a colleague whose son had died, he wrote:

> Although we know that after such a loss the acute stage of mourning will subside, we also know we shall remain inconsolable and will never find a substitute. No matter what may fill the gap, even if it be filled completely, it nevertheless remains something else. And actually this is how it should be. It is the only way of perpetuating the love which we do not want to relinquish.
>
> (Freud 2003, 386)

Thus, rather than experiencing the detachment he theorized, Freud eloquently described the enduring bond to his beloved child after her death.

Erich Lindemann's classic 1940s clinical study built on Freud's idea of mourning. He identified what he felt were the eight symptoms associated with acute grief: somatic distress, irritability, angry outbursts, not accepting the reality of the loss, preoccupation with the lost loved one, distancing from others, feelings of guilt, and difficulty focusing and making decisions. He posited that mourners would recover from acute grief after they allowed themselves to acknowledge their memories and pain.

Melanie Klein's (1940a, 1940b) object relations theory presented a different perspective on mourning. Klein placed less emphasis on detachment from the lost loved one, instead highlighting the need for reparation. In her view, death evokes painful and destructive fantasies toward the dead: the world previously experienced as good and safe is now infused with aggressive and rageful urges. Klein thought of mourning as a time of repair, during which unleashed destructive fantasies are recaptured and a positive internal relationship with the lost object is reestablished.

The British analyst John Bowlby (1969, 1973, 1980) made significant contributions to our understanding of grief and mourning in his study of attachment. In examining the effects of losing one's mother in childhood on later development, he emphasizes biology rather than psychology. According to Bowlby, attachment is a protective biological mechanism that has evolved to ensure survival. Bowlby (1980) describes grieving as a process in which the mourner moves through four phases: a numbing phase, a yearning or searching phase, a disorganization and despair phase, and finally a reorganization phase, where individuals redefine their identity and place in the world. Elizabeth Kubler-Ross (1969) built on Bowlby's idea of stages of grief with her well-known five psychological stages in the process of accepting one's own death: denial, anger, bargaining, depression, and acceptance.

Bowlby joins Klein in emphasizing that aggression is a necessary part of healthy mourning. Yet where Klein views aggression as a result of an inborn paranoia, contempt, and desire for triumph over the object, Bowlby views it as a natural reproach and protest for having been abandoned. He relates that a goal of mourning is to become consciously aware of the aggression toward the deceased rather than displacing it onto others. He emphasizes that if the individual doesn't receive or imagine retaliation for his or her aggression, it does not necessarily need to lead to guilt. Numerous authors have described this ongoing nature of the attachment to the lost loved one (Bowlby 1980, Rubin 1985, Baker 2001).

Edith Jacobson (1965) introduced the notion of reunion fantasies in her writing about adult patients who imagined a magical reunion with a parent who died when they were young. Didion, in her 2006 book *The Year of Magical Thinking*, describes how such fantasies continue throughout life. In spite of the finality of her husband's death, she maintains an ongoing conviction that he might still return to her. Paul Maciejewski and his colleagues (2007) conducted a study with 233 people who had experienced the death of a parent, child, or spouse. They found that the predominant feeling was not depression, disbelief, or even anger but instead yearning.

The early view of mourning as a process of gradual detachment does not hold true for most contemporary theorists and clinicians. John Baker (2001, 70) writes, "A continuing internal relationship can coexist with the development of new object relationships, which in turn enrich the inner world in their own unique ways, [leading to the] . . . coexistence of inner attachments in the mourning individual, even long after the death of the love object." Robert Gaines (1997) conceives of mourning not as "decathecting"—breaking the bonds between the survivor and loved one—but in terms of "creating continuity." He writes that the mourner's capacity to preserve a connection with the deceased loved one protects the mourner from melancholia, or pathological mourning. Indeed, Irvin Yalom and Morton Lieberman (1991) conclude that the experience of profound grief does not lessen the likelihood of finding meaning after the loss and of subsequently experiencing healing and personal growth. Similarly, Robert Neimeyer (2001) describes that moving through grief requires "meaning reconstruction," that is, maintaining one's ties to the loved one and at the same time rebuilding one's personal narrative and integrating the reality of the loss.

In chapter 1 of this volume, Kerry Malawista and Linda Kanefield highlight that the task of normal mourning is to preserve rather than to sever the internal relationship. In other words, the bereaved needs to hold on to the memory of the loved one and, at the same time, reinvest in new goals. Mourning is a complicated task that requires the living to assimilate the loss, maintain a positive internal connection to the lost person, and continue to find meaning in other areas of life. As Victor Frankl (1984) explains, our survival in situations of loss depends on our ability to find meaning in our grief. Through the process of mourning, we seek to become wiser, stronger, more empathic, and more compassionate.

Culture, family history, and personal beliefs powerfully influence the bereaved individual's unique experience of mourning. For example, in some cultures, grief is treated as a private event. Emotions are expected to be silently contained, and a high premium is placed on "moving on," "bucking up," and "putting it behind you." In other cultures, grief is highly emotional, demonstrative, and public. For many, religious beliefs and rituals are a central component to the process of grieving and can help create a soothing and comprehensible narrative.

In these rituals, we can see that mourning is a highly social process. Supportive others help ameliorate the feelings of stigma and isolation that stem from the unique circumstances of each death (Fowlkes 1991, Hagman 1996, Sussillo 2005). The communal dimension of mourning reveals itself in the mourner's ongoing need to remember and share memories with others. Meaning is always derived in part from the relationships within which the loss is nested. Reminiscing is an important way to keep loved ones alive. In this way, painful feelings of loss can dissipate gradually and make room for an array of deep and complex feelings in relation to the person who died.

Of course, while sadness is a universal response to loss, no two people grieve in the same way. Many seek therapy during periods of mourning to alleviate feelings of aloneness and pain. Therapists can help differentiate normative feelings of grief and loss from a more intractable depression.

However, while one moves on with life, the pain of loss never disappears. As we will see throughout this volume, time does not heal all wounds. For those who have suffered a devastating loss, the world is irrevocably changed. It is as though we continue to live on parallel tracks, one leading us forward toward new experiences and relationships while the other carries the memories and connections to those we have lost. This is the place we refer to here as the middle-distance.

TRAVERSING THE MIDDLE-DISTANCE

In this book, we consider the process of working through grief to be transitional and developmental, wherein we gradually weave together the threads of loss into a narrative of separation, reconstitution, and a renewed sense of self, buoyed by new hope for the future. In the aftermath of a loss, the mourner finds herself in a transitional space, a state Kerry Malawista and Linda Kanefield refer to as the "faraway nearby." They describe it as a kind of middle-distance that provides a mental holding place in which to accomplish the work of mourning.

In this middle-distance, the mourner is caught between two worlds: in one, the lost person is still accessible, a specter just out of reach whose presence is palpable and real, and in the other, the world is irrevocably changed and rendered nearly unrecognizably void, the absence of the other the omnipresent backdrop for all experiences. In this faraway nearby place, the mourner can at times feel very close to the lost one. Like a phantom limb, the loss is experienced more as an acute sense of an invisible presence. We think we've glimpsed that person just around the corner; we make a cup of tea for him; we can't wait to get home to tell him how unhappy we've been since he died. Simultaneously, we are subjected to grief that can take us unawares. Such grief washes over us in waves and leaves us gasping in its wake.

For the clinician, this process has bearing on our sense of self-as-therapist. Loss and grief unfold on multiple planes—the middle-distance to be traversed is, in a sense, inhabited by the memory traces of those people, places, and parts of ourselves—of our "therapist-selves"—now lost to us. Finding the words to capture this complex experience and beginning to rework the narratives of our selves are essential to mourning.

In some ways, we inhabit the faraway nearby as a timeless place that allows for the gradual reconstitution of a world in which the loss is simultaneously absent and omnipresent. In this psychic space, the mourner can begin to integrate the reality and finality of the loss in small doses that ebb and flow in and out of our awareness. We go about our day momentarily shifting our awareness from the process of mourning to the ordinary work of day-by-day living and back again. This rhythm is important because it helps titrate the recognition of the loss and thus protects from overwhelming feelings of despair. This is the reason that we often prefer to return to work as soon as possible after a loss—to find ourselves again in the familiar patterns of who we are at work. Sometimes, however, we struggle to reorient ourselves in a world that is familiar yet permanently changed.

If one remains too deeply in the illusory world or retreats too hastily from the space of mourning without some gradual recognition of the reality of the loss, then one may live with a permanent dread of confronting the death. At times, we find we are loath to give up the pain of loss because it binds us still to whom or what we've lost—both a lifeline and a resurrection wish. We must learn, over time, to tolerate some awareness of the pain of the loss in order to go on living and to find renewed pleasure in life.

TOWARD A NEW DIALOGUE

In the pages that follow, as we examine personal experiences of grief and bereavement, we invite you to explore with us the landscape of the middle-distance. We draw on the image of the faraway nearby as a way to organize our understanding of the therapist's experience of loss. We have sought to infuse life into such experiences, some of which continue to haunt us and to inform our work today. Most importantly, we hope to open the door to a candid dialogue about what we therapists think and feel when we are in caught in the inevitable process of mourning.

NOTES

1. For readers interested in delving deeper into this topic, we direct you to several leading books that we have included in our bibliography.
2. Portions of this chapter appeared in Malawista, Adelman, and Anderson (2011).

REFERENCES

Archer, J. 1999. *The Nature of Grief.* New York: Routledge.
Baker, J. E. 2001. "Mourning and the Transformation of Object Relationships: Evidence for the Persistence of Internal Attachments." *Psychoanalytic Psychology* 18: 55–73.
Boswell, James. 1791. *The Life of Samuel Johnson.* New York: Penguin, 2008.
Bowlby, J. 1969. *Attachment and Loss.* Vol. 1: *Attachment.* New York: Basic Books.
——. 1973. *Attachment and Loss.* Vol. 2: *Separation, Anxiety, and Anger.* New York: Basic Books.
——. 1980. *Attachment and Loss.* Vol. 3: *Loss, Sadness, and Depression.* New York: Basic Books.
Buechler, S. 2000. "Necessary and Unnecessary Losses: The Analyst's Mourning." *Contemporary Psychoanalysis* 36: 77–90.
Didion, J. 2006. *The Year of Magical Thinking.* New York: Random House.
Fowlkes, M. R. 1991. "The Morality of Loss—The Social Construction of Mourning and Melancholia." *Contemporary Psychoanalysis* 27: 529–551.
Frankl, V. E. 1984. *Man's Search for Meaning: An Introduction to Logotherapy.* 3rd ed. New York: Simon and Schuster.
Freud, S. 1913. "Totem and Taboo: Some Points of Agreement Between the Mental Lives of Savages and Neurotics." In *The Standard Edition of the Complete Psychological Works of Sigmund Freud [SE],* ed. J. Strachey, 13:vii–162. London: Hogarth.
——. 1915. "Thoughts for the Times on War and Death." *SE* 14:274–300.
——. 1917. "Mourning and Melancholia." *SE* 14:237–258.
——. 2003. "Sigmund Freud to Ludwig Binswanger, April 11, 1929." In *Letters of Sigmund Freud, 1873–1939,* ed. E. L. Freud, trans. Thomas Roberts. New York: The Other Press.
Gaines, R. 1997. "Detachment and Continuity." *Contemporary Psychoanalysis* 33: 549–571.

Hagman, G. 1996. "The Role of the Other in Mourning." *Psychoanalytic Quarterly* 65: 327–352.

Jacobson, E. 1965. "The Return of the Lost Parent." In *Essential Papers on Object Loss,* ed. R. V. Frankie, 233–290. New York: New York University Press, 1984.

Klass, D. 1996. "Grief in Eastern Culture: Japanese Ancestor Worship." In *Continuing Bonds: New Understandings of Grief,* ed. D. Klass, P. R. Silverman, and S. L. Nickman, 59–70. Washington, D.C.: Taylor and Francis.

Klein, M. 1940a. "Love, Guilt, and Reparation." In *The Writings of Melanie Klein,* vol. 1, *Love, Guilt, and Reparation, and Other Works, 1921–1945,* 306–317. New York: The Free Press, 1975.

——. 1940b. "Mourning and Its Relation to Manic-Depressive States." In *The Writings of Melanie Klein,* vol. 1, *Love, Guilt, and Reparation, and Other Works, 1921–1945,* 344–369. New York: The Free Press, 1975.

Kubler-Ross, E. 1969. *On Death and Dying.* New York: Touchstone.

Lindemann, E. 1944. "Symptomatology and Management of Acute Grief." *American Journal of Psychiatry* 101: 141–148.

Maciejewski, P. K., B. Zhang, S. D. Block, and H. G. Prigerson. 2007. "An Empirical Examination of the Stage Theory of Grief." *Journal of the American Medical Association* 297, no. 7 (February 21): 716–723.

Malawista, K., A. J. Adelman, and C. L. Anderson. 2011. *Wearing My Tutu to Analysis and Other Stories: Learning Psychodynamic Concepts from Life.* New York: Columbia University Press.

Neimeyer, R., ed. 2001. *Meaning Reconstruction and the Experience of Loss.* American Psychological Association: Washington, D.C.

Rubin, S. S. 1985. "The Resolution of Bereavement: A Clinical Focus on the Relationship to the Deceased." *Psychotherapy* 22: 231–235.

Sussillo, M. V. 2005. "Beyond the Grave—Adolescent Parental Loss: Letting Go and Holding." *Psychoanalytic Dialogues* 15: 499–527.

Verghese, A. 1998. *The Tennis Partner: A Doctor's Story of Friendship and Loss.* New York: HarperCollins.

Walter, C. A. 2003. *The Loss of a Life Partner: Narratives of the Bereaved.* New York: Columbia University Press.

Willock, B., Bohm, L. C., and R. C. Curtis, eds. 2007. *On Deaths and Endings: Psychoanalysts' Reflections on Finality, Transformations, and New Beginnings.* New York: Routledge.

Yalom, I. D., and M. A. Lieberman. 1991. "Bereavement and Heightened Existential Awareness." *Psychiatry* 54: 334–345.

PART I

THE THERAPIST'S
EXPERIENCE OF LOSS

IN THIS section, our authors explore grief and loss from three different vantage points. In our first chapter, Kerry Malawista and Linda Kanefield approach the experience of loss through the lens of artistic representation, fictional narrative, and neurological and psychoanalytic understanding. They suggest that rather than moving through "stages" or "phases," mourning is more like a Möbius strip—a form both simple and elegant that has no beginning or end but rather weaves around itself in a continuous loop. With this perspective, there is no clear endpoint to grief nor any specific goal for mourning. Instead, the mourner finds herself in a transitional space, a state Malawista and Kanefield refer to as the "middle-distance."

As we discussed in the introduction, the realm of the middle-distance provides a psychic holding place where the mourner can gradually assimilate and integrate the reality of the loss while still maintaining a phantom presence of the loved one. For the mourner, life progresses without the deceased, yet at the same time the memory of the loved one remains right alongside, always in one's peripheral vision. One need only turn one's head slightly to catch a glimpse—a reminder that can bring a stab of pain or a cherished memory. We will return to this notion of the middle-distance as a way to capture the mourner's dual experience of the loved one as simultaneously present and irrevocably lost.

Judith Viorst describes the primary themes uncovered over the course of sixteen interviews with analysts who were invited to discuss their personal experience of terminating with long-term patients. All but one of her interviewees acknowledged that ending treatment invariably elicits feelings of loss. She highlights that this is an intimate relationship from both sides of the couch. Each analyst organizes and makes sense of these feelings in a unique way that then affects their clinical decisions during the termination. Each participant is subject to a range of feelings that can complicate the process of ending treatment. She brings the hopeful idea that during the termination phase both patient and analyst have new opportunities to mourn.

In the next chapter, Sandra Buechler describes the oft-unacknowledged reality that we really do miss our patients when they go, whether they plan to leave or end treatment abruptly, or, in some instances, when they die. She introduces the idea that when a treatment ends we lose the opportunity to become the person we glimpsed in ourselves with that particular patient. What was unique and only possible within this distinct patient-therapist dyad is now gone. It will never again be the same two people in the room together in quite the same way. Our imagined future is forever altered by the loss.

Buechler addresses the question that each of our authors in this section touches on in one form or another: How are we to behave in the face of such a loss? She writes that, within our profession, there is a general reluctance to acknowledge the gratifications we receive from our patients or the benefits we as therapists gain from our work. We are taught to be wary of allowing our own needs into the room. Buechler demonstrates how this complicates the grieving process. Though we may not admit it, the loss of a patient is inextricably linked with the loss of a certain kind of personal satisfaction, or as Buechler calls it, "joy."

CHAPTER 1

FROM THE FARAWAY NEARBY

Perspectives on the Integration of Loss

KERRY L. MALAWISTA AND LINDA KANEFIELD

GEORGIA O'KEEFE'S 1937 oil painting *From the Faraway Nearby* depicts the remains of an elk's skull and antlers above a range of pink and white mountains in the desert. The painting, like its title, captures the dualities of life: the haunting idea that something can be both distant and, at the same time, dangerously close. O'Keefe's painting is filled with contradictory images—light, representing life, and bones, the marker of death. It denotes the dual experience of something that is simultaneously present and immediate yet absent and elusive. Curiously, the canvas lacks a middle-distance, an artist's term for the space between the foreground and the background. In O'Keefe's painting, objects appear either starkly nearby or eerily far away. As we view the painting, we are jarred and confused by the absence of the middle-distance. Visually, we try to make sense of the odd perspective: we seek to comprehend whether we are near or far from the juxtaposed images of life and death. The absence of this middle-distance on the canvas unsettles us, and we try to create a middle realm that would allow the apparent contradictions inherent in life and death to coexist and comingle more quietly.

As in the painting, so it is in life: a middle-distance is necessary. Experientially, we need to navigate a middle-distance to absorb and integrate death. At times, the middle-distance is the perch from which we safely encounter our lost loved one. From this perspective, we can glimpse the past in the distant background, evoking a time before the death. Without the middle-distance, we are assaulted by the starkness of our loved one's absence in the foreground. At other times, from this perch we can see the possibility of calmer, more serene times in the future, when we are no longer haunted by the intrusive shock of our loss. The middle-distance is not only the position from which we can gain perspective; it is also the emotional and private place in which the deceased temporarily, or even enduringly, resides. When we feel their presence, they are there, not completely gone from our awareness but not alive in the way we have known them to be. Our relationship to the middle-distance is a dynamic and compelling one. Our capacity to periodically visit there—or allow our lost one to reside there—is critical in coping with a recent death.

This duality of life and death is familiar to most people who have experienced a personal loss. Over the years, our conversations, shared reactions, and struggles generated by our personal losses have led us to this chapter. These conversations have served as support and consolation and eventually led to the desire to organize our musings with the hope that it might be useful to us as therapists, as well as others, allowing us to make sense of how loss affects us privately and in our work. Our understanding of this aspect of life became the background for a more focused inquiry and exploration. It became clear to us that any notion positing a rigid or linear progression through grief, implying a static outcome to its resolution, is entirely inadequate. Likewise, a return to life and its pleasures does not signify a completion of mourning as much as it does a capacity to tolerate this duality.

The intrinsic paradox that a deceased loved one can be concurrently experienced as both present and elusive guides our exploration of mourning and our struggle to make peace with grief. How do we make sense of this seemingly irreconcilable contradiction that someone is dead but not gone from our internal world? We believe that the space between the psychological foreground and background, what we call the middle-distance, may serve as a psychological waystation where the bereaved struggles to integrate the loss and form a new cohesive self-narrative.

In fact, we contend that mourning can be understood as a process through which the death is first experienced in the foreground, as a raw, unintegrated trauma, then in the middle-distance, where memories are gradually woven together into a coherent picture. Then, over time, the loved one is internalized, new self-narratives are created, and the loss recedes to the background. This capacity to exist in the middle-distance, to bear unbearable feelings, is healthy yet often undervalued. It is a dynamic and nonlinear process that allows for movement, permeability, and integration, and it unfolds over the course of one's life. For example, someone who has lost a parent may revisit the loss and continue to feel that parent's presence at developmentally significant times, such as a wedding, a birth of a child, or a graduation.

While grief generally proceeds along this trajectory, we focus primarily here on the middle-distance experience. At the same time, we also appreciate that every loss is different. For example, in coping with the death of a child or the early loss of a parent, one faces unique challenges in mourning. For most parents, a child is experienced as an extension of oneself, as is the parent for a young child. Parents often look at their children and see the promises of their future. In ordinary parenting, these dreams for the future help buffer the blow of life's inevitable disappointments or setbacks. However, when a child dies, the loss is dual—the very real loss of the child as he or she has been known and the loss of the imagined future for and with the developing child. With no new or anticipated memories to weave into the current self-narrative, one may remain in the middle-distance.

In this chapter, we rely on a variety of points of view. We draw on our personal voices as well as on the more universal voices that emerge from other losses. As we explore the movement toward integration, we incorporate the words and vision of artists and the thinking of psychoanalysts and neuroscientists. For us, these seemingly disparate standpoints, like the ever-changing perspectives from which we all experience a death of a loved one, come together to provide a more complete notion of loss and grief.

CONTRIBUTIONS FROM PSYCHOANALYTIC THEORY

The psychoanalytic understanding of grief begins with Freud's "Mourning and Melancholia" (1917). With considerable sensitivity, he explores how the loss of a loved one is dealt with through one of two processes: mourning or melancholia. Both allow for the gradual "bit by bit" (245) withdrawal of attachment from the loved one. Freud considered mourning to be normal, a process that when "completed" (245) allows for the freedom to form new attachments. Melancholia, a more complex process, is characterized by unconscious ambivalence, a loss of self-esteem in the bereaved, and by self-reproaches shifted away from the loved one onto the self. In melancholia, there is an ongoing and consuming struggle to loosen the tie to the object.

Freud brings our attention to subtle questions about the process of mourning. With Freud's insights in mind, we consider mourning a continually evolving process rather than one defined by reaching a distinct endpoint. Although the deceased is never completely relinquished, the bereaved is not necessarily melancholic. The distinction between a normal process of mourning and a pathological one need not be as absolute as Freud originally posited. In fact, he later questioned some of his earlier assumptions about mourning being a finite process (2003).

Rather, life is compromised by how limited, inhibited, or emotionally shut down one becomes while traversing this middle-distance. The intensity of the intrusive thoughts and the unrelenting or all-encompassing nature of the loss also affect the degree of anguish one experiences during this process. These feelings of grief exist on a continuum of experience, not as a dichotomy. Even denying aspects of the loss, especially when traumatic, does not intrinsically indicate pathology. Instead, the ongoing presence of a lost loved one in the periphery provides stability when the world is threatening to fragment. Such continuity, a thread to the deceased, allows the bereaved to maintain self-cohesion through the passage of time in the middle distance. Memories of lived experiences with the deceased provide this thread.

The concept of disavowal is one way to understand what occurs psychologically when we are in this middle-distance. In 1924, Freud described disavowal as a psychotic defense against overwhelming feelings of grief following the death of a significant loved one. Later, however, in *An Outline of Psycho-Analysis* (1938), Freud argues that not only psychotic patients but all individuals have the capacity to deny and accept simultaneously an unwanted reality. He came to see disavowal as ubiquitous and not necessarily an indication of pathology. Indeed, we all continually blur fantasy and reality, sometimes emphasizing one reality when the other is too painful to confront.

In fact, fantasy and playacting all require imagination and the suspension of reality. Winnicott refers to this when he explores the landscape of "playing and reality." While not directly referring to mourning, he notes that "no human being is free from the strain of relating inner and outer reality" (1971, 13) and suggests that it is a psychological "intermediate experience"—or, in our words, the middle-distance—that provides a respite from this tension. Disavowal protects the mourner from overwhelming pain. In this way, the individual may acknowledge the reality of the death but not yet completely integrate the meaning and acceptance of the loss until the truth can be tolerated fully.

In our view, the deceased's enduring presence in the middle-distance is adaptive for the mourner. It is a way to preserve one's sense of self in the face of disruptive loss or trauma. Philip Bromberg's (1998) work describing "the multiplicity of self" and dissociation may help us understand what occurs in this transitional or intermediate space. Bromberg describes dissociation as a "complex system of discontinuous and shifting states of consciousness" (251). He notes that it "is not inherently pathological, but it can become so. . . . It is intrinsically an adaptational talent that represents the very nature of what we call 'consciousness.' Dissociation is not fragmentation" (244). In other words, it is a way to protect one's psyche by having an alternate way of experiencing, a way of staving off an unbearable reality. A familiar form occurs in acute grief, when mourners often are able to function in the outside world—describing all the facts of a loved one's death, or planning a service and burial—while nonetheless still expecting the deceased to return to them. In other words, they function as if in a dissociated state, having not yet integrated the loss as a traumatic piece of a personally comprehensible self-narrative.

Certainly, a death, especially that of a child, poses a significant threat to the experience of the self as whole and intact. The bereaved moves between states of acute grief and adaptive functioning. Bromberg writes that "it is the ability to stand in the spaces between realities without losing any of them; the capacity to feel like one self while being many" (256) that allows the integration of experience. This movement between psychological spaces captures our idea of the middle-distance and the flexible nature of the permeable boundaries between the bearable and unbearable states of mind that we experience during mourning—the acute sensation that someone is gone but still present.

Melanie Klein places the process of mourning into a developmental context. She notes that the longing to "save and restore the [lost] loved ones" (1940, 349) is heightened because it evokes an infantile and painful awareness that the mother can, in fact, be lost. Therefore, according to Klein, the loss of a loved one deeply threatens the stability of the internal world. To stave off the danger of the inner world collapsing, there must be a gradual renewed link to the external world. These links, in which the reality of the loss is encountered, serve to restore psychic equilibrium. Klein notes: "Without partial and temporary denial of psychic reality, the ego can not bear the disaster by which it feels itself threatened" (1940, 349).

Otto Kernberg describes how he came to question some generally assumed characteristics of "normal" grief and mourning after his own "deep personal mourning experience." He states, "perhaps mourning processes do not simply end, but rather, evolve into something more lasting or permanent" (2010, 601). Through a process of identification, he notes, there is a continuing, active internal relationship with the deceased. Gathering insight from work with patients and interviews with friends and colleagues, he observes that most who experience a loss retain the "conviction that the person [who has died] was still there, in some unreal world" (605). Through evocative art, photographs, or burial sites, or "in the transitional space of [the treatment] relationship" (615), the bereaved attempts to experience the lost loved one as still present. Kernberg notes that in these ways, the process of mourning can strengthen the bereaved and ultimately "enhances the capacity for loving."

THE IMPORTANCE OF NARRATIVE

Struggling with our own losses gave us a deeper understanding of Schafer's work on historical reconstruction and self-created narratives in therapy. Working through earlier experiences, including those of loss, requires reconstructing our history. As Schafer (1982) states most simply, "Reality is mediated by narration" (235). We revise, we remember differently, and the "facts of the past, the facts of the here and now exist only in narrated versions of them" (195). Schafer posits that we construct "multiple histories" determined by the context of the retelling. In the middle-distance, we are continually reinterpreting, reorganizing, retelling, and striving to create a new and cohesive story about ourselves after the loss.

When a traumatic loss harshly disrupts the story that we tell others and ourselves, we are no longer held together securely by the story's thread. Thus, a revision is essential to construct a new version of who we are and who we will be. New meaning must be made to incorporate the loss. The more traumatic the death, the more challenging the task of revising the narrative such that it provides continuity with the past, acceptance of the present, and an anchored sense of self to meet the future. The creation of this new narrative promotes a sense of agency. This is especially critical when enduring a profound loss, which can generate often paralyzing feelings of passivity or powerlessness.

Not only does the disorganization in narrative after a traumatic death affect the way we understand our self and our history, but it is also transmitted across the generations. As Main (2000) found in her extensive research on the transmission of attachment patterns between parents and children, unresolved mourning in the parent results in a corresponding attachment style in the child. In fact, the narrative style of the parent is predictive of the child's attachment style—regardless of the nature of the parent's experience—and demonstrates how critical it is for the loss to be integrated so that adaptive development can ensue. Thus, a cohesive narrative is not only important to the bereaved but has a direct effect on the next generation.

Creating an unbroken narrative is necessary for the integration of grief. Malawista, Adelman, and Anderson (2011, 203) evoke the struggle to forge a new, reparative narrative. Describing the experience of the middle-distance, they write:

> It is the small, ordinary moments—a word, a gesture, a song—which bring another surge of grief. . . . You are gone. . . . I imagine I am a war veteran who lost a limb. I continue to feel pain where there is an absence. An essential part of me is missing . . . you are my phantom limb. I continue to feel that you are there, but you are not. . . . Even though you are gone, you haunt my days, so I seek the comfort of sleep, but you pursue me in my dreams at night. Then I realize it's not you haunting me—I haunt you. I see you around every corner, in every encounter, in every face. . . . Although it makes no sense, I wait to hear from you or from some messenger you will surely send to me.

These words depict the middle-distance in which we locate ourselves in mourning. From this position, we can function in multiple states of mind, with the impression that the lost beloved is suspended, hovering in the periphery. Joan Didion beautifully captures this feeling in her book *The Year of Magical Thinking* (2005), where she describes the outward appearance of accepting her husband's death while internally denying the reality of this loss, holding on to the fantasy that he will return. This phantom sensation of the loved one's continued presence mitigates the pain of the otherwise unbearable trauma.

A FICTIONAL NARRATIVE

The duality of life and death is often the subject of fiction. Writers of novels use narrative to expand and deepen our understanding of the complexities of universal emotions. Don DeLillo's novel *The Body Artist* (2001) provides a gripping study of grief and mourning. In it, a young woman, Lauren Hartke, attempts to navigate this middle-distance in the weeks and months following the death of her film-director husband, Rey.

DeLillo explores the tension as Lauren tries to absorb the reality of Rey's death while simultaneously sensing his presence at every turn. DeLillo writes, "[Lauren] stepped slowly through the rooms. She felt him behind her when she was getting undressed, standing barefoot on the cold floor, throwing off a grubby sweater, and she half turned toward the bed" (33). Later, he describes her endless searching: "She looked. She was always looking. She could not get enough" (85). Lauren struggles with who she is now that she is no longer Rey's wife. "She looked at her face in the bathroom mirror and tried to understand why it looked different from the same face downstairs, in the full-length mirror in the front hall . . . she thought, why do I look different?" (63). She reads the loss in her face, reflected back to her in the mirror, as a profound rupture.

Lauren attempts to regain her equilibrium by reconstructing a new narrative for herself, one that encompasses a future without her husband. She encounters "Mr. Tuttle," a person (or apparition) who emerges as if he had been hiding upstairs. The reader is left to wonder whether Mr. Tuttle is an actual person or a projection of Lauren's grief. She imagines that Mr. Tuttle comes from cyberspace. He represents this "in-between" world, a link to her mourning that does not exist in time: "She thought maybe he lived in a kind of time that had no narrative quality" (65). It is as if Mr. Tuttle has no spatial or temporal reality. Lauren imagines that he lives in "overlapping realities" (82), what we call the middle-distance. As the story develops, it becomes clear that Mr. Tuttle is the embodiment of Rey. As Lauren progresses through mourning, Mr. Tuttle serves as the link that allows her to linger in the middle-distance. Like Rey, he exists in this transitional space: no longer outside yet not completely inside. Similarly, Lauren cannot move forward without Rey nor explore a past that does not include him. Mr. Tuttle "knew how to make her husband live in the air that rushed from his lungs into his vocal folds—air to sounds, sounds to words, words the man shaped fatefully on his lips and tongue" (62). She pleads, "Talk like him. I want you to do this for me. I know you are able to do it. Do it for me. Talk like him. . . . Say whatever comes into your head, just so it is him. . . . Do Rey. Make me hear him" (71). Through the existence of Mr. Tuttle, Lauren is able to maintain this duality that Rey is both dead yet still here, always hovering right nearby, looming in her peripheral vision: "[Lauren] saw something out of the corner of her eye. She turned her head and nothing was there" (76).

Lauren, no longer able to see or touch Rey, is in a constant state of dislocation, though she is not delusional. In this way, Mr. Tuttle acts as a kind of internal emissary, summoned, as it were, by her unconscious to help her traverse the middle-distance, to move from holding on to letting go. "She began to understand that she could not miss Rey, could not consider his absence, the loss of Rey, without thinking along the margin of Mr. Tuttle" (82). She is afraid that without Mr. Tuttle she loses Rey, that memory alone is not sufficient to contain her longing for her lost love. In this way, DeLillo illustrates how Lauren begins the process of integration and, ultimately, the acceptance of Rey's death. At the end of the novel, when Lauren looks in the room, she sees it is empty, a state she can now tolerate. She realizes that both Rey and Mr. Tuttle are truly gone. It is through the emptiness of the room that she starts to reclaim life and is able to notice the details of the room: "The light was so vibrant she could see the true colors of the walls and floor. She'd never seen the walls before. The bed was empty" (124).

CONTRIBUTIONS FROM NEUROSCIENCE

In the last decade, recognizing that all emotional experiences have a bodily component, psychoanalysis has begun to bridge the gap between the pathos of the mind and the science of the brain. Thus there may be a neurological anchor or analogy to our understanding of grief. The death of a loved one, as Malawista et al. describe above, can be experienced as a phantom limb that continues to feel pain, in spite of its absence. The concept of the phantom limb is a complex one that has been extensively researched. Ramachandran (1998), a neurologist, studies patients who have lost limbs yet continue to describe vividly the lost arm or leg as still attached to their body. Even though the nerves supplying the arm or leg are severed, they still experience pain. The brain, faced with tremendous sensory conflict, continues to experience the limb as present—in other words, as a phantom limb. To study this phenomenon, Ramachandran ingeniously created a "mirror box" that allows the patient to see the reflection of the healthy arm as the missing one. When asked to move their existing fingers, the patient has the sensation that the phantom limb is moving. When the phantom arm is visually perceived, the pain ceases. A therapeutic repetition of the illusion that the arm exists ultimately relieves the pain.

Interestingly, the more traumatic the loss, the more vivid and persistent the phantom limb remains. In fact, Ramachandran (1998) notes that a vivid phantom is experienced by over 90 percent of all patients who have lost a limb. Some phantom limbs are present for days or weeks but then gradually fade from consciousness. Others persist for years, even decades. It is as if, initially, the traumatic loss of a part of the body is almost impossible for the brain to integrate. In this way, the amputated limb continues to exist in the middle-distance long after it is gone. Analogously, it is the same when we lose someone who is essential to our view of ourselves, such as a parent losing a child; we psychologically experience a "phantom existence" of a lost loved one.

Pally and Olds (1998) and Turnbull (1999) describe Ramachandran's research with patients who suffered a right-hemisphere stroke resulting in damage to the parietal cortex. Many of these stroke victims deny their disability, a condition known as anosognosia. When asked to perform tasks using the left side of the body, they ignore their handicap and instead give convoluted excuses to explain their inability to perform that task.

Historically, this reaction was explained as having a psychological basis in denial, where a patient could not tolerate a traumatic alteration of the self. However, the origin of this phenomenon is not purely psychological but rather organic. Unlike those with right-brain strokes, patients with left-brain strokes rarely display anosognosia. The different roles of the right and left hemisphere illuminate this finding. The left hemisphere is the interpreter of data and is primarily concerned with making sense of all the bewildering sensory inputs with which we are flooded. It then orders them into a coherent belief system based on what was previously known. The left hemisphere culls through all the data it knows about the self and protects that version of the self against a clashing storyline. By limiting the number of possible interpretations, the brain protects the self from being overwhelmed by all the explanations or from being paralyzed by indecision in new situations. When events occur that are inconsistent with our experience of our self, the left hemisphere either denies the incompatible information or confabulates to achieve coherence, even at the expense of reality.

For this reason, Ramachandran locates psychological defensive strategies such as denial in the left hemisphere. Through his experiments, he demonstrates that the right hemisphere detects when the overwhelmingly contradictory data threaten the current narrative and demand integration. Patients with anosognosia no longer have this "detector," so they continue to deny what is literally right in front of them. The left hemisphere of the brain, without the input of the right hemisphere's "detector," continues to see the body as whole and intact despite all contradictory evidence. Similarly, Basch (1983, 134) describes this process in psychoanalytic rather than neurological terms. He writes that "reality testing makes a potentially painful percept available to preconscious thought . . . but, at the same time, bars the way to making those connections with past experience that would force a confrontation with the meaning that that percept has for the self."

It may well be that when profound grief strains our ability to cope or comprehend, the brain functions much like Ramachandran describes. In an attempt to keep traumatic knowledge at bay, the mourner may give the outward appearance of emotional composure even while feeling internally adrift. Nevertheless, in facing grief, there are moments when reality necessarily intrudes, or, in neurological terms, when the right-brain "detector" steps in. When this occurs, the carefully constructed barrier is broken, allowing grief to seep into the interior world. No matter how effective the disavowal, the trauma and pain still return at unanticipated moments. This is a necessary yet exquisitely painful part of the grieving process. Although distressing, the failure to tolerate these breakthroughs of grief poses other risks. If disavowal leads to the avoidance of full participation in life, in order to not be reminded of the trauma or feel the loss, life can become overly limited, isolated, or deadened.

In our effort to integrate a jarring loss, it is critical to create a new and comprehensive narrative out of past experience. Cozolino (2002) writes about the malleability of memory and the therapeutic importance of reworking painful memories in a constructive way. He integrates psychoanalytic theory, the importance of narrative, neuroscience, and treatment when he writes: "From the perspective of psychotherapy, however, the plasticity of memory provides an avenue to the alteration of neural systems. . . . The introduction of new information or scenarios about past experiences can modify affective reactions and alter the nature of memories" (100). Perhaps, when it comes to the trauma of loss, the back-and-forth experiences of recognition/denial and acceptance/dissociation may provide a path for incremental neural flexibility that allows for the eventual integration of the loss. As Cozolino notes, there can be therapeutic healing when there is "increasing levels of affect tolerance and regulation and the development of integrative narratives" (28). The middle-distance allows the space for this integration to occur.

CONCLUSION AND IMPLICATIONS FOR TREATMENT

The trauma of loss is universal. The nature of a particular loss, its position in the course of ordinary developmental expectations, and the degree to which it reverberates with earlier losses all affect one's sense of self. Yet we are inevitably destabilized in the aftermath of a significant loss. Amid painful feelings, we struggle to integrate such disruptive experiences of loss into the narrative of who we are and who we will become. At times, we adaptively attempt to regain our psychic equilibrium by disavowing our loss or by dissociating our grief. It is during this time of adjustment that the mourner exists in a psychological middle-distance, constantly striving to feel whole, even while the deceased lurks like a phantom just out of reach.

The capacity to traverse the middle-distance is critical. Its very presence allows for movement, permeability, and integration of loss in a bearable way. It allows us time to grapple with constructing a new and coherent storyline of ourselves. Even after the process of mourning appears complete, a part of the mourner may linger in this middle-distance. While this capacity to experience the middle-distance comes naturally for many, there are times when unacknowledged or unconscious feelings about the deceased, such as anger or shame or even guilt about anger, might interfere with the process. Ordinarily, however, the middle-distance brings us closer to the deceased one, a place we seek to return to again and again. It is as though we hope to retrieve the memory of something lost, beloved, and profoundly familiar. This idea is expressed in Georgia O'Keefe's (1934) description of her home at Ghost Ranch: "Such a beautiful untouched lonely-feeling place, such a fine part of what I call the 'Faraway.' It is a place I have painted before . . . even now I must do it again."

When therapists experience a profound loss, we too revisit our loss again and again, as we struggle to integrate and make sense of the trauma. It is often during this prolonged and private sojourn of mourning that we return to work. Inevitably, we stumble upon the realm of the middle-distance in our consulting room. We might struggle to focus on our patients' subjective world, where we find comfort in the distraction their stories provide. At other times, however, our patients confront us with our loss and catapult us back into our raw, unprocessed grief.

Just as parents cannot always shield their children from realities that are developmentally overwhelming, so too there are times when we are unable to shield our patients from our own significant life events. Patients may differ in what they know of our actual loss and vary in how attuned they are to us, both consciously and unconsciously, depending on each patient's unique sensitivities and on the particulars of each therapeutic pair. With one patient, for example, we may suddenly find ourselves vulnerable and unmoored, thrusting us headlong into our grief. With a different patient, a sympathetic remark about the loss we have endured may be intended to protect us from pain and may spare both patient and therapist the discomfort of feeling bereft or abandoned. Another patient's angry insistence that we could not possibly be emotionally available to do the work of therapy may amplify our awareness of the loss as it coexists with our ability to carry on in a productive way. Ordinarily, we are comfortable with our professional and our personal selves and do not need to focus on the permeability and overlap between these aspects of our identity. At times of personal loss, however, the boundary between these aspects of our identity is ruptured. Out of necessity, we encounter the classical roots of our profession, which posit the ideal of the anonymous analyst. A personal loss compels us to recognize the impossibility of this stance as we accept our own feelings of vulnerability, pain, confusion, or guilt.

For each of us, it can be a challenge to use our clinical knowledge and experience, as well as our self-awareness and strength, to help our patients navigate the new and often painful territory that our personal losses create in the work. Psychological and neurological information, as well as the art of fiction and prose, illuminate our efforts to make sense of ourselves in the grip of loss. Ideally, such an experience expands our capacity to resonate with our patients' traumatic losses and gives us a deeper appreciation of their challenges as they rework their own narratives and move toward greater integration. Like the observer of

Georgia O'Keefe's painting, we are constantly in pursuit of the missing perspective—the middle-distance.

NOTE

We thank Catherine Anderson, Paula Atkeson, Kathy Beck, Judy Chused, Nancy Goodman, Eileen Ivey, Aimee Nover, Shelley Rockwell, Richard Waugaman, and Robert Winer for their thoughtful reading of and helpful comments on earlier versions of this chapter.

REFERENCES

Basch, M. F. 1983. "The Perception of Reality and the Disavowal of Meaning." *Annual of Psychoanalysis* 11: 125–153.

Bromberg, P. 1998. *Standing in the Spaces*. Hillsdale, N.J.: Analytic Press.

Cozolino, L. 2002. *The Neuroscience of Psychotherapy: Building and Rebuilding the Human Brain*. New York: Norton.

DeLillo, D. 2001. *The Body Artist*. New York: Scribner.

Didion, J. 2005. *The Year of Magical Thinking*. New York: Random House.

Freud, S. 1917. "Mourning and Melancholia." In *The Standard Edition of the Complete Psychological Works of Sigmund Freud [SE]*, ed. J. Strachey, 14:237–258. London: Hogarth.

——. 1924. "The Loss of Reality in Neurosis and Psychosis." *SE* 19:181–188.

——. 1938. "An Outline of Psycho-Analysis." *SE* 23:141–207.

——. 2003. "Sigmund Freud to Ludwig Binswanger, April 11, 1929." In *Letters of Sigmund Freud, 1873–1939*, ed. E. L. Freud, trans. Thomas Roberts. New York: The Other Press.

Kernberg, O. 2010. Some Observations on the Process of Mourning. *International Journal of Psychoanalysis* 91, no. 3: 601–619.

Klein, M. 1940. "Mourning and Its Relation to Manic-Depressive States." *International Journal of Psychoanalysis* 21: 125–153.

Main, M. 2000. "The Organized Categories of Infant, Child, and Adult Attachment: Flexible Versus Inflexible Attention Under Attachment-Related Stress." *Journal of the American Psychoanalytic Association* 48: 1055–1095.

Malawista, K., A. J. Adelman, and C. L. Anderson. 2011. *Wearing My Tutu to Analysis and Other Stories: Learning Psychodynamic Concepts from Life*. New York: Columbia University Press.

O'Keefe, G. 1934. *Rotating O'Keefe Exhibit*. Fort Worth, Tex.: National Cowgirl Museum and Hall of Fame, 2010.

Pally, R., and D. Olds. 1998. "Consciousness: A Neuroscience Perspective." *International Journal of Psychoanalysis* 79: 971–989.

Ramachandran, V. S., and W. Hirstein. 1998. "The Perception of Phantom Limbs." *Brain* 121: 1603–1630.

Schafer, R. 1983. *The Analytic Attitude*. New York: Basic Books.

Turnbull, O. 1999. "Review: *Phantoms in the Brain: Human Nature and the Architecture of the Mind* by V. S. Ramachandran and S. Blakslee." *Neuropsychoanalysis* 1: 269–272.

Winnicott, D. W. 1971. *Playing and Reality*. London: Tavistock.

CHAPTER 2

EXPERIENCES OF LOSS AT THE END OF ANALYSIS

The Analyst's Response to Termination

JUDITH VIORST

A PATIENT is nearing the end of a lengthy analysis. The fantasy is that his analyst, who has a pair of tickets to an Isaac Stern concert, offers him one of the tickets as a gift. At the concert hall, he sits beside the recipient of the analyst's other ticket, who turns out to be none other than the analyst's lovely, and unmarried, daughter. They talk, they start to date each other, they fall in love, and soon they are happily married—living, of course, not too far from daddy-analyst.

A typical patient's fantasy? Not quite. The fantasy belongs not to the patient but to the analyst. At the end of an hour one day, the analyst found himself caught up in this pleasant reverie, which, he explains, "both took care of my fatherliness and met the needs of my patient to hold onto me."

Firestein (1978), in his fine study of termination, characterizes the terminal phase of analysis as that period when the focus is on the issue of ending a highly significant relationship. Both the patient and the analyst experience separation reactions, he writes, and both—to varying degrees—experience "what, for want of a better description, could be called grief" (215).

Reactions to termination may also occur before the subject is ever discussed; they may, indeed, impede its being brought up. And reactions to termination may continue after the analysis is done, for in defining "the work of termination" as "the patient's and analyst's emotional experience of the end of their customary relationship," Firestein's study indicates that this work continues after the final hour (212). Thus, before, during, and after the formal termination phase, responses to termination may arise. And although it is certainly true that termination may evoke in the analyst feelings of gratification at a job well done—or feelings of relief at being rid of an especially trying case—it usually also evokes feelings of loss.

Buxbaum (1950, 190) writes that "to resolve the countertransference becomes a major part of the analytic process of termination." I believe this chapter will show that the need to identify, resolve, and digest one's losses is a significant technical issue for the psychoanalyst during the terminal phase. I believe it will also show that, in dealing with aspects of loss, analysts may find that they can utilize their responses for their own—as well as their patients'—further development.

A NOTE ON PROCEDURE

To obtain the material for this discussion, I solicited interviews of approximately one and a half to two hours in length from twenty analysts. Sixteen analysts from three analytic institutes—eleven supervising and training analysts, one teaching analyst, three recent graduates, and one candidate—agreed to be interviewed. Of the four who declined, one said the project did not interest him, one had no time available in the near future, one expressed concern for his patients' privacy, and one expressed concern for his own privacy: "It would be," he said, "like going into analysis with you."

What he meant was that a frank examination of his responses would involve a substantial degree of self-revelation. And, in fact, the interview setting, with its assurances of total anonymity (the sex of some patients and analysts and some small identifying details have been changed) evoked in a number of analysts not only thoughtful comments but a confessional, emotionally charged response.

In the analyst's work with patients, such emotionally charged reactions are examined and contained, not acted out; between the analyst's affects and the cool, observing analytic eye is stretched the creative tension of the analysis. The interview situation, in contrast, seemed to provide an opportunity to *express* as well as to *analyze* these affects. Anger and guilt and frustration and disappointment, along with sorrow, were openly manifested as we spoke of loss at the end of an analysis.

There was no sustained attempt in these interviews to collect information about standards for termination (such as modification of a harsh superego, increased tolerance of affects and instincts, or removal of pathogenic defenses) or styles of termination (whether or not, for instance, the analyst proposes termination, sits the patient up, or becomes more "real"). Nor did I explicitly investigate whether loss experiences were different for different age groups (certain patterns suggest themselves, but further work remains to be done in this area) or whether loss experiences with candidates were different from those with noncandidates. On this last point, however, I did gain the impression that for most of the analysts interviewed, analysis was analysis and losses were losses, whether or not the patient being terminated happened to be a candidate.

The focus remained on the analyst's experience of loss at termination, although the fairly unstructured interviews allowed for a good deal of free association. And although one might at times be tempted to discern further meanings in some of the material, and although—as this wasn't analysis—certain responses were surely left unsaid, every person interviewed made a serious effort at self-examination.

I believe that most of the analysts spoke with a high degree of frankness and that they spoke individually in ways that they would never speak publicly or collectively. I also believe that because of the isolation of their work, they found pleasure and relief in talking about it.

A DEFINITION OF COUNTERTRANSFERENCE

Whether some or all of the loss reactions to be described should be called "countertransference" depends on one's definition of this complicated and controversial word. Countertransference was originally perceived as an impediment to analysis (Freud 1915) and later as a potentially valuable tool. Surveys of the literature by Cohen (1952), Tower (1956), Racker (1957), and others show that it has been defined in a number of different and often contradictory ways.

Tower, for instance, differentiates countertransference from other kinds of responses, including empathy. He reserves the word countertransference "*only* for those phenomena which are transferences of the analyst to his patients" and which are unconscious, based on the repetition compulsion, and directed toward significant persons from the past (1956, 227–228). Searles (1979), on the other hand, includes in his definition of countertransference both the analyst's empathic experiencing of the patient's feelings and the analyst's own affective reactions, including primitive feelings of jealousy, murderous rage, and fear, evoked over the course of the work.

It is clear that countertransference can be viewed very narrowly or very broadly. For the purpose of this discussion, I propose to take the broadest view, defining countertransference as all of the analyst's feelings and attitudes toward the patient. Those who insist, however, on a stricter definition may prefer a more general term like "counterresponse." In any case, what is offered here are the *analyst's reactions*: his or her experiences of loss at the end of analysis.

ASPECTS OF LOSS

Only one analyst interviewed claims no problems with loss at termination. "Professionalism," he remarks, "defends against loss." At the opposite end of the spectrum is the analyst who maintains that "partings are always traumatic" and ought to be eased whenever possible. Eased for the analyst—not just the patient. To do this, he explains, he rarely goes "from four to zero"—he tapers off his patients' hours instead. And he always strives "for a perfect ending, for a really pleasant parting," over the course of which "we become increasingly real for each other." He also eases his sense of loss through the fantasy that he'll marry each woman patient and become the intimate friend of each man. And finally, he notes, when he finds himself focusing on the monetary loss, he knows he's defending against the pain of parting.

Although there is no consensus that partings are always traumatic, virtually all the analysts interviewed find some terminations a time of significant loss. And most say there is some sense of loss—though not of traumatic proportions—in all terminations.

"I cannot stop with a patient without a feeling of loss," observes Dr. A. "I cannot imagine not having some such feelings." In dealing with such loss, he comments, experience helps and so, of course, does self-knowledge. "How do I manage? Sometimes better than others."

Dr. B concurs and adds that although "it's a one-sided relationship, there are nevertheless very strong feelings of intimacy. It requires tremendous control to hold oneself back, to use the countertransference to interpret but not to express. And the reality that it's going to end makes these feelings even more intense." He pauses for a moment and then musingly recalls, "One of my analysts was crying when I left."

Balint (1950, 197) describes a comparable emotional response, one he says occurs at the end of a successful analysis when "the patient feels that he is going through a kind of re-birth into a new life, that he has arrived at the end of a dark tunnel, that he sees light again after a long journey, that he has been given a new life." In Balint's words, "It is a deeply moving experience; the general atmosphere is of taking leave forever of something very dear, very precious—with all the corresponding grief and mourning. . . . Usually the patient leaves after the last session happy but with tears in his eyes and— I think I may admit—the analyst is in a very similar mood."

Dr. C says that termination is always an experience of loss to him because "the feelings are real—the feelings are not synthetic. To call an analytic relationship a professional one is merely a way of annotating its objectives and its course, but it doesn't affect the quality of the relationship."

Dr. D describes "the sense of letdown, the empty feeling" that he and so many of his colleagues observe in themselves at the time of termination, and he identifies this as an experience of loss. He explains the nature of this loss by pointing out that analysis is a rich but limited relationship—"the patient doesn't really know you, and in many ways the patient is someone you don't know at all." It is not until the terminal phase, when "what is left are two adults no longer meeting on an archaic basis," that a real relationship is possible, that these two relative strangers are ready to know each other—"and then they must part." He adds with a sigh that his is a "tough profession, because if the analysis isn't successful it's hard to see them go. And if it *is* successful, it's hard to see them go."

Dr. E tells how, gradually, over a long span of years, he learned to let himself feel fully and mourn his own losses. Now, during termination, he says, "I sit in my office, my eyes full of tears half the time. And it's nothing that I fight—I let it happen."

Dr. F, though conceding that certain obsessives may be easier to part from, notes some sense of loss at all terminations. One indication that it is time for termination, she observes, is the ease and comfort and smoothness of the work together. "And this is the dilemma," she adds, "that just when the patient becomes a great pleasure to work with, you have to let go."

Sylvan Keiser points out that "the analyst must be sufficiently attuned to his own unconscious to be able to decide whether he has . . . a reluctance to give up the personal enjoyment of the analytic relationship" (Robbins 1975,

166–167). And indeed, some analysts interviewed, addressing themselves to this point, speak of the special sense of loss in terminating with patients who are pleasing to work with.

Dr. G, for instance, says she finds it hard to part from those patients she calls "lively"—that is, from patients who have a sense of humor, "who don't show the usual deference," and "who give me a view of life I might never otherwise have gained." And Dr. H describes the particular feelings of loss in terminating with those patients who are "so creative, so brilliant, so in touch with their feelings, so motivated for change." In discussing such a patient, he notes that "each analytic hour was a pleasure; when termination approached, I was really sad—I realized I was going to miss him tremendously." Furthermore, this patient was fairly famous and moved in rather heady circles, and "I got vicarious pleasure from all the stories he would tell—they were such a delight."

The loss of daily contact with a mind and a milieu that were—to be quite honest about it—a turn-on; the loss of daily contact with a famous, intelligent person whose high esteem for his analyst (unlike the esteem of less discerning patients) felt plausible, non-neurotic, and highly flattering; the loss of daily contact with someone who, just a few years older than Dr. H, could represent some kind of ego ideal—all of these were significant losses indeed. And so, in the terminal phase, when the patient exhibited a resurgence of earlier symptoms, Dr. H became involved in analyzing the old pathology as if it were an ongoing conflict instead of seeing it for what it was—a defense against the impending termination. Finally, he understood the loss that he—Dr. H—was defending against and dealt with it for himself and for his patient.

For the youngest group of analysts, the sorrow of losing a patient may be heavily interlarded with the joy of having—at last—a completed case. There is also the consolation that with years and years of professional life ahead, other patients will fill the departing one's place. Changes in the insurance system and nonexistent waiting lists may make these less consoling. But even without these concerns, young analysts may find themselves having to learn—as did Dr. A—"how to become more comfortable with loss."

Early in his career as a child analyst, Dr. A treated a young patient from latency into adolescence, serving—because the boy's parents were divorced—as the significant male figure in his life. Working with him, Dr. A could "redress some things" he wished had been different in his own history, and because of his overinvestment he was tempted, during the termination phase, to continue the analytic work a bit further. He had a legitimate pretext—the boy had just begun getting into some prehomosexual activity. Although Dr. A was well aware that "all kids have to go through this," he nonetheless struggled with the wish to keep him in treatment until it was resolved.

In order to let him go, Dr. A says, he had to accept the fact that some things have to be resolved on your own, that "to hold on too long was just as harmful as not holding on at all." To let him go, he says, he had to recognize that "this was not the last child I was going to treat or my last opportunity to do something successful."

But what about elderly analysts, whose opportunities may in fact be narrowing? Are terminations more difficult for them? Are feelings of loss more intense in the later decades? For Dr. I, the answer—so far—is no.

A vital and healthy woman who has reached her seventh decade, Dr. I is taking no new analytic cases because—as she quite matter-of-factly explains—"I don't follow as well. I'm much more forgetful. I don't feel nearly as sharp as I once was." Although she is currently terminating the last training analysis she will ever conduct, she feels no particular sense of loss, for this case has involved "special sacrifices," there are still some (nontraining) analyses yet to complete, and there is plenty of other work to fill her schedule.

Dr. I seems truly untroubled by the loss of her last candidate. Dr. B offers another point of view. Over the past several years, he observes, "I've had to renounce more and more," including the very deep pleasure he found in parenting. His patients have come to play an increasingly important part in his life, and his partings from them have become increasingly difficult.

Similarly, another elderly analyst remarks, "When I was younger, I had less difficulty separating from my patients. I could write papers. There were other ways I could broaden my experience. But now my patients give me something to do." "Occupation is very important for elderly analysts," he adds. "It is difficult not to feel useful."

In a doggedly upbeat essay, Eissler (1975, 147–148) highlights the contributions that aging may make to the practice of psychoanalysis. He notes, however, that if the elderly analyst keeps on aging, "he gradually loses all those contemporaries to whom he had become attached in the course of his life. . . . The impoverishment of love objects will often lead to a greater cathexis of his professional life . . . indeed, in rare cases his patients may be the sole love objects left him." Under such conditions, writes Eissler, the "optimal distance between the analyst and the patient may be lost and because of the undue gratification the emotional atmosphere may lead to the patient's fixation on the treatment situation." He stops just short of the obvious point that it also may lead to the *analyst's* fixation or at least to some problems with loss at termination.

Loss in the terminal phase may surely be felt—at any age—as the loss of a love object. But there may be other significant losses as well. Sometimes the countertransference response is to the loss of certain identified-with parts of a patient, or of what Searles (1979) calls the "therapeutic symbiosis," or of some especially gratifying role that the work permits the analyst to play.

Weigert (1952, 471–472) writes about the "goal-inhibited tender closeness of psychoanalytic intimacy" in which infantile emotional attachments are relived. "The analyst may tacitly allow the patient to use analysis as a sanctuary, a refuge . . . and in the countertransference the analyst may vicariously enjoy a protective permissiveness that he could never experience in relation to his own parents." This empathic identification with the protected part of the patient may pose a problem with loss at termination.

Searles (1979, 374), from his special point of view, emphasizes the positive side of this kind of identification when he writes about "therapeutic symbiosis," in which the analyst participates at a feeling level in what the patient is feeling and a "process of mutual rehumanization" occurs. He also emphasizes "the patient's own therapeutic strivings toward the analyst" and the fact that the patient to some extent may wish and indeed be able to "cure" the analyst. According to Searles, the analyst as well as the patient may experience separation anxiety in the face of the end of this symbiotic relatedness.

Dr. G makes a similar point. She speaks of a reluctance to let go of those special patients who provide her with what she calls a "holding environment." With one woman whose capacity to do this "was very precious to me," Dr. G recalls her own unwillingness to relinquish the pleasing feeling "of her taking care of me." This reaction was expressed in the analysis by her letting her patient waste large amounts of time; she also did not "forthrightly and persistently cut in on certain kinds of nongrowth behavior." It was not that she failed to interpret, but "my wishes to hold onto the status quo rendered my interventions ineffectual."

Termination, then, can mean the analyst's loss of gratifications having to do with feeling protected and safe. It can also mean the loss of certain other gratifications having to do with playing the great protector, with playing the role—the "very flattering role," Buxbaum (1950, 186) reminds us—of "the wise, foreseeing, almighty analyst."

Indeed, there is a wide range of roles that analysts may enjoy over the course of their analytic work with patients. In his discussion of countertransference, Sandler (1976) notes that the patient attempts to actualize unconscious fantasies by pressing certain roles on the analyst. The analyst, he adds, possesses a free-floating role responsiveness that makes him susceptible to accepting such roles. "Naturally some analysts will be more susceptible to certain roles than others" (46). And some of these roles may provide a gratification to the analyst that is difficult to relinquish at termination.

Some of the analysts interviewed refer to role loss and role susceptibility. Dr. J, for instance, is now in the terminal phase of his work with a successful older man who came into treatment because of dissatisfaction with his career, marriage, and parenting. Over the course of the analysis, the patient has become more able to take pleasure in his accomplishments, and Dr. J has observed that he—Dr. J—derives considerable pleasure from helping the patient appreciate himself. Dr. J has become aware that in this countertransference role he is playing the loving son that he never has been, that he is doing what he has longed to do—and has never been able to do—for his own "unworthy" and devalued father. He confesses to fantasies that his patient, eternally grateful, will "publish my books, lend me money, sponsor me." And he says that termination is requiring him to work through, at a deeper level, his anger and disappointment regarding his own father. It will also, of course, require him to relinquish his gratifying good-son role, the loss of which, he now recognizes, "made me not eager to push termination forward."

Analysts may sometimes be susceptible to a role precisely because it is one they have played before and because in accepting this role they recapitulate a relationship important in their own as well as the patient's history. The impending loss of this role may thus arouse anxiety in both participants.

Dr. K, in the terminal phase of his work with a chronically depressed woman, became caught up in his patient's concerns about damage and intactness, concerns expressed in the fantasy that her wholeness depended on the analyst's presence and that the end of analysis would mean the end of that wholeness. Like his patient, Dr. K's mother had assigned him the role of being her "completion" and had viewed any separation from him as damaging. And Dr. K became aware that "I was being terribly thick; I was missing obvious things in the analysis" in an unconscious effort to avoid the harm that termination would bring to his patient = mother. By analyzing his countertransference, Dr. K was able to terminate the analysis and also to relinquish what he terms "my omnipotent fantasy of being responsible for my mother's well-being."

A different aspect of loss that termination presents to the analyst may appear in cases described by Annie Reich (1951, 28) as those "in which the activity of analyzing is used in some way for extraneous unconscious purposes" and where the patient "is not a real object but is only used as a fortuitous tool." The analysis, for instance, may on occasion serve the analyst as a tool for furthering professional ambitions—expressed, perhaps, as the wish to impress a senior colleague by doing a brilliant analysis on the colleague's child. Or there may be a wish to win a competitive victory over one's classmates by conducting a quick analysis and graduating, or to please authority figures at the institute with a "complete" and "correct" analysis. For obvious reasons, these issues seem to come up more often among the younger analysts, as in the example given by Dr. L.

Dr. L's first case was a woman with an obsessional neurosis and strong masochistic tendencies. After three and a half years, analysis had yielded some degree of character change, though a stubborn demand for her father's love remained. When she started talking about termination, both Dr. L and his supervisor decided she'd gone, for now, as far as she could. A termination date was set for six months in the future, at which point Dr. L began feeling guilty.

He was, for many reasons, extremely happy to see her leave—she came at too early an hour in the morning, she paid him an exceedingly low fee, and he found her masochism to be particularly unpleasant. Yet, as he faced the end of the case, he believed that he had short-changed her. He wanted to tell her the treatment had been a fraud. He felt that he had used and misused her to forward his professional ambitions. He felt very guilty.

In exploring this guilt, Dr. L was forced to look at a more deep-seated guilt, which was tied to a piece of as yet unexamined behavior: his search for mentors who, in exchange for what he called "ass-kissing" conduct, would assure him that he was indeed a good boy. Eager for such assurances from his current institute mentors, eager "to do it right and be a good boy," he had analyzed his patient in a rigidly "correct" and orthodox way. As a result, he explains, his work had been too cautious, constricted, and unimaginative.

Completed case or not, Dr. L decided he couldn't remain so damagingly complaint. "Fuck it," he said, "I won't play this game anymore." In the final months, his analytic work grew far less rigid—"I analyzed it *my* way and wrote it up honestly." His patient, in turn, began to speak of early oral issues involving her mother, which clarified her demands for her father's love. By the end of the analysis, Dr. L was feeling quite good about his work. And he says that he now is no longer inclined to seek mentors.

For Dr. L, the search for the approbation of mentors was a way of absolving old feelings of guilt. But if he was to become a good psychoanalyst, he had to let go of that approbation. "I've been very comfortable since then without the help of mentors," he observes. "I guess I never realized how much of my work with that woman served as a focal point in resolving this issue."

Analysis may also be used as the tool of the analyst's therapeutic ambitions—expectations, often unrealistic expectations, that must be given up at termination. Relinquishing one's perfectionism, one's savior fantasies, or one's overestimation of analysis may prove a difficult loss in the terminal phase.

In "After the Analysis . . ." Schmideberg (1938) talks about the fantasies of patients who believe that, having been "fully analyzed," they will be "blissfully happy, perfectly balanced, superhumanly unbiased, and absolutely free from" guilt, anxiety, aggression, pregenital interests, polygamous tendencies, bad habits, and neurotic symptoms (122). Schmideberg notes that although many analysts can readily analyze a patient's skepticism regarding treatment, such "overestimation of analysis, so long as it is not too glaringly absurd, is more easily condoned because it is flattering to the analyst and coincides with his own idealization of analysis" (132). She later adds that "the great possibilities of analytic therapy are likely to stimulate the ideas of grandeur inherent in us all" (142).

Offered Schmideberg's observations for comment, Dr. M nods her head in recognition and admits with a rueful smile, "I shift uneasily in my seat." She then discusses what for her is the most significant termination loss— "relinquishing my view of what the patient could have possibly become, reconciling myself to what the patient doesn't get worked through in the analysis." "In a way," muses Dr. M, "I'm always searching for the Holy Grail—for the resolution of problems that don't get resolved." She talks about her wish to analyze what she calls, quoting Winnicott, the patient's "true self"—that early, helpless, absolutely vulnerable self that so rarely reveals itself in an analysis. Without the analysis of this true self, Dr. M believes, an analysis is to some degree incomplete—not in the rigid, perfectionistic sense of "I have failed to purge you and make you pure" but in the sense that the therapy has failed to provide a setting of such safety that the patient can run the risk of revealing this self.

Dr. M describes a patient who came to her in her late forties, a depressed woman who had severe problems with adjustment and coping and who was involved in a disastrous affair. Over the course of the analysis, this patient ended the affair, entered into a relationship with a much more appropriate and emotionally supportive man, and found work as a highly gifted dance therapist. Nevertheless, she stubbornly maintained her great resistance to becoming aware of, and thus being able to tolerate, any of her own negative feelings.

"In her own work," comments Dr. M, "she had a fantastic ability to recognize other people's symbolically expressed pain and to help them get some relief from it without having to spell it out. She could accept in her patients what she couldn't accept in herself. She could get her patients to accept a kind of relief from her that in our work she refused to accept from me."

In supporting this patient's wish to terminate after seven or eight years of analysis, Dr. M had to make her peace with the fact that "this was it." The patient had found useful work and had found love, and "though I found it unbelievable that I could formulate things so clearly and she could continue to ignore them," says Dr. M, "my head had gotten sore from being banged against a stone wall."

The work with this patient, explains Dr. M, crystallized something for her about her "search-for-the-Holy-Grail tendencies" and about the limits of analytic work. She urges herself to consider the metaphor of a gnarled tree, which becomes twisted in certain ways as a young sapling and which no kind of horticultural effort will straighten out. Yet, yet . . . "I haven't totally given up the search." So, at terminations, she confronts the incompleteness of the work, her failure to analyze the patient's true self, her sense of loss at again not being able to find—for her patient and for herself—the Holy Grail.

Dr. C, voicing a similar view—at one point with tears in his eyes—talks about those patients whose early devastating experiences with separation leave them impaired in certain ways that analysis cannot really hope to resolve. To accept that analysis with these patients has certainly been helpful but has not met the magical expectations either of the patient or of the analyst is, for Dr. C, a significant aspect of the loss at termination. He has dealt with some of this sense of loss by becoming more involved in working with children, who, he says, are considerably more accessible to help with such early traumas. A former patient of his, having learned of his success with young children, expressed the envious wish that he could have done as much for her—an adult. Dr. C, consoling both of them, responded gently, "If it hadn't been for you I couldn't have done it."

Sometimes the issue is not the analyst's overly high expectations of analysis but the analyst's overly high expectations for the patient. And at termination analysts may have to part with goals they have for their patients that the patients simply don't have for themselves.

Dr. F, for instance, struggled with this issue in the terminal phase of her work with a woman she describes as "a crackerjack intellectually, who opted for something quite below her capacity because her family relationships and her genuine wish for a quieter kind of life were more important to her than her professional ambitions." Dr. F indicates that she was well aware of what *she* would have opted for and that she did try to steer her patient in that direction. It is not always clearly cut, she points out, whether a decision to settle for less is attributable to a neurotic fear of aggression and competition or to an appropriate choice of lifestyle. Thus, in the analysis, "there was quite a thorough investigation of what, if any, was the patient's pathology—and of how my own values interfered." Dr. F at last accepted the idea that her patient indeed had made the right decision and that "she probably won't, at age sixty-five, say, 'Why didn't my analyst kick me in the behind?'" She also accepted that, out of appropriate respect for her patient's autonomy, she must let go of her higher goals for her patient.

Therapeutic ambitions may be an issue at termination if *life goals* have not been distinguished from *treatment goals*. In his discussion of this subject, Ernst Ticho (1972, 315) defines life goals as those "the patient would seek to attain if he could put his potentialities to use" and treatment goals as those concerned with the "removal of obstacles to the patient's discovery of what his potentialities are." The latter, claims Ticho, are realistic goals of the analytic work. The former are not. The analyst who fails to make a distinction between these two goals and who fails to relinquish the expectation that the patient's life goals can be achieved in the analysis will either feel a sense of disappointment and anxiety at termination or will detain the patient too long in analysis.

Annie Reich (1951, 28) makes the further point that the analyst's therapeutic ambitions "can lead to . . . hostility against the patient who fails to give his analyst the narcissistic gratification of becoming cured by him." Dr. D develops this theme as he looks back with amusement and horror at his response to the termination of his first analyzed case.

His patient, a professional woman in her late thirties, had come for treatment after being hospitalized for a month with severe depression. She was living with her mother, who drove her back and forth to work, she had no social life outside her family circle, and her only sexual experience had been a one-time intercourse at age seventeen. By the end of treatment, the connection between her oedipal conflicts and her tie to her mother had been analyzed, and she was able to move out of her mother's home, live independently, and enter a quite satisfactory sexual relationship with a man. Although she had steadfastly refused to analyze her transference wishes regarding Dr. D—using a maddening vagueness as her chief defense—the patient announced in her final hour, without any vagueness at all, "I always had the idea that I was going to marry you, but it's not going to be." She told him that she would remember him on her deathbed, thanked him, and left.

Dr. D agrees that by any reasonable set of standards the results of this analysis were "fantastic." Indeed, on the basis of this completed case, his institute invited him to graduate. There were, however, certain highly narcissistic wishes that Dr. D had not fulfilled through this case. Rather than relinquish these wishes and make his peace with their loss, he did an outrageous thing: He refused to graduate.

Why did he do it? He was furious, he says, with his supervisor, who, like his own mother, matter-of-factly accepted his accomplishments without any praise, enthusiasm, or pleasure. He was furious, too, with his patient, whose farewell line about marrying him had persuaded him that, if only she had allowed it, he could have analyzed those transference wishes. And, of course, he was furious—probably most of all—at himself, "for failing to produce the perfect analysis, for failing to tie up everything in a knot."

Although Dr. D's therapeutic ambitions did not seem to impair his excellent work with his patient (who went on to marry and to handle many life difficulties with great fortitude), his behavior at termination, he acknowledges with a sigh, "was an incredible piece of self-destruction." It delayed his graduation and slowed by several years his promotion to a teaching and training analyst. But it also, not surprisingly, prompted him to examine his narcissism and then to seek further help through a second analysis.

Whereas narcissistic wishes are surely expressed through the analyst's therapeutic ambitions, Schmideberg (1938, 138) suggests that "narcissistic gratification . . . is not the most important motive in excessive ambition for one's patients." The more important motive, she contends, is the analyst's superego drive: "The analyst feels he must improve his patient . . . as he should have improved himself."

Schmideberg's comments must resonate with those analysts who regret what they haven't accomplished in their own analyses. For as they let go, in the terminal phase, of some hopes and dreams they have harbored for their patients, they also may finally have to let go of some hopes and dreams they have harbored for themselves.

One analyst spoke regretfully of mistakes he had made in his life, mistakes he expected analysis to repair, mistakes in some ways similar to those of a patient with whom he had recently terminated. For both himself and his patient, part of the loss to be dealt with in the terminal phase was the loss of this hope that the mistakes could be undone. "What I had to work through once again," he remarks, "was the fact that I had to accept them. What I had to work through once again was the fact that I can, that I have to, live with my imperfections."

THE INTEGRATIVE FUNCTION OF LOSS REACTIONS

The end of every analysis is a time when, to some extent, something must be relinquished, let go of, lost. But it also may be a time during which the analyst—as well as the patient, of course—can work through, or work through again, his or her reactions to loss.

Ernst Ticho (1972, 328) suggests that "countertransference difficulties play a larger part in the termination phase than in other phases of the analysis." I believe these interviews show why this may be true. For they show that termination involves many different kinds of loss—the loss of a whole, real object; the loss of some identified-with part of the object; the loss of a healing symbiotic relatedness; the loss of some especially pleasing role; the loss of a host of professional and therapeutic ambitions; and the loss of the analyst's dream of his or her own perfection.

Termination may, indeed, entail significant loss experiences. But if properly understood, the many different responses to loss can serve as valuable tools in the work with the patient. And, if properly understood, they can also serve as valuable tools in the analyst's continuing self-analysis.

In an early discussion of countertransference, Freud (1910, 145) writes that "no psychoanalyst goes further than his own complexes and internal resistances permit." Decades later, in "Analysis Terminable and Interminable" (1937, 248–249), he states that "the special conditions of analytic work do actually cause the analyst's own defects to interfere" and recommends that analysis become "an interminable task."

Gitelson (1952, 4), elaborating on Freud's point, notes that "no analyst enters upon the analysis of another person without residual potentialities for reaction either to the patient, the patient's material, the patient's transferences, or the patient's real attitude toward him as a real person." However, he adds, "a countertransference reaction, if the analyst is 'open' enough to analyze it, can be an integrative experience along the long road of interminable analysis" (7).

It is this integrative aspect of the analyst's response to loss that I found of particular interest in my research. In several of the interviews the analysts—often to their own surprise—traced how they had used a patient's termination phase to resolve some piece of their own unfinished business:

- to work through the oedipal denigration of the father (Dr. J);
- to relinquish the wish to undo the mother's castration (Dr. K);
- to deal with guilt without resorting to self-betraying acts of reparation (Dr. L);
- to convert certain magical strivings into a useful and gratifying sublimation (Dr. C);
- and, in the case of Dr. D, to confront and tame his self-destructive narcissism.

Gertrude Ticho (1967) notes that among the activities that analysts can engage in to forward their own self-analysis, "the most important, as well as the most rewarding, activity is the continuous self-investigation of countertransference phenomena" (314). And even if self-analysis fails to produce any truly new insights, there is a "working through of repetitive patterns with deeper and more extensive understanding" (316).

It is no doubt true that the experience of loss in the terminal phase can call forth countertransference resistances, which may, if left unanalyzed, result in holding the patient in treatment too long or in premature dismissal to avoid the pain—the analyst's pain—at the loss.

But Anne Reich reminds us that "the special talent and the pathologic" are often two sides of the same countertransference coin (1951, 29).

And Gitelson reminds us that countertransferences exist in every analysis, enabling the analyst—if he or she can perceive and integrate them—to become a "vital participant in the analysis with the patient" (1952, 10).

NOTE

Permission received to republish from *Psychoanalytic Inquiry* 2 (1982): 399–418.

REFERENCES

Balint, M. 1950. "On the Termination of Analysis." *International Journal of Psychoanalysis* 30: 196–199.

Buxbaum, E. 1950. "Technique of Terminating Analysis." *International Journal of Psychoanalysis* 31: 184–190.

Cohen, M. 1952. "Countertransference and Anxiety." *Psychiatry* 15: 231–243.

Eissler, K. R. 1975. "On Possible Effects of Aging on the Practice of Psychoanalysis: An Essay." *Journal of the Philadelphia Association of Psychoanalysis* 2: 138–152.

Firestein, S. K. 1978. *Termination in Psychoanalysis.* New York: International University Press.

Freud, S. 1910. "The Future Prospects of Psychoanalytic Therapy." In *The Standard Edition of the Complete Psychological Works of Sigmund Freud [SE],* ed. J. Strachey, 11: 139–152. London: Hogarth.

——. 1915. "Observations on Transference Love." *SE* 12:159–171.

——. 1937. "Analysis Terminable and Interminable." *SE* 23: 211–253.

Gitelson, M. 1952. "The Emotional Position of the Analyst in the Psychoanalytic Situation." *International Journal of Psychoanalysis* 33: 1–10.

Racker, H. 1957. "The Meanings and Uses of Countertransference." *Psychoanalytic Quarterly* 26: 303–357.

Reich, A. 1951. "On Countertransference." *International Journal of Psychoanalysis* 32: 25–31.

Robbins, W. S., reporter. 1975. "Termination: Problems and Techniques." *Journal of American Psychoanalytic Association* 23: 166–176.

Sandler, J. 1976. "Countertransference and Role-Responsiveness." *International Review of Psychoanalysis* 3: 43–47.

Schmideberg, M. 1938. "After the Analysis . . ." *Psychoanalytic Quarterly* 7: 122–142.

Searles, H. 1979. *Countertransference and Related Subjects.* New York: International University Press.

Ticho, E. 1972. "Termination of Psychoanalysis: Treatment Goals, Life Goals." *Psychoanalytic Quarterly* 41: 315–333.

Ticho, G. 1967. "On Self-Analysis." *International Journal of Psychoanalysis* 48: 308–318.

Tower, L. 1956. "Countertransference." *Journal of the American Psychoanalytic Association* 4: 224–255.

Weigert, E. 1952. "Contribution to the Problem of Terminating Psychoanalyses." *Psychoanalytic Quarterly* 21: 465–480.

CHAPTER 3

MISSING MYSELF

SANDRA BUECHLER

WHEN I was with Barbara,[1] I almost believed in God. God was one of the few explanations for her radiance that made any sense to me. Her face had its own light. It had, in fact, a whole complement of weather conditions. Brief showers would sometimes magically give way to sunshine. No matter how long clouds prevailed, I always knew the sun would eventually shine through. This continued throughout my three-times-per-week treatment of her, which lasted for more than a decade.

I couldn't look at her smiling face without feeling joyful, though not sure why. I firmly asserted what her future held, as though I saw it clearly. I *knew*. I allowed myself brief fantasies of growing old beside her.

I was quite aware that I was different from my usual self when I was with her. But it didn't really feel so much like I had changed. Rather, the world seemed different, and I had just responded naturally to it.

Barbara's lively beauty was a secret from herself. I found it astonishing that she thought she was plain. It gave persuasive testimony to the power of the unconscious—both hers and mine. Looking in the mirror, Barbara could only see herself through her mother's eyes. I let myself hate her shadowy monster mother. This, too, was an unusual self-indulgence. But it seemed necessary for me to hate the woman who fed on Barbara's life so greedily. Hating Barbara's mother helped me feel I wouldn't let myself do something similar.

In some ways, Barbara reminded me of other strong women whose self-esteem has been battered. Barbara was too old to start her life again but not old enough to accept its tally as final. She was in her forties, newly self-aware enough to realize she should have married a soulmate but too spent to start looking for one. She found me, instead.

Barbara was an accomplished, beautiful woman who often saw herself as an unintelligent, ugly nobody. Shame was her lifelong companion.

When I was with Barbara, I was sure of myself. I knew my job as well as I knew my name. It was my job to help Barbara push her mother out of the way when she looked in the mirror. I needed to introduce her to her own smile, and how it radiated aliveness, and the pinpoints of light dancing in her eyes.

Losing Barbara meant losing the person I could be when I was with her. I focus on this loss here. I hope to understand what I have lost, besides her presence. Who could I have been, if Barbara hadn't left, to create herself elsewhere? For her sake, I am glad she left. A new life awaited her, full of professional and personal opportunity, in a rich intellectual environment well suited to bring out her gifts. I am genuinely happy for *her*. But what about *me*?

I used to believe that losing patients was bearable so long as we cut our losses to their minimum. If we could retain the inner object, we could bear the loss of the external object. In other words, if unresolved anger, regret, guilt, or any other negative feeling didn't keep me from having a good relationship with the internalized Barbara, I should be able to bear losing her actual presence in my office. This thought used to comfort me more than it does now. Experience has led me to two unavoidable conclusions.

1. I miss Barbara's body. No "inner object" has her fragrance or fills a chair the way she did.
2. I miss becoming all the Sandras I would have become for her sake.

Rilke (1934, 69–70) tells us that loving is "a high inducement for the individual to ripen, to become something in himself, to become world, to become world in himself for the sake of another person; it is a great, demanding claim on him, something that chooses him and calls him to vast distances." Thus, the child takes her first steps toward the arms of someone she loves, someone who also loves her. I don't believe that she takes her first steps toward the idea of someone but, rather, toward their arms. Throughout life, we become a world for the sake of another person. When I do treatment, I count on this. Over time, I have become a more convinced interpersonalist. Growth is always interpersonal. At least partially, it is both *toward someone* and *for someone*. Although at times it may be possible, I think it is less likely for us to grow for the sake of the idea of someone rather than for a *real* other. When a loving mother holds her arms wide open, she invites her toddler to brave first steps. Excited joy carries the child forward, forgetful of past bruises and brushes with pain and fear. I believe this never changes. Only love gives us the courage it takes to cover the vast distances of our first and last steps.

In treatment, the two of us create a world, one with its own phrases, memories, rituals, and jokes. It is fully alive so long as we are together. Hopefully, when we part something remains, but it is not the same. Barbara won't surprise me tomorrow. I won't change for her sake tomorrow. We won't invent a new phrase. We won't look forward to being together next week or think about what we should work on in the future. I might try to grow, some, for the sake of the *idea* of her, but it is not the same high inducement as it would be if she still brought her unmistakable ambience to my office.

WHILE SOMEONE ELSE IS EATING

> About suffering they were never wrong,
> The Old Masters: how well they understood
> Its human position: how it takes place
> While someone else is eating or opening a
> Window or just walking dully along . . .

> —W. H. Auden, "Musée des Beaux Arts"

Many have commented about the incongruity of loss against the backdrop of others leading their daily lives, unaware of the tragedy next door. We have the urge to shout, to break the silence and disturb the peace. It feels sacrilegious that everyday life continues unbroken. It seems an offense, an affront to the dead.

Yet when Joan Didion's husband, John, died and the doctor was hesitating about telling her, the social worker said it was okay to tell her, since "she's a pretty cool customer." As she left the hospital, she "wondered what an uncool customer would be allowed to do. Break down? Require sedation?

Scream?" (2005, 15–16). I think that, in general, society gives us conflicting injunctions about our responses to death. It's wrong to look too cool, but it is also wrong to lose control entirely. Of course, the expected response differs a great deal depending on the nature of the situation. But, often, it seems inappropriate to be unaffected but equally inappropriate to be totally unhinged.

But for us, as clinicians, when we lose a patient, how are we expected to act? And what are our own expectations of ourselves? Speaking for myself, I know I feel obligated to keep confidentiality; for example, I would not discuss with the next patient the termination of the patient who had just left. Even if the two know each other in some way, I would never say, "Boy, I am going to miss her!" It is precisely this problem, that confidentiality requires us never to talk to one patient about another, that convinced Ferenczi he had to abandon his experiment with "mutual analysis." We may choose to disclose other aspects of our lives, but we can't talk about our experience with one patient to another—or for that matter to anyone else, for the most part.

I think the pull, here, is to be a kind of "cool customer," in Didion's sense. But this can come at a cost. Perhaps the feel and meaning of it is different for each of us, but I will try to describe my own experience. I remember a last session with a patient I had seen for more than ten years. It was a "good" termination, in that the treatment had been helpful, and we were able to spend some time looking back and reflecting on our work together. Still, there was the inevitable sadness, along with many positive feelings. In the midst of actually saying goodbye, the buzzer sounded, announcing the next patient's arrival. I remember having a brief moment of embarrassment, as though I had been caught at something. Later, I questioned myself about this reaction. What was there to feel ashamed of?

I think, for me, buzzing in the next person before the departing patient left felt like I was being too "cool" a "customer." I was transitioning too smoothly. In Auden's language, I was "just walking dully along." I was resuming ordinary life before the body was cold, so to speak. Perhaps it also felt a bit like showing off, as though I were demonstrating that I could just move on. We are back in elementary school: someone is painfully taking their leave, and I am smugly announcing that I already have someone else to sit with in the cafeteria.

THE SHOCK OF EXPECTED LOSSES

In summarizing some first-hand reports of responses to a death, Joan Didion (2005, 46) suggests, "the most frequent immediate responses to death were shock, numbness, and a sense of disbelief." It seems very meaningful to me that human beings often respond to a death with surprise, in some sense, even when it has been long anticipated. Similarly, the termination of a treatment can have a surprising effect on the clinician, even if it had been planned well in advance. Perhaps the surprise is a reaction to grief's unexpected intensity. Or, maybe, when we anticipate losses we are thinking about them in the abstract, but when they happen, their concrete meanings become evident.

No matter how well planned a termination may be, I might still feel a shock when Monday morning, ten o'clock, rolls around and, for the first time, no one is at the door. Yes, I knew about the termination of the patient who used to come at ten on Mondays. But what I knew was the abstract *idea* that he was gone. It is only at ten on the first Monday after termination that I am shocked by the *actuality* of his absence from my life.

For me, the aspect of a treatment's termination that is hardest to realize is its impoverishment of my own self-experience. It is far easier (though it may be painful) to understand the loss of the patient. What is most difficult is to comprehend that because of this ending I myself am diminished. Some of my selves are gone. Persons I was becoming may never exist. This can be extremely hard to grasp, let alone accept.

I began treating one patient when she was still a teenager. On and off, we worked together until she was in her early thirties. I have not heard from her for many years now. I miss her. She was a lively, vibrant presence. I miss her physicality as well as her personality. But my sense of loss of *her* is laced with feelings about losing the part of *me* that she evoked. In her presence, I could revive an adolescence, in me, that had been interrupted by life events. In fact, it was hard to be over eighteen with her, though I did manage it some of the time. But her throaty laugh and twinkling eyes, her hearty health, kindled a younger, fuller-bodied me. Along with missing her, I miss that Sandra. It may be possible for me to access this self-state without her. But, with her, it was as natural, as simple, as breathing.

Writing about her is one of the few ways I can access her. The clinician does not have available grief's usual cleansing rituals. Whereas sadness over a loss can sometimes draw human beings closer together, losing a patient is a very solitary experience. Usually there is no one we can talk to who also knew the patient. We have no opportunities to reminisce, to share funny or touching moments with someone else who also had funny and touching moments with her. My experience with my patient existed in a kind of parallel universe. While we worked together, each of us was also knowing other people and living our lives. No one in my life ever met her, and no one in her life ever met me. People from her life could pass me in the street, and we would not recognize each other.

This means that some of the human repertoire for bearing loss is unavailable to me. I can't laugh or cry with her friends, her parents, and the partner and children she may or may not have. I can't imagine how she looks now. When I try, my mind's eye sees a woman much younger than she must be. My eye sees someone in early adulthood, but my mind knows that in reality she is approaching middle age. Even my memories of her are confused. Usually an old snapshot of someone can be compared with more recent shots. Remembering someone gains meaning when it can function as a prelude or harbinger of the person she became. But I may never know the woman my patient became. And I may never know the woman I could have become in her facilitating presence. We grow differently with each patient we treat. A treatment's termination interrupts our growth as much as it does the patient's. In fact, since termination is usually (hopefully) timed to suit the patient's needs, it may be particularly ill timed to suit our own.

The interpersonal viewpoint holds that the analyst grows along with the patient and that each analytic "couple" is unique. So when my everlastingly teenage patient left treatment, I lost the partner that would have helped me bring out some aspects of myself. And I lost her, and these aspects of myself, in a more total way than would be the case in any other context. I am prohibited from the comforts of reminiscing about her with anyone who knew her. I may never know who she became or did not become. I can't even know whether or not I will ever hear from her or hear about her. I think some of these unique aspects of the treatment relationship can exacerbate the shock of the actuality of a termination. Being prepared for the idea of ending a treatment by talking about it for a period of time may not adequately prepare us for the actuality of what it is like when it occurs. Perhaps, in a sense, we are never really prepared for significant losses. But the frame, boundaries, and peculiarities of the treatment can add to the effect of the loss, for both partners.

This is further complicated when the patient is in the field. In one sense, the separation may never be absolute, because information about the other may be easy to access. But in another sense, confidentiality takes on the greatest significance. For example, when I treat someone who is in training, that person has to be able to rely on my utmost adherence to confidentiality. I may be supervising his best friend, teaching his class, and having lunch with a member of the committee that will decide whether he will graduate this year. My patient must be sure that I can keep our work entirely separate from all my other interactions.

Those of us who have been in this role repeatedly are accustomed to its challenges. What I feel is less often recognized is the effect on the analyst of the compartmentalization that our role encourages us to use. In a sense, it might be easier for me to navigate some social situations, conferences, and meetings if I could "forget" whom I have analyzed and what I know about them. Of course, that is not possible or even desirable. But there are moments when it certainly would be convenient.

What this can mean in practice is that when I terminate treatment with someone in the field they enter a kind of limbo. Termination never attains the clarity it can reach with other patients. It may, then, be even harder to grieve. When we are not sure a loss is permanent, the uncertainty can bolster our reluctance truly to accept it. That may actually delay or interfere with grieving. With people in training it is unusually important that I can keep information about them in a separate "box," yet it is more difficult than usual.

I probably lose more potential "selves" when someone in the field terminates. Who I was becoming with them probably had more dimensions. It is likely that there were moments when we lived together on a theoretical plane. At other moments, the implication that we know people in common hung in the air, usually unelaborated but present. A mutual understanding of the hardships and joys of analysis could be assumed, to some extent. I think that, at least for me, more "channels" are open in me when I treat people in the field. This widens my potential gains from the work but also my losses when it is over.

Elsewhere (2004, 2008) I have written about the similarities between a treatment's termination and a death. Here I would like to highlight a difference between them. When a patient wants to terminate, there is often a pull on the clinician to agree with it. Sometimes the patient implies that resistance on the clinician's part must be self-serving. This is likely to be true, to some degree, since the treatment serves some of our needs. But I think it is often the case that a termination can be welcomed and agreed upon. It is, in a way, a graduation. We can both be happy for the ratification of our accomplishments together. Of course, there are times when patients want us to ratify more than we feel has been truly accomplished. But in more fortunate moments, a termination is an occasion of mixed sadness and joy.

On the other hand, while death can sometimes bring relief, I think it is not generally associated with joy. It is true that some cultures celebrate wakes, and many funeral services, conducted as a part of a religious observance, include some form of celebration of the life that was lived. But (usually) we are not asked to agree with death, as we are (more often) with termination. I think this adds a moral dimension to how we conduct the end of a treatment. Colleagues often ask consultants how to "handle" a patient who wants to terminate. They want to figure out the "right" stance. Generally, death does not ask for or wait for our agreement. Of course, there are exceptions. But I think the clinician is unusually likely to run into certain moral dilemmas. Patients ask us to advise them objectively as to whether they should terminate a treatment we have a stake in (in many senses). While there are times the clinician wants the patient to terminate before the patient wants to end the work, more often it is the patient who first expresses the desire to leave.

So, with termination, the clinician has to make complicated clinical and ethical judgments, deal with losing the patient, and deal with losing further development of some of her own potential "selves." In my view, quite a tall order!

GRIEVING APPROPRIATELY

The narrator in Philip Roth's *Portnoy's Complaint* (1969) was mystified as a boy by how his mother could survive when she never sat down and ate. At meals, she was always standing and serving others. Like the self-sacrificing mother, the analyst often feels expected to be solely invested in the patient's welfare. This raises very complicated issues. Previously (2010), I have suggested that the analyst's investment needs to be primarily non-narcissistic. What self-interest in the analyst is compatible with doing good work? How is this "appropriate" self-interest manifested at the end of the treatment?

Put another way, I think the deals we make unwittingly in a treatment often go unnoticed until the end, when they become impossible to ignore. If a patient brings me access to parts of the wider world, or parts of myself, that I wouldn't know on my own, I am likely to become acutely aware of this at termination. Of course, more concretely, the financial aspect of the arrangement can also become a focus when the treatment ends.

So often I hear clinicians feeling shame and guilt about any self-interest they have. Especially when the patient mentions termination, we often are desperate to hide our own investments. We find rationales (or rationalizations) for why the *patient* needs the treatment to continue. We may become highly anxious lest the patient figure out that we need the income, or the hours toward our analytic requirements, or the pleasure the patient brings us, or the self-development the work affords us, or other gratifications.

This reluctance to admit our gratifications complicates the grieving process when the work ends. There are feelings we can't permit ourselves. For example, we can't be angry on our own behalf. We can't heed Dylan Thomas's advice not to go gently into that good night. If we have anxiety or fear about losing too many patients, we certainly can't express that. If we feel shame that we lose more patients than we imagine our colleagues lose and believe this reflects our inferior clinical talents, we had better cover this up. If we think that we lose patients because we don't really put effort into our work, we are likely to want to hide that, too. If losing a particular patient evokes painful loneliness, we are likely to try to keep that to ourselves as well. Just what aspects of our feelings on our own behalf are within bounds?

Most often, I would suggest, we are allowed to feel sad and to say we will miss the patient. We may feel it is acceptable to feel happy that the treatment has come to a "successful" conclusion. If the termination is abrupt and decided upon by the patient without our input, we may feel entitled to express anger, in some form. If the patient suddenly decides to terminate, we can certainly express surprise.

From another angle, therapists have no trouble admitting to vicarious traumatization, nowadays. But what about other vicarious feelings? What about vicarious romance, ambition, achievement, lust, revenge, or joy?

And how do we let go of all the glimpses of other professions and, more generally, of other lives that we are privileged to experience? What about the education about relationships that we often get from our patients and bring into our own personal lives?

THE CLINICIAN'S NON-NARCISSISTIC INVESTMENTS

When earlier I suggested that our investment in a treatment should be non-narcissistic, I do not mean to proscribe self-interest. To me, a non-narcissistic investment means that we shouldn't need to use the outcome of the treatment to prove our own worth. I believe that our task is to be fully, but not narcissistically, invested. But what kind of investment in a treatment is non-narcissistic? In other words, what can we allow ourselves to want from doing treatment, without abusing our position? This section will briefly spell out several benefits clinicians can derive from our work, without using patients to prove our worth.

PURE JOY

> satisfaction is a lowly
> thing, how pure a thing is joy.

> —Marianne Moore, "What Are Years?"

The first benefit of clinical work I will mention is the joy it can bring. Elsewhere (2008), I have called joy "the universal antidote" because I see it as the emotion that can modulate all our negative feelings and make them bearable. What brings each of us joy is personal and a product of our own histories. Yet joy itself is a universal feeling. It functions as an antidote in that joy can potentially counterbalance anger, anxiety, fear, sadness, regret, shame, guilt, and loneliness. Thus, if anger is fundamentally a response to an obstacle, joyous experience tells us that some obstacles can be overcome. The joyous feeling of having what it takes to triumph can modulate the feeling of being insufficient, a painful aspect of shame, anxiety, and fear. Joy balances the sadness of losses with the uplift of gains. Joy connects us to one another, overcoming our loneliness. In short, while all of the negative human feelings may bring us down, moments of joy lift us back up. Joy is uniquely suited to be the universal antidote, in that it makes all of the pain in life more tolerable. But what exactly is joy, and how can we get joy from doing clinical work?

Here are some descriptions of joy: "Joy, then, is what we experience in the process of growing nearer to the goal of becoming ourselves" (Fromm 1976, 106). "Joy is often accompanied by a sense of harmony and unity with the object of joy and, to some extent, with the world" (Izard 1977, 271). Schachtel (1959, 42) defined "real," as opposed to "magical" or omnipotent, joy as "a feeling of being related to all things living." Heisterkamp (2001, 839) contrasted anxiety and joy: "Whereas anxiety reflects psychic distress in connection with problems of structuring, joy is the expression of successful (re)structuring. It is the feeling of self-discovery, of a new beginning, and of self-renewal."

It seems to me that these authors are suggesting that two significant sources of joy come from being able to connect to humankind as a whole and being able to know our selves more profoundly. I have explored these more fully elsewhere (2008, chap. 5). Here I highlight joy's role as an aspect of the clinician's non-narcissistic investments in treatment.

Many authors, both analytic and nonanalytic, have described the joy of identifying with humanity as a whole or with life itself. Frankel (2003, 22) put it simply when she said, "We experience joy when we feel a sense of oneness and connectedness." Treatment gives the clinician many opportunities to identify with life. In another paper (2002, 618), I wrote about a moment with a patient where I let myself enter the patient's world, losing track of myself, floating into the experience. I think these moments are not uncommon in the clinician's daily life. For one instant, we are free of the constraints of time, place, and identity that usually define us. There can be a kind of joy in this unmoored state.

But probably just as frequent are the moments in treatment when we come to a heightened awareness of our own individual identity (as well, perhaps, as the patient's). Biancoli (2002, 597) put it this way: "authenticity is encountered along the road to individuation, and repeated experience thereof should occur in analysis on the part of both the analysand and the analyst." Treatment gives both participants endless chances to know themselves through contrast with another person. The assumptions we each make about life, about ourselves, and about others are highlighted when they differ with the assumptions made by the other participant. Thus, a patient discovered how competitive he expects people to be by experiencing me as not interested in competing. When another patient told me the story of a professional meeting she attended and I wondered out loud why she didn't voice her opinions, she pointed out that, alternately, she might have preferred to remain quiet. I was, on the other hand, assuming that something inhibited her from speaking. Each of us has had an opportunity to know ourselves and the other person through contrast. A profound and accepting knowledge of oneself and another can bring joy.

More generally, treatment can bring us the pleasure of watching and furthering transformations. Karen Maroda (2005) and I (2005) wrote about these "legitimate gratifications" from the work we do. Maroda argues for our honesty about the personal satisfactions that doing treatment affords us. The intimacy we experience with patients is a major component of these satisfactions. I highlight how much we may need to see underdogs triumph over adversities. We tend to want the "little engine" to feel it "could." It is likely that personal experiences inclined us toward reveling in these triumphs, and then our training probably reinforced these tendencies. What gratifies each of us the most is, of course, a function of our particular character predispositions, life experiences, and personal and professional backgrounds. But the wish to be of help to others, the need to feel hopeful about human potential, and the privileging of courage are likely components of our motivations.

VOYAGES TO INNER SPACE

A second benefit of clinical work is its fascination. Nina Coltart (1996, 27) was completely unabashed in her praise of her chosen field: "One of my strongest and deepest reasons for wanting to be a therapist was that, ever since early childhood, I could think of nothing that gave me more intense enjoyment than listening to people telling me their stories." She goes on to proclaim, "We have the most interesting job in the world." While this assertion would be hard to prove, I certainly join her in the spirit of her enthusiasm. Doing treatment affords us endless chances to be curious. I love how two poets have described the satisfactions of being interested in our selves and other people. The first, Mary Oliver ("When Death Comes," 1992, 269), firmly asserts

> When it's over, I want to say: all my life
> I was a bride married to amazement.
> I was the bridegroom, taking the world into my arms.

I think it is fair to say that clinicians, in general, would like to be brides married to amazement. It seems to me to be such a wondrous goal, to retain open-eyed curiosity.

The second poet, Jason Shinder ("Coda," 2008, 278) explains why he feels connected to a fellow poetry lover. After naming some of the similarities that are not the deepest sources of their connection, he says "it is / that you're my friend out here on the far reaches / of what humans can find out about each other." Clinicians and our patients certainly occupy those far reaches more often than most.

I remember being a college sophomore and attending a lecture in which a therapist talked about some of his clinical experiences. The stories were endlessly fascinating to me. I was genuinely amazed and put the feeling in the form of the question: "Can it be that he is actually paid for doing that?" Later, I reflected that this was the perfect profession for me, since each hour is different from the last. While not the only reason for my love of clinical work, the chance to be curious is a significant benefit.

Joy and curiosity seem to me to foster our non-narcissistic investments in clinical practice. *They involve us in the work itself and not in any particular outcome that would enhance our own pride.*

Elsewhere (2004), I suggested that paranoia and curiosity exist on a continuum. That is, extreme paranoia is the diametric opposite of extreme curiosity. In paranoia, all uncertainty is abolished. A theory is held to be absolutely true. It explains all otherwise unexplained phenomena. Thus, for example, a paranoid person who is troubled by upsetting thoughts might conclude, "I am having these thoughts because they are communicating to me via the airwaves," rather than, "I really don't know why I am having these thoughts."

The clinician is confronted with a potentially overwhelming array of unexplained information and observations. Often, the patient is begging for an explanation of them. Armed with a vast array of possible theoretical explanations, some therapists give in to the temptation to explain by oversimplifying. Holding our theories lightly, keeping curious wonder alive, can take great determination. But it allows us bring more open-mindedness to the process and invite the patient to engage in curious exploration.

I think the challenge of holding theories lightly has potential benefits for us. Curiosity is a tough taskmaster. But if practiced with passion, it can contribute to our humility. Wonderment can make us aware of the exceptions to our theories and help us stay generally alert. Hungry curiosity can sharpen our appetite for our chosen work and contribute to our motivation to retain (or regain) empathy for our patients.

I have come to view the analyst's empathic relatedness in treatment as a struggle to retain and regain emotional balance (2004, 2008). An intense feeling, such as acute shame, throws the analyst off kilter. But then access to another feeling facilitates bouncing back. Resilience, born out of a marriage of curiosity and love, allows one to regain access to a wide range of feelings. Referring to curiosity is my way of talking about Schafer's "analytic attitude." While engaging in an interpersonal interaction, curiosity helps us look at the exchange at the same time as we are living it out. Access to this attitude is as important for the patient as it is for the analyst, in my judgment. Both participants need to cultivate their capacity to be curious.

Love is what can inspire fervor for life itself and for a particular patient's richer life. It can be manifested in a sudden intensification of emotional availability. Just the patient's use of a phrase familiar to us both can remind me of expansive, loving feelings I have had for the patient in the past. We could say it kindles a more responsive self-state in me. Overcome by rage, regret, loneliness, shame, fear, or sorrow, our responsive range is narrowed, and we can't access other emotions, with their rich affective resources. For example, in a state of intense rage I can't fully resonate with sorrow. But just as a strong emotion can temporarily throw the balance off, so can fervent feelings restore it.

I have always been fascinated by artists who seem to me to express some of emotion theory's central tenets in what they create. For example, the fifteenth-century artist Albrecht Dürer captured a vital truth in his portrayal of melancholia as an imbalance of the "humours." In countless mythologies, human beings and gods are rescued by love. As analysts, we too can be restored to our full resourcefulness, by curious love. In his witty and wise essay "On Love," Adam Phillips (1994, 40) describes the conjunction of knowing and loving in psychoanalysis: "'Transference,' 'repression,' 'fetishism,' 'narcissism,' 'the riddle of femininity'—all these key psychoanalytic concepts confirm the sense that in psychoanalysis love is a problem of knowledge. That lovers are like detectives: they are trying to find something out that will make all the difference."

In the Bible, to "know" someone is to have sexual intercourse with them. An example can be found in Genesis (4:1): "And Adam knew Eve his wife, and she conceived." Knowing, like love, is a potentially fruitful form of penetration. In psychoanalysis, knowing is the form of loving that allows both participants to conceive themselves anew. Heinrich Zimmer (1948, 6) wrote that "the true dilettante will be always ready to begin anew." To me, beginning anew is a way of describing resilience, the capacity to recover emotional balance. In that sense, the analyst must be a true dilettante, ever ready to begin again, to love through curious knowing and know through profound love.

CHANCES TO ATONE

Clinical work provides unceasing opportunities to atone. The need to overcome guilt, regret, and secret shame stems from sources that are unique to each of us. Doctoring these wounds heals a breach. We become more whole, at peace, at one.

Elsewhere, I have described (2008) some of the ways doing clinical work can capitalize on our need to atone. Briefly, whatever we regret can motivate us to modulate unrecognized harmful impulses in ourselves and develop greater wholeness or integrity. Every clinical hour is an opportunity to make up for something, to own up to something, to "make good."

I think the wish to atone can enhance the clinical will. In other words, the profound wish to compensate for something can strengthen the determination to help people. Supervisors are prone to frown upon this motive in clinicians. I remember one such supervisor who advised young clinicians, "It is fine to *want* to help but problematic to *have* to help."

This sounds sensible, yet can we really tell the difference? It seems to me that a genuine longing to atone can contribute to the clinician's non-narcissistic investment in the work. Of course, it could also motivate a narcissistic wish to appear saintly. But still it can spur us on to want to render real service, regardless of the form it takes. In Gail Hornstein's (2000, 39) fine biography of Frieda Fromm-Reichmann, she quotes from Joanne Greenberg's descriptions of the noted analyst. Greenberg said that Fromm-Reichmann "would have swung from the chandelier like Tarzan if she thought it would help" her patient. I am sure that such dedication can help analysts atone, no matter what we might be atoning for. The chance to atone can be counted as one of the blessings that the profession offers.

BECOMING EXPERT LOSERS

In her beautiful poem, "One Art," Elizabeth Bishop (1979, 215) advises us to practice losing things. When we become good at it, we will be able to bear more and more significant losses. She tells us that "the art of losing isn't hard to master." Bishop directs us to "lose something every day." As analysts we have ample opportunity to put her suggestions into practice. Given that every treatment relationship ultimately ends, we all eventually become highly experienced losers. This capacity can come in handy in our other walks of life.

The philosopher Seneca once said that we spend our whole lives preparing to die. I take this to mean that we spend all our lives learning how to be good losers. By definition, at the time of our deaths we lose everyone we have known and everything we have ever been. How can we gain facility at losing?

Teachers, pediatricians, and other professionals also eventually lose everyone they encounter. But analysts lose aspects of *our selves* with each patient who terminates. I think it is fair to say that our professional losses more closely resemble the most devastating personal losses aging brings to human beings. When my patient John and I terminated treatment, I lost John *and* the Sandra I was with John. It is true that other professionals may feel particular clients bring out certain aspects of them, but nowhere is this more fully realized than in the analytic relationship. In analysis, a patient and I may co-create a Sandra that I hardly recognize. When that patient leaves, I may never see that "Sandra" again in exactly the same form. The loss of the "Sandra" I was with John heightens the pain of losing John. This is one reason why we have so much trouble with the termination phase. Often, we do termination badly, because we feel unready to lose the part of ourselves that a treatment conceived.

I have practiced Bishop's "art" for a long time. I can't tell how much facility I have gained. I still feel uninhabited when people leave. When the door closes for the last time, I feel smaller than usual. It is this moment that gives the term "shrink" its meaning for me.

As I age, am I better at losing friends because of the many patients who have left me? Perhaps I have gained a surer sense that however diminished I am, I can still survive. It seems to me that to practice Bishop's "art" we must be able to put up with the absurd. It doesn't make sense that someone began my Mondays, Wednesdays, and Fridays, for twenty years and, now, I don't know if they are still alive. In his poem titled "Grief," Matthew Dickman (2008, 228) captures this quality. He imagines making two piles, one of the names of people who have died, and another of those who still live. He muses about "how reckless it is / how careless that his name is in one pile and not the other." While I can usually explain why a patient moved from one pile to the other, there is always a lingering absurdity about it. As those who people my personal life switch piles, I will certainly be quite familiar with this absurdity.

In a more general sense, I would say that part of the non-narcissistic benefit of being an analyst is our great familiarity with life's rhythms. Comings and goings are always in the air. In theory, at least, we get used to them. Someone new comes to us, and we get used to being with each other. We accustom to a scent. It isn't new any more. Briefly foreground, it fades to background, and then, perhaps suddenly, it is gone. For a while, I can still imagine it, but I know that even that may not last for long.

Because of my vast experience losing people, am I better able than most to move away from the scent of someone gone and move toward the scent of someone new? Confidence has given me an edge. I have faith in myself as a good loser. "Good" in that I am usually aware of what I have lost. Practice has made me believe I will survive, although the "I" that survives will be diminished.

I think familiarity with gaining and losing may prepare me for making non-narcissistic investments in life. In a particularly striking analogy, Mitchell (1986, 153–181) suggested that one of life's challenges is to be able to expend effort building sand castles, knowing they will not last. Some are handicapped in their ability to build, because they can't care about what is temporary. Others are unable to realize that the castle won't be there forever. It is a human achievement to be able to create lovingly a fleeting castle.

As analysts, we have many chances to get used to investing profoundly in temporary shelters. Of course, constant exposure to this situation doesn't affect us all in the same way. Some of us actually become less able to build sand castles with gusto. Some insist on the castle's permanence, fighting termination until the patient insists on it. Others burn out, barely able to make wan efforts to build a castle they know won't last. But, despite these negative outcomes, there also exists the possibility that we can learn to accept the absurdity of lovingly carving turrets that won't outlive the tide.

The analyst who has become expert at loss, who can put her whole self in a temporary relationship, has some of the emotional equipment necessary to make non-narcissistic investments in patients' lives. That is, surviving the loss of Barbara (the patient I mentioned at the beginning of this chapter) may help me invest in the next person whose face almost makes me believe in God. To put it another way, every time I lose a Barbara, I have another chance to learn how to care more about her life than I care about her enhancement of *my* life. Every Barbara I lose, and every Sandra-with-Barbara I lose, gives me practice at painstakingly patting each grain of sand into its place. From the very first moment, I know what the tide will do. From the very first moment, I see the tide leveling my castle. With one eye (and one "I") I see its inevitable destruction, and with the other eye (and "I") I still create it.

ON BALANCE

Eventually we lose every treatment partner we ever have. While we may retain some of the personal qualities we developed in these relationships, we lose aspects of ourselves that only came alive in a very specific interpersonal context. Nevertheless we have opportunities for many joys, including the joy of participating in the lives of people that we come to care about. We get to take countless voyages into boundless inner space. We have many chances to fight for our own emotional balance, to atone for our own misdeeds, to retain and regain empathy, and to develop our capacity for losing gracefully, even losing parts of ourselves.

NOTE

1. Several details have been changed to protect the patient's confidentiality.

REFERENCES

Auden, W. H. 1940. "Musée des Beaux Arts." In *The Art of Losing: Poems of Grief and Healing*, ed. K. Young. New York: Bloomsbury, 2010.

Biancoli, R. 2002. "Individuation in Analytic Relatedness." *Contemporary Psychoanalysis* 38: 589–612.

Bishop, E. 1979. "One Art." In *The Art of Losing: Poems of Grief and Healing*, ed. K. Young. New York: Bloomsbury, 2010.

Buechler, S. 2002. "Joy in the Analytic Encounter: A Response to Biancoli." *Contemporary Psychoanalysis* 38: 613–622.

——. 2004. *Clinical Values: Emotions That Guide Psychoanalytic Treatment*. Hillsdale, N.J.: Analytic Press.

——. 2005. "Secret Pleasures: A Discussion of Maroda's 'Legitimate Gratification of the Analyst's Needs.'" *Contemporary Psychoanalysis* 41: 389–395.

———. 2008. "Modeling Self-Exposure: Discussion of Papers by Andrew Morrison and Donna Orange." *Contemporary Psychoanalysis* 44: 101–104.

———. 2010. "Developing a Sense of Professional Competence in Analytic Training." Paper presented at the Clinical Services Meeting, William Alanson White Institute, September 28.

Coltart, N. 1996. *The Baby and the Bathwater*. Madison, Wis.: International Universities Press.

Dickman, M. 2008. "Grief." In *The Art of Losing: Poems of Grief and Healing*, ed. K. Young. New York: Bloomsbury, 2010.

Didion, J. 2005. *The Year of Magical Thinking*. New York: Random House.

Ferenczi, S. 1988. *The Clinical Diary of Sandor Ferenczi*. Ed. J. Dupont. Cambridge, Mass.: Harvard University Press.

Frankel, E. 2003. *Sacred Therapy: Jewish Spiritual Teachings on Emotional Healing and Inner Wholeness*. Boston: Shambhala.

Fromm, E. 1976. *To Have or to Be*. New York: Harper and Row.

Heisterkamp, G. 2001. "Is Psychoanalysis a Cheerless (Freud-Less) Profession?: Toward a Psychoanalysis of Joy." *Psychoanalytic Quarterly* 70: 839–870.

Hornstein, G. 2000. *To Redeem One Person Is to Redeem the World: The Life of Frieda Fromm-Reichmann*. New York: The Free Press.

Izard, C. E. 1977. *Human Emotions*. New York: Plenum.

Maroda, K. 2005. "Legitimate Gratification of the Analyst's Needs." *Contemporary Psychoanalysis* 41: 371–389.

Mitchell, S. A. 1986. "The Wings of Icarus: Illusion and the Problem of Narcissism." In *Relational Psychoanalysis*, vol. 1: *The Emergence of a Tradition*, ed. S. A. Mitchell and L. Aron. Hillsdale, N.J.: Analytic Press, 1999.

Moore, M. 1941. "What Are Years?" In *The Art of Losing: Poems of Grief and Healing*, ed. K. Young. New York: Bloomsbury, 2010.

Oliver, M. 1992. "When Death Comes." In *The Art of Losing: Poems of Grief and Healing*, ed. K. Young. New York: Bloomsbury, 2010.

Phillips, A. 1994. "On Love." In *On Flirtation*. Cambridge, Mass.: Harvard University Press.

Rilke, R. M. 1934. *Letters to a Young Poet*. New York: Norton, 1984.

Roth, P. 1969. *Portnoy's Complaint*. New York: Random House, 1986.

Schachtel, E. G. 1959. *Metamorphosis*. New York: Basic Books.

Schafer, R. 1983. *The Analytic Attitude*. New York: Basic Books.

Shinder, J. 2008. "Coda." In *The Art of Losing: Poems of Grief and Healing*, ed. K. Young. New York: Bloomsbury, 2008.

Thomas, D. 1952. "Do Not Go Gentle Into That Good Night." In *The Poems of Dylan Thomas*. New York: New Directions.

Zimmer, H. 1948. *The King and the Corpse: Tales of the Soul's Conquest of Evil*. Ed. J. Campbell. Washington, D.C.: Bollinger Foundation.

PART II

WHEN A PATIENT DIES

There are things that happen everyone says
Could not be helped, there was nothing
Anyone could do. I am trying to believe that.
I try not to say every morning when the line
Of trees sharpens the bedroom window: If only.
If only I would have, he might have.

—"Trying To," Wendy Barker

EVERY TREATMENT begins with the knowledge, whether conscious or unconscious, that this is a relationship that is bound to end. At the same time, it often begins with the "fantasy of forever" (Robert Winer, personal communication). These interwoven themes form the backdrop and can influence the course of treatment, although one may not know how, until the end. For both patient and therapist, anticipating this future loss becomes part of the process and may be alternately avoided, denied, or minimized. The intersection between how patient and therapist contend with loss lies at the heart of the treatment and ultimately affects the course of the termination.

The death of a patient brings into relief the unique and highly complex quality of the therapeutic bond. The private nature of this work requires that the relationship remain set apart from our day-to-day lives, both for patient and therapist alike, yet at the same time, the intimacy of treatment makes the relationship an essential and meaningful one. When a patient dies, we may ask ourselves whether it is appropriate to attend the funeral or express our condolences to family members who often do not know us or, sometimes, even know of our existence. We often tell our colleagues that we have lost a patient, yet our mourning process unfolds largely in the shadows. As a profession, we have no customs or rituals to mark such a death. We may be inhibited by feelings of shame, as though having strong feelings for our patients is taboo. We feel bereft, but unlike with any other loss, the world may not recognize that we are mourning. The following four chapters bring us into the consulting room to share our authors' experiences at the time of their patients' death.

Anne Adelman movingly describes the painful and complicated mourning following a patient's unexpected and sudden death. She brings us through the process of coming to know and then, sadly, having to lose her patient. In this chapter, Adelman describes how, over the course of treatment, her patient Irina had discovered the wish to hold on to old suffering, "preserving the history of her pain" through artifacts and relics. Together they understood that this was Irina's way to preserve the integrity and validity of her experience: "I am here. This happened to me." In a similar way, in the aftermath of this patient's death, Adelman discovers in herself a parallel wish, the wish to hold on to a relic, a book that her patient had loaned her. She writes of "a secret sense of pleasure in still having the book with me, along with a pang of guilt: I wanted to hold onto something of hers, claim a part of her for myself, but I worried, as well, that having it was a subtle crossing of an analytic boundary." In this way, Adelman illustrates how patient and therapist form a bond that becomes increasingly meaningful and vital to each of them. She further points out that in the face of a patient's death the therapist lacks access to ordinary customs that mark and help to contain the loss. She writes, "The universal rituals surrounding death could serve the function of making her [Irina's] death real and begin to dissipate the feeling I had had in my office, that she was there one day and then, not the next." Thus, she highlights the unique and solitary nature of mourning the loss of a patient.

In the following chapter, Arlene Richards poignantly describes the grief she experienced following the death of a child patient whose parent had prematurely terminated her son's therapy the year before. Richards was haunted by her feelings of helplessness, which interfered with her ability to mourn and reawakened memories of earlier and painful losses. She suggests that "rather than viewing mourning as a process of moving through the defined stages of denial, rage, sadness, and acceptance, all of these emotions are experienced in doses, separated by periods of functioning in the world." Richards examines a number of defenses that protect an individual from feeling overwhelmed in the face of loss. Like all of our authors, she emphasizes that mourning is made bearable by the ability to share it with others.

In "When a Patient Dies," Sybil Houlding describes a five-year period in which three of her patients died. She examines the effect of these losses in light of her personal and professional development as well as in terms of the phase of the treatment each patient was in when they died. In each case, she struggles with alternating feelings of grief and anger. At the time of the third death, she begins to feel a dearth of psychic energy, almost as though she could not access the resilience that had sustained her through the earlier losses. A letter of thanks that she receives from a family member highlights her wish to feel "acknowledged as someone who had sustained a loss," a role each clinician struggles with in the face of a patient's death. Houlding also brings to light how a death in one's practice evokes earlier experiences of loss and informs how the therapist works through the grieving process.

The complexity of the therapist's response to a patient's suicide is discussed in Catherine Anderson's chapter, "When What We Have to Offer Isn't Enough." Here we read about how a close-knit community of colleagues provided the essential support to help weather a patient's suicide—or, in one case, a rash of suicides. Anderson explores the range of feelings the therapist may encounter, including isolation, shame, fear, and guilt. She writes, "We likely search, often obsessively, for any signs that we could have missed, feeling numbed with shock. Perhaps we rage against our helplessness—as well as the patient who caused it—and feel deep, isolating professional and personal shame."

In this section, each author traverses the middle-distance, lingering with the painful question of whether they could have done more, even somehow prevented the death. As therapists, we recognize our own wish to "have enough" for our patients—to ward off fate and protect them from mortality. We are repeatedly confronted with our limitations and fallibility in the face of inevitable loss, yet at the same time we are bolstered by the gains and growth that our patients may ultimately achieve.

CHAPTER 4

THE HAND OF FATE

On Mourning the Death of a Patient

ANNE J. ADELMAN

Death Speaks: There was a merchant in Baghdad who sent his servant to market to buy provisions and in a little while the servant came back, white and trembling, and said, "Master, just now when I was in the marketplace I was jostled by a woman in the crowd and when I turned I saw it was Death that jostled me. She looked at me and made a threatening gesture. Now, lend me your horse, and I will ride away from this city and avoid my fate. I will go to Samarra and there Death will not find me." The merchant lent him his horse, and the servant mounted it, and he dug his spurs in its flanks and as fast as the horse could gallop he went. Then the merchant went down to the marketplace and he saw me standing in the crowd and he came to me and said, "Why did you make a threatening gesture to my servant when you saw him this morning?" "That was not a threatening gesture," I said, "it was only a start of surprise. I was astonished to see him in Bagdad, for I had an appointment with him tonight in Samarra."

—"Appointment at Samarra," retold by W. Somerset Maugham (1933)

IRINA'S[1] GHOST has settled into the chair across from mine, in the exact spot that Irina occupied, three times a week, for nearly three years. I glance up and see her deep eyes dance at me; her smile is wry and sad. "You see," I hear her say, "it's just as I told you—if there's only a 1 percent chance that something bad will happen, it will happen to me." Her thick hair cascades around her. With an intense gaze, she wills me to undo the spell cast by her abrupt death and restore her to life.

It is only now that I understand that Irina, a lively woman in her forties and mother of two, had been preparing for death throughout her life—a checkerboard life marked by disruptions, disappointments, and loss. Irina was passionate and resilient in the face of adversity. Like a bold, vigorous trek through an exotic land, her therapy afforded far-reaching vistas colored by the rich memories she conjured from a lost childhood in a distant country. She would regale me with lively stories about her early years before a revolution tore apart her homeland and led her to flee permanently. Other times, she would invite me into her intimate thoughts like a warm host beckoning a willing and trusted guest into sacred rooms. We were joined together in a shared effort to find our way through the unmapped territory of her story of survival and renewal. I thought that with an assiduous and steadfast therapy, she would be able to break free from the constraints of her traumatic history and gather the full force of her intelligence and self-determination. I was right. Until, all of a sudden, things went horribly wrong.

During a routine physical exam, Irina was diagnosed with cancer. Fortunately, as diagnostic testing proceeded, her prognosis became increasingly favorable—she had a cancer that was typically treatable. Surgery was performed successfully, and in her sessions, we drew a joint breath of relief. Then, less than four months later, she died.

I was driving when I first heard the news. Stunned, I pulled the car over. My mind flashed on Irina's crooked smile and worried eyes as she left our last session. She had been preparing for what was expected to be a minor medical procedure. Instead, she never left the hospital. The procedure, a postsurgery follow-up meant to eradicate any residual cancer cells, had gone mysteriously wrong. No one seemed to know precisely what happened. Perhaps I never will.

That day, my mind was a jumble. I wondered, "What did I miss? How did it happen?" I had the sudden and distinct thought that she had known all along that she was going to die; she had simply enacted an elaborate charade by transforming herself from a healthy and vibrant woman into the caricature of an optimistic, curable cancer patient.

In my office the next Monday, I was bereft. I mentioned Irina's death to my close colleagues, but I found it hard to express my thoughts. At the hour of her usual session, I was alone. Staring at an empty chair, I sat there helplessly. I wondered if my other patients could sense her absence as palpably as I felt it. I remembered that she herself had always been tremendously aware of them and had opined about them, at times with glee, at times with malice, but always with enough punch to signal that she longed to be my one and only.

I stood and pulled out her file. Irina had given me several photographs that were meaningful to her, ones of herself with her husband, mother, and children—her universe's nodal points. In one photo, Irina is two years old. She is bedecked in a gorgeous frock with a bow in the back and another wide white bow in her hair. At her side is a statuesque young woman whose chin is tilted defiantly upward. This is her mother. She is holding her daughter's hand, yet she is remote, standing much taller than her small daughter and looking fiercely away, in the direction of the camera. She is seemingly unaware of the small figure beside her who clings tightly to her hand. Encircling the little girl's waist is the arm of her beloved nanny, whose face cannot be seen in the photograph.

As I examined the photo, the faces smile back at me. I was struck by Irina's vivacity, as I often had been in our sessions. The photograph captured her essence: her bright smile, her sea of black hair, and her dark eyes with pools of sadness and pain hidden far below. In life, her eyes had expressed what she could not put into words; now, I felt as if I were gazing through to her soul. The grief she had endured over the course of her life flooded through me.

A few days later, I arrived at a large, elegant hotel to attend the memorial service. A stream of people flowed through the doors. A poster-size photograph of Irina, looking radiant and alive, gripped me. A slideshow projected images of her with family members, on trips abroad, at formal gatherings, and in repose. Fascinated, I stared at the screen. Every photograph was calling out to me in some way. I felt her whisper: Here I am on that trip, right after I found out about what he'd done; here I am after we fought; there's that expensive jacket I bought that I didn't really want, I told you about that, remember? Here are my mother and father; see how she is looking at me, smiling with a frown? See how he seems dazed, absent? There's my stepmother; do you see her kind smile? And, here, here I am with my children.

As the slides slipped by one after another, I remembered a letter she had brought in just a few weeks ago from one of her children. Her daughter had drawn a picture of herself as a tree growing in a garden and her mother as the water sprinkling down on her, nourishing her. Now, I gazed at her daughter sitting in the front row, crumpled, tearful. It was uncanny to watch the scenes of her life—details of which she had spoken so many times—unfold before me here. I felt that I was looking at them as if from behind her eyes.

As I waited for the service to begin, I tried to match faces with names I had heard over the years. For the moment, I had stepped out of the confines of the therapy space and into the life—and death—of my patient. This was a glimpse into the patient's everyday world that analysts rarely get. I was oddly out of place, acutely aware of my unique relationship with her. In therapy, Irina had told me things about herself that she rarely gave voice to outside of the consulting room: how she'd felt when she woke in the middle of the night, how deeply she had buried her anger and hurt, how she'd feared she had failed her children, how shameful she had felt about the cancer. The topography of her inner landscape lay, stilled, within me.

I also felt grief for her children, siblings, parents, husband, and relatives. Wishing neither to expose herself nor to overburden others, she had kept most of her thoughts and feelings hidden from them. Perhaps what was most disconcerting about the memorial service was my sense that she had foreseen with eerie precision the events that I was now witnessing.

When Irina learned she had cancer, fearing the worst, she called to request an additional session. She said she had opted for surgery to remove the detected lump. That decision had been easy. Resolving what to say about her illness, and to whom, troubled her the most. To her, cancer seemed an overwhelming humiliation. Her body, now poked, prodded, and examined in excruciating detail, was violated and no longer in her control. The tumor represented a flaw on the surface of the perfectly smooth veneer she wished to present to the world. She pictured her postsurgery body disfigured, no longer intact. To be scarred exposed a defect. She spent much time fretting over whether she would be able to conceal her scar.

Feeling diminished and exposed, she could not imagine that her family and friends might provide comfort and support. Indeed, it was just the opposite; she dreaded their reactions and imagined that her cancer would be used against her to diminish her standing in her community. She pictured the intrusive questions others might ask—an image that was closely followed by the wish to pull out her frying pan and start swinging. The rageful feelings she summoned up provided her with only the barest protection from her underlying sense of vulnerability, hearkening back to the years of early loss and abandonment that the cancer had reawakened in her.

Irina detailed for me what the doctors had told her. The news seemed positive, and she had every reason to be optimistic. The type of cancer was considered to be at low risk for recurrence. Nonetheless, she agonized over the possibility of the worst outcome, convinced that she was the outlier, destined for catastrophe.

In anticipation of her surgery, Irina readied herself for death. She wrote letters to her children and her husband and placed them in safekeeping. She put her affairs in order and left specific instructions with the one family member in whom she had confided. Although I wondered whether she was perhaps exaggerating the actual danger she was in, I sensed the power of her conviction that her chances of survival were slim.

In one session prior to her surgery, Irina said that she had thought about writing a letter to me but had not been able to. We talked about what might have been in the letter had she written it, and she expressed to me, tearfully, her feelings that her therapy had affected her life deeply. She told me she had never before had someone in her life that she trusted absolutely. She laughed, remembering her recurrent wish to quit therapy whenever she was annoyed—by something I'd said, by the constraints of my schedule and my fees, by the thought that she was still in therapy while her husband had declared himself "cured." She acknowledged that she felt changed by the work we'd done together. In therapy, she had begun to repair both broken relationships and broken aspects of her self.

In the following session, she mused about her death. It seemed as though her diagnosis, in spite of its optimistic prognosis, gave her the freedom to contemplate what she had most feared. She pictured the life that would go on after her imagined death. She expressed her fears that her husband would be overwhelmed by the demands of the household and children. They carried on what she thought of as a sham, behaving as if he were the strong one, king of his castle, while she alternated between the roles of queen and handmaiden. In reality, she knew he was utterly dependent on her. Imagining the woman her husband might remarry if she died, she felt a wave of fury. She spoke tearfully about her daughters, sensitive and troubled girls who relied on their mother as their rock; she viewed them as highly vulnerable and poorly equipped to cope with loss.

Most of all, she pictured her funeral: masses of people, curious, saddened, but unable to comprehend who she had been and how she had felt. She bristled at their imagined oratories and at the gossipy gratification people would derive from her funeral. Her fantasies were rooted in her perception that she wielded an unusual power in her social sphere because, unlike the other women, she held herself apart, keeping her cards close to her chest, knowing all, revealing nothing. She saw herself as an object of both idealization and intense speculation. Poised, perfectly groomed, socially gracious, highly efficient, never late, never self-revealing, she knew that she prompted gossip and envy of her wealth, her position, and her seemingly happy marriage. She pictured her funeral as a huge event that people would be talking about for weeks afterward.

Before her surgery, Irina was told that, while recurrence was unlikely, further postsurgery treatment might be recommended. Irina tolerated the surgery well and recovered quickly. Afterward, she was given the positive news that no further treatment would be necessary after all. However, the germ of the idea had formed in her mind that only the follow-up treatment would fully protect her from recurrence. Unable to absorb the positive outcome of her surgery, she could not shake her conviction that she needed that follow-up treatment. She said that she could not bear the thought of being haunted forever by the specter of future recurrence.

Her physician attempted not only to reassure her but also to indicate to her that doing the follow-up treatment could bring with it its own risks. In session, Irina and I talked about her determination to pursue postoperative treatment, to outwit fate and stave off her vision of her inevitable, imminent death. She remained convinced that only this final treatment would reassure her that she had done everything she could. Only then, she felt, would she be able to consider herself free from risk. I felt torn during these discussions with her, wanting to help her take stock of the options available to her and to consider deeply all of the risks involved (Bernstein 1987). She brushed it off, viewing it as no more dangerous than swallowing a couple of Tylenol. I was concerned about her exposing herself to an apparently unnecessary treatment, but it seemed that I could make no inroads in the face of her resolve. In spite of the visible fatigue that had set in during her illness, her inner strength and persistence never faltered. She was determined to seek out and eradicate any stray cancer cells that might still be lurking in her body. She would not rest until she had done everything in her power to ensure that the cancer would never return.

It was a sad irony that Irina's sudden and wholly unanticipated death was the result of rare complications related to this follow-up treatment. We had both been confident that the worst was already over, that she was, as she put it, just buying herself the "premium insurance plan"—that her life would now resume fully and richly and absolutely free of the fear of cancer. Her sudden death startled and derailed me. I felt deeply sorrowful, knowing full well how intensely she had been fighting for her very existence. In our work together, we strove to find meaning in her life. In her absence, I was alone in my effort to make sense of her unfathomable death.

Now, at her service, I could not shake the ghostly echo of that session with her, just a few weeks earlier. Every detail was as she imagined, down to the pastries and tea being served in the foyer. The eulogies were brief and, I felt, failed to do justice to her intense personality and the untimeliness of her death. In my thoughts, I returned once again to the idea that Irina had needed to rehearse her own death, as if she were preparing, both consciously and unconsciously, for its occurrence. I began to wonder again, for the hundredth time, about her death.

Irina had been given an excellent, positive prognosis. She was practically cured. So why did she die? The medical answer was straightforward enough: an unexpected reaction to a generally well-tolerated treatment. But as her therapist, the more meaningful question was: how could I understand her death in the context of her life?

Irina had grown up in a wealthy family in South America, at the height of an aristocracy that was soon to be dealt a bitter blow. Her father had lived abroad and was highly educated and accomplished. Dashing and charismatic, he held an exalted place in their community, and his reputation was as treasured in the family as his wealth. Her mother, from a poor and uneducated background, was nonetheless a stunning beauty who quickly learned to conduct herself in a manner befitting the family's status. It was from her nanny that Irina received tenderness, affection, and physical ministrations. Her mother was far more erratic in her care, alternating between benign indifference, bouts of affection, and at times violent outbursts of rage.

As a young girl, Irina had despised being made to wear dresses. Her mother scolded her for being a tomboy, sitting with her legs spread apart or clambering to the roof of a car in pursuit of her younger brothers and their friends. She told me, "As a girl, I felt somehow my privacy could be invaded. My mother would not respect my boundaries. I was very conscious that I had body parts that I didn't want anyone to see. Being myself meant feeling exposed . . . My mother could somehow make me feel completely naked."

Physical beauty, according to her mother, was a woman's sole source of power. Her mother drew on what Irina came to view as superstitious, primitive beliefs and practices to keep herself and, by extension, her daughter, beautiful and lithe. For example, she showed Irina how to press sideways, hard, against a wall, to keep fat from building on her thighs. Irina looked askance at this practice, yet privately she worried greatly about her body, and every blemish stood out to her as a black mark of imperfection.

Irina's parents had a difficult marriage, and her father was away from home much of the time. When Irina was eleven, her parents divorced, and her father moved to the United States. The children would visit him there on school holidays and summer vacations. A year later, political unrest swept through her country and destroyed the very fabric of the society that had accorded them such status. From being revered, they now risked violence and persecution. On their way to the airport for what they thought was a holiday to visit their father, Irina and her siblings were told that they would not be returning to their country but were to live with their father and his new wife permanently. In this abrupt way, Irina was separated from her mother; she did not see her again until many years later. Her mother stayed behind in the midst of political turmoil, with diminished resources and little security.

Irina did not get along with her new stepmother, whom she experienced as critical and shaming. She was sent to a nearby boarding school and avoided returning home. During her adolescence, Irina felt as though she was raising herself. For example, she told me, "When I needed my first bra, I took myself by the hand, telling myself ok, now you have to do this, it's time, you need this thing. But there was nobody to go with me, so I just took myself." Later, as she got older, Irina began to understand her rage at her father, believing that he had chosen his new wife over his eldest daughter and offered her no more protection and security than he provided to her mother.

Torn from her family, her roots, her country of origin, from her mother and her mother tongue, Irina was taken hold by a nascent sense of fatality that became a core organizing principle: everything I have will be taken away, everyone I love will be lost to me, the worst that can happen will happen. This became the mantra she used to stave off hope, which she feared would only lead to bitter disappointment. She came to believe that she could rely on no one but herself. Despite this belief, however, she held onto her sense of self through a powerful tie to her cultural identity, which rooted her firmly in the midst of transition and change.

When her mother eventually rejoined her family, managing to leave their country and emigrate to the United States, Irina noted with surprise that she felt very little emotion at their reunion. She discovered in herself a cold, hard nub that seemed to insulate her from her family. She had learned how to present a gracious and well-put-together façade that concealed the part of herself that had turned to stone.

Nonetheless, she yearned for a partner, and she felt she had found one in Miguel. She was drawn to him because of his boldness and charisma. Unlike other men she had known, he seemed unafraid of her power. Her own self-sufficiency had come to feel to her like an immense stone wall erected around her that would be too high or daunting for anyone to scale.

Irina's marriage, however, was fraught with both passion and profound conflict. Irina rediscovered in Miguel the omnipotent childhood father she had lost, along with, as she would gradually come to know, the ineffectual, unfaithful father she had come to scorn. While she was no longer alone, her marriage extracted a huge price. Her husband was uninhibited in his criticisms of her physical appearance and body. He demanded of her a loyalty and faithfulness to him that was not reciprocated. He required that his needs be met first, while she was to delay or forgo gratification of her own wishes and desires. On a deeper level, however, Irina also understood that he depended on her completely, and she gratified his need to appear powerful and in control.

Irina came to therapy at a point in time when the life she had struggled to knit together threatened to come completely unraveled. After twenty years of marriage, Miguel confessed to her that he was in love with another woman and was considering a divorce. This confession, gradually followed by others, led Irina to question whether she had ever truly been safe with him. For months, Irina doubted herself and him and wondered whether she was crazy to give him another chance. She said, "If I forgive and take a step closer, I feel diminished, who I am, what I'm made of, my pride. How can I move forward when he has made me feel disposable? How can I tell him it's ok to shit on me?"

In our first meeting, Irina wept while she described her marriage, now in shambles. She related to me her conviction that every significant relationship was bound to end in betrayal and pain. Through tears of rage and despair, Irina warned me nonetheless never to counsel her to leave her marriage or even to raise it as a possibility. While this came up again and again in a myriad of ways, I was struck then by the defiance and challenge in her gaze, which I later recognized as the trademark symbol of her fierce determination and independence. Over the course of our work, however, I came to understand that her bravado served to conceal her childlike yearning for affection from someone she could depend on—someone who would neither let her down nor abandon her nor take advantage of her. These opposing pulls, of independence and of reliance, of confidence and mistrust, of self-sufficiency and neediness, defined the poles of her inner world.

From the beginning, Irina and I seemed to resonate with each other, and as the therapy progressed, our mutual respect deepened. It was important to Irina that I experience her in this warm, positive way. She feared that if she were to reveal the full range of her emotions, the therapy would implode, like so many of her other relationships had. She needed to trust that we liked each other enough for her to risk exposing the shattered, deeply concealed aspects of herself. This was the warp and weft of the therapy.

Irina carried herself with dignity, but she could break someone in two with a cold stare or a disdainful sniff. She teased me relentlessly: she despised my yellow bag and was critical of my hairstyle. She poked fun at me for speaking softly in the waiting room, throwing me off guard by saying, "What, are you whispering again or is something wrong with your voice?" If I was surprised, she would tease me for that too, relishing her own capacity to create imbalance or even chaos. I came to understand that Irina's teasing served multiple opposing functions: staving off feelings of closeness while at the same time creating an atmosphere of familiarity, disempowering me while simultaneously revealing how closely she scrutinized me, testing my ability to withstand her destructive and aggressive urges, dismissing me while attempting to remake me into a more ideal object worthy of her love and affection.

Eventually, we also understood that when she was confronted with changes, however subtle—whether it be my new hairstyle or a picture slightly askew on my wall—or too far from her ideal view of me, she felt disoriented. She told me, "I can't feel as close to you when you put your hair up, it's like it's 'not-you.' Like my mother, who is normally polished, stylish, elegant. If she is disorganized or confused, I can't bear to be around her because it's like 'not-her'—the mom I knew isn't there anymore." Her sense of the other as a stable presence was thus deeply challenged by her ever shifting internal experience of the other. She felt she had not been held and thus lacked the capacity within herself to hold others in her mind in a constant and enduring way.

Irina tried to shield me from her rage. She talked openly and colorfully about her wish to tear someone limb from limb or hit them on the head with her frying pan, but she also laughed at my interest in these feelings, saying, "You probably would love to be a fly on my wall when Miguel and I are fighting. You wouldn't believe it's me." Her own rage felt enormously powerful, wild, and destructive, and she deeply feared losing control. Her anger could erupt at a moment's notice, and she had no hope that anything useful or healthy could ever be derived from that place. If her anger became unleashed, she feared destroying all those whom she held closest to her. She dreaded that she would replicate, through rage, her early experiences of abandonment.

Cancer, for Irina, inflamed the scars of these old traumas. Losing a sense of wholeness and control over her destiny evoked multiple earlier traumatic losses: of the stature of her family in her homeland, of disruptive separations from her parents. The disjointedness that she had experienced previously in relation to her mother, or in the therapy with me—the feeling she called "not-me"—had become a feeling of internal collapse and, at its most intense, a feeling of annihilation. The cancer, in spite of its relatively minor and highly treatable nature, felt like a death knell to her.

During the funeral, I glanced over at her parents, sitting at opposite ends of the front row. Her mother was weeping silently, while her father, ashen, sat slumped in his chair. How, I wondered, could fate be analyzed? What did I miss? How did it happen? I realized that those twin reactions were spun together from my feelings of responsibility, on the one hand, and, on the other, my profound sense of loss of this meaningful and unique relationship I had had for so long with Irina.

The analytic relationship is extraordinarily intimate and authentic (Coen 1994). We know that for many patients it can feel like the closest and most unconditionally accepting relationship they have known. In many ways, this was true for Irina. In her experience, every significant person in her life had failed her through abandonment or betrayal. She strove to create in me a steadfast, constant, and genuine presence and refused to tolerate artifice. "You know me," she would say, "and you know the situation. I want to know what you would do with Miguel. Could you forgive him? Do you think you would?" She let me know immediately if she detected the slightest hint of disingenuousness and demanded that I respond to her with immediacy and absolute truth.

The more our patients demand that we become authentic in their presence, the more engaging, dramatic, and alive the treatment relationship comes to feel. Such was the case with Irina. She would accept interpretations from me only if they were embedded in genuine interactions between us. On countless occasions, she would request that I respond to her questions from my "soul" and not just from my good, solid analytic training. If

I responded to a question with a hint of evasion, she would immediately stop me with a smirk and the comment, "There you go, putting your shrink hat on." I learned not to get caught in the "catch-22" that would unfold if I deflected her questions in the direction of pursuing her own thoughts: she could not think her thoughts in my presence if I did not acknowledge the reality that I had thoughts of my own.

With her sudden death, the treatment came to an abrupt halt. She walked out of my office on a Wednesday, and I fully intended to see her again the following Monday, restored to her former self. But instead, she was suddenly gone. There would be no termination, no opportunity to resolve transference and countertransference issues, no goodbye. I was alone, silenced and silently devastated by the loss of my patient. Her death overtook the security of the treatment, which as her analyst I had been charged to protect, and left me raw and defenseless, to struggle on my own with the meaning of her therapy and of her death, of my loss and of my grief. I wondered, how do we end the therapeutic relationship when the patient dies?

Without a patient, who is the analyst? When a husband dies, wife becomes widow; when a parent dies, daughter becomes orphan. Just as we have no term to refer to a parent whose child has died (K. Malawista, personal communication), we also have no term to speak of the bereft analyst. Analysts do not often speak or write of the meaning of the analytic loss (Buechler 2000), perhaps because it requires that we acknowledge how deeply we come to feel about our patients.

In some ways, my interrupted work with Irina placed in the foreground the dilemma that analysts face in every treatment relationship: where do we draw the line between the analytic alliance and the bond of love that ties us to our patients? Over the course of thousands of hours of listening to our patients and trying to understand them, empathy grows and becomes love. To be empathic demands deep care as well as carefulness. Just as patients experience their analysts as unique and cherished, so do analysts take special care of their patients, in a way that is unlike any other relationship they have. As Pinsky (2002, 201) writes, "the psychoanalytic situation is carefully constructed to induce an extraordinary intimacy that is its reason to exist; it is through this singular human connection—an intimacy that intends separation—that the work is accomplished and the endpoint reached." This is not to say that it is not transference or that there is no hate; rather, to tolerate and accept our patients' transference, including love and hate, envy and despair, destruction and desperation, is an exceptional form of love.

This may be why it is so hard for analysts to speak frankly and candidly about the actual work that goes on in the consulting room (Buechler 1992). We are accustomed to describing our work in its revised state, as a more or less coherent, acceptable, and comprehensible narrative. Nonetheless, in spite of, or alongside of, our efforts to develop a lucid analytic voice and cohesive account of our treatment, aspects of our work with patients remain elusive and hard to define. Just as we are different parents to each of our children, each of our patients requires us to be a different analyst. With our background, training, and experience as analysts to scaffold us, we must acquire the flexibility, willingness, and wherewithal to be attuned to our patients' various needs.

We all hope to see our patients through a meaningful treatment and a successful termination. Over the course of what we might generally consider to be a desired outcome, the process of termination allows for both individuals in the analytic dyad to work through feelings of anger, hurt, and loss, as well as love; to consolidate an understanding of the meaning of the work that has unfolded; and to acknowledge together the shared tapestry that has been created over the course of the treatment (Viorst 1982; reprinted in this book). However, it is not uncommon that treatment is interrupted abruptly, such as when a patient decides to leave; runs out of money, time, or steam; moves to another location; or simply loses interest. Often, though not always, we have the opportunity to pick up cues of an impending termination, even before the thoughts may be fully cognizant to the patient, and attempt to address them in a way that we hope might be useful to the patient.

A treatment aborted can sometimes feel like an analytic failure, in spite of our best efforts to consider the ending in light of the patient's particular personality organization. Our only tool is our analytic ear, and while potent and vigilant, it is not foolproof. Limentani (1982, 438) points out that "'unexpected' terminations are likely to create painful conflicts in the analyst . . . feelings of guilt are inevitable, as are rationalizations and pleas of justification." We cannot help but wonder how the treatment may have broken down and whether it might have been salvaged in some way.

What of the treatment interrupted by fate? Are we not still left with the response that characterizes most deeply our analytic stance, that is, to question whether there was something we missed, something that eluded us, something we could have done differently that would have led to a different outcome? We have no second chance; still we are bound to examine, because we are compelled to make meaning out of chaos and confusion. We are accountable to our patients. They place their psychological well-being, their internal life, their hopes, ideals, and fears, in our hands. We cannot guarantee what the outcome will be. We cannot guarantee that there will be no mistakes, no failures, no omissions or blind spots. But we are accountable.

The circumstances of Irina's death raise analytic questions as well as medical ones. The diagnosis of cancer naturally arouses in everyone the fear of illness and eventual death; for Irina, this fear grew extreme and insistent. In reality, Irina's cancer was curable and not life threatening; so should have been the subsequent treatment she sought following the successful and complete removal of the tumor. Yet, in a cruel paradox, the lengths that she went to protect herself ultimately—and unpredictably—led to her sudden death.

Irina was fiercely determined to survive the cancer, as she had already survived a multiplicity of traumatic events and threats to the integrity of her self. Her sense of herself was organized around her capacity to pull herself up by her bootstraps, to rebound in the face of despair and make herself over into a stronger and ever more resilient version of her self. She felt she could meet the challenge of cancer with the same defiance with which she met the world—a defiance that mirrored her internal sense of being forever tested by the tribulations that befell her. The discovery of her cancer became, for her, an opportunity to defy the ultimate challenge. Elevating the idea of cancer and death to nearly phobic proportions underscored the need for defiance.

Every phobia serves as a defense against some perceived internal danger; irrational fear is rendered increasingly powerful by the opposing force of the dangerous wish that necessitates the defense. It is possible, for example, that the fear of death belied suicidal thoughts—thoughts that one might expect in the face of excruciating shame. Or, perhaps, thoughts of her own death stood in lieu of thinking about the deaths of others—an expectable fantasy in the face of hidden rage.

For Irina, the diagnosis of cancer occurred at a time in her life when she was reeling from profound disappointment in her marriage. Cancer became a tragic recapitulation of earlier events in her life. Because she kept her illness a secret, she bore it in solitude and silence. Therapy had become a place where her feelings of shame and worthlessness could be understood, but she had only just begun to give voice to feelings of powerlessness and rage. Thoughts of suicide—or homicide—were never in her conscious awareness;

the closest she came were in her fantasies of wielding her frying pan or in her preoccupations with her own death. Indeed, she clung fiercely to survival as her most potent revenge.

But could her defiant insistence on survival have bespoken a different form of revenge? Imagining the pain her death would inflict on others could allow her to strike back at those who had harmed and misused her. I wondered also whether her over-responsiveness to the idea of her own death, opened up by the discovery of her tumor, was the counterpoint to her own unexpressed wishes to die, which she could not approach in any conscious way. By pursuing further treatment for the cancer, did she throw herself headlong into harm's way because she could not endure giving voice to her own wishes to die?

Whether or not she may have unconsciously held this fantasy of revenge through death will never be known; that I cannot know offers acute and painful proof that the therapeutic work was left permanently incomplete. I cannot help but wonder whether indeed the treatment did miss something essential. Irina had feared the risk of the possibility of the cancer recurring, while I had questioned the risk of her pursuing follow-up treatment. Yet, I had been familiar with Irina's streak of defiance—just as she had defied me ever to question her staying in her marriage, just as she had defied medical advice, she had also defied, at times, my efforts to offer her deeper insight into her mind. Early on, she had put me on notice: there were places I was not to go, questions I was not to ask, doors in her psyche I could not open.

Like Somerset Maugham's merchant who lent his horse to his servant to escape his appointment with death, could I, too, have been an unwitting accomplice? Throughout the therapy, providing her with an authentic response to her experience was essential to engage her in a meaningful treatment. But now, in the face of the real threat of her cancer and my genuine wish to keep her healthy, did my own bias toward questioning the necessity of follow-up treatment inadvertently intensify her defiance? My analytic neutrality and her explicit demand (dare?) that I never advise her to leave her marriage made it easy to avoid that trap, but perhaps my sincere concern for her health had blinded me to a more fine-tuned focus on the possible meanings of her defiance itself.

Could I, then, have been any more successful in helping her escape her appointment in Samarra? I will never truly know. In the end, however, whether she was motivated by an unconscious wish to annihilate herself and disappear from the world in order to punish her betrayers or whether she was driven, instead, by her fierce, healthy, and sound attachment to life at any cost—or whether both of these were equally powerful driving forces within her—her death was random, arbitrary, and terrible. It could neither have been foreseen nor prevented—no more so than Oedipus could have escaped his own fate. What I was left with, then, was the terrible awareness of my own helplessness to protect her and shield her from harm (Pinsky 2002). The sad and disquieting truth was that there was nothing I could have done to prevent Irina's death.

While these questions are almost unbearably painful, they are also part of the legacy left by the sudden death of a patient. The bereft analyst's grief requires working through an understanding, albeit incomplete and uncertain, of the process of death. We are always engaged in the work of examining the process and deriving what understanding we can from the meaningful interplay of internal conflicts and external factors. But in the aftermath of a patient's death, we are left with grief, and we are also left to try to make sense of the treatment and, finally, to preserve its meaning.

Over the course of our work, we turn frequently to our colleagues, teachers, and supervisors, as well as our own analysts, to help us make sense of the work when we feel at sea. The community of our colleagues traditionally offers us support, encouragement, engaging discussion and debate, and the promise of ever deepening our ways of thinking and understanding. In this instance, however, I discovered a certain kind of gap that could not easily be traversed. While many therapists experience such losses—treating patients who are terminally ill, patients who become ill during the course of treatment, patients who go off to fight wars, patients who die unexpectedly—we do not have a language to speak about it. It is both a universal experience and a deeply painful one, yet it is also awkward and risky to talk about. It hints of unresolved countertransference, of subtle and complex boundary issues, of personal feelings we have for our patients that may be outside of the sphere we regularly talk about when we talk of therapeutic alliance. As Buechler (2000, 82) points out, "the analytic culture dictates, sometimes in subtle ways, the emotional reactions deemed 'appropriate' and acceptable." These analytic "mores" may interfere, then, both with how we speak of loss within the analytic dyad and how we are able to mourn the loss of our patients.

While it is generally acknowledged that every therapeutic encounter changes the therapist as it also, hopefully, changes the patient, years of training and careful analysis teach us to keep our feelings for our patients in check. We learn to care for our patients rather than ourselves. It is not unusual for analysts to find it difficult to cancel sessions when we are ill; we worry about leaving our patients during a vacation or while we are away at a conference. In a planned termination, we trust that there will be time for both patient and therapist to work through feelings of grief over losing the other and feeling alone, but when the death of the patient is unexpected, the working-through aspect of the termination is curtailed, and what remain are feelings that perhaps elude the language of analytic discourse.

While all grief has an intensely private quality, the exceptional nature of the analytic relationship sets the analyst apart from other mourners. The analytic relationship, uniquely private and protected, is kept in the shadows. The analyst has no readily identifiable place amongst the mourners who are left behind in the wake of death.

When Irina died, I was acutely aware that I held secrets about her that no one else in her life could know. I knew, too, that Irina had a hiding place for some of her secrets, a place where she kept letters, photographs, and other artifacts, a compilation of the evidence of years of anguish she both wished to destroy and simultaneously to memorialize. Often, in therapy, she would speak about her secret shrine of pain, and we would wonder together about the self-punishing quality of revisiting these heartbreaking mementos. She would come to the edge of the decision to destroy them but then would pull back, unable to allow herself to be released from their irresistible and painful hold on her. It was as if, by preserving the history of her pain through these relics, she also asserted the integrity and validity of her experience: "I am here. This happened to me."

Over the course of her treatment, her secret cache was in a sense unpacked, examined, and entrusted to my safekeeping, in the hope that, as she gained in strength, self-understanding, and self-acceptance, she could gradually relinquish her attachment to her painful memories and start anew, stronger, clearer, at peace. Instead, her death came in the midst of the process of sifting through the traumatic debris, and it was left in shambles. What we had begun to unpack could be neither repacked nor discarded. I had become the safe-keeper of secrets that had no proprietor.

Sitting in the room where Irina's memorial service was being held, I remembered suddenly that she had once loaned a book to me. It was a compilation of stories by a South American author about emigration to America, and it held multiple meanings to her. In particular, she had found meaning in a story about a young girl who had been separated from her mother and sent to live with foster parents, to whom she grew deeply attached. When this girl was reunited with her mother, she felt the loss of her foster mother more profoundly than she had ever consciously registered the loss of her mother, and she could not reattach. I remembered that a few weeks earlier, we had talked about the book, and I had decided to hold onto it a little longer, to be able to think more about the multiple aspects of her experience that she was trying to convey to me through the book.

Now, I discovered in myself a secret sense of pleasure in still having the book with me, along with a pang of guilt: I wanted to hold onto something of hers, claim a part of her for myself, but I worried, as well, that having it was a subtle crossing of an analytic boundary, an echo of my discomfort at attending her service. While I listened to others speak about her, I could in no way openly acknowledge our relationship. In addition, while I was a stranger to most of the people in the room, many of them were not strangers to me, because I had met them over the course of many hours of listening to Irina, as she laid out the roadmap of her life and peopled it with many of the individuals who were now in the room with me.

I wondered whether I belonged there, and for whose benefit I had attended the service. There had been no question in my mind about attending when her husband asked me to, and I knew in part I was there out of my respect for her, my wish to provide solace to her family, and my sense that she would have wanted me to be present. But also, I was there because it was necessary for me, in seeking meaning, to be among those who knew her and were mourning her death. As her therapist, I could not mourn in public, but I could be present and hold her in my thoughts. The universal rituals surrounding death could serve the function of making her death real and begin to dissipate the feeling I had had in my office, that she was there one day and then, not the next.

In the consulting room, analytic time is different from real time: it is demarcated by session hours that contain within them a whole world created by the patient in our presence; threaded together, they form the whole of the analytic work. Analytic time can confound the process of grieving because it inevitably leaves open the possibility that the patient will return at a future hour. Even when we terminate with patients, we say, "The door is always open." There is an implicit promise that there will always be an hour made available for a returning patient. Indeed, even when patients in ongoing treatment do not come for their session for one reason or another, it is still their hour. Thus, being absent is just another way of being present in the treatment, and we can be fairly sure the patient's absence will be talked about, worked through, understood.

When a patient dies suddenly, the hour remains as if suspended in time. When Irina died, I was faced with the dilemma of what to do with her hours. I wondered whether I would allow myself to fill her hours, preferring almost to keep them open for her, in memoriam. On the other hand, not only was it unbearable to hold the hours open, it was also impractical. My analytic work is also my business and my livelihood, and I could no more enshrine her hours than she could enshrine her pain. Likewise, I struggled with the final bill and my reluctance to send it to her husband. Did her death invalidate the analytic contract? Perhaps I had yet to resolve the sense of guilt I carried—over my own helplessness, my inability to protect her, my having received from the work we did together something precious of my own, my being alive while she was not. In the end, I did send the bill, along with a note. The analytic frame rested on the structure provided by the contract: we had settled on a fee, a schedule, a consistent and predictable procedure, those factors that are the unvarying heartbeat of any analytic work—our own human effort to counter fate. The meaning of the work could endure only within the framework established by those procedures.

In the stillness of my office, Irina's ghost settles in, as softly as the background hush of the heater. I imagine that the cushions in the chair she sat in still carry the faint impression of where she sat. But no, she had preferred to smooth down the pillows, fluff them a bit, brush off the lint, and straighten the picture hanging on the wall as she went out, closing the door behind her.

NOTES

The author would like to thank Sharon Alperovitz, Angela Martin, Deirdre Callahan, Tesa Conlin, Martha Dupecher, Joanie Lieberman, Angela Martin, Elizabeth Rees, Shelley Rockwell, and Bonita Winer.

1. The case discussed here is disguised so that the privacy of the people involved is assured.

REFERENCES

Bernstein, A. 1987. "Love and Death: Letting Go." *Modern Psychoanalysis* 12: 195–206.
Buechler, S. 1992. "Stress in the Personal and Professional Development of a Psychoanalyst." *Journal of the American Academy of Psychoanalysis* 20: 183–191.
——. 2000. "Necessary and Unnecessary Losses: The Analyst's Mourning." *Contemporary Psychoanalysis* 36: 77–90.

Coen, Stanley. 1994. "Barriers to Love Between Patient and Analyst." *Journal of the American Psychoanalytic Association* 42: 1107–1135.

Freud, S. 1917. "Mourning and Melancholia." In *The Standard Edition of the Complete Psychological Works of Sigmund Freud*, ed. J. Strachey, 14:237–258. London: Hogarth.

Limentani, A. 1982. "On the 'Unexpected' Termination of Psychoanalytic Therapy." *Psychoanalytic Inquiry* 2: 419–440.

Pinsky, E. 2002. "Mortal Gifts: A Two-Part Essay on the Therapist's Mortality. Part I: Untimely Loss." *Journal of the American Academy of Psychoanalysis* 30: 173–204.

Viorst, J. 1982. "Experiences of Loss at the End of Analysis: The Analyst's Response to Termination." *Psychoanalytic Inquiry* 2: 399–418.

CHAPTER 5

LITTLE BOY LOST

ARLENE KRAMER RICHARDS

> All things go
> downward.
> Even the rocks
> settle and sink,
> even the flowers bow.
>
> —Gregory Orr, *Orpheus and Eurydice*

SO EURYDICE welcomes her lover, the great musician Orpheus, to hell. She comforts him with the idea that everything animate must die. But, she adds, even inanimate things change, get used up, get lost, disappear. This death of the inanimate is even more horrible than the death of the musician, even more horrible than the death of the beloved. The death of the inanimate, of the natural, makes it clear that not even nature, not even earth is eternal. Everything gives way to entropy. If entropy is the great law, then death is comforting. In this way she says that death, to her, is freedom.

After what I thought was a very successful two-year treatment of a nine-year-old boy I will call Jack, his single mother said she could not afford to continue and abruptly ended the therapy. Jack himself wanted more. A year later, I learned from the newspaper that another boy in a video game parlor had murdered him. The knowledge haunted me and eventually led me to give up my child therapy practice altogether. Recently, I passed the building where he lived and felt a deep sadness. I hope to convey the various ways I have dealt with my grief for this child and the consequence of having failed to mourn him adequately for the two decades since his death.

His slim, elegant, young mother, whom I will call Ms. Green, told me in our consultation that she wanted to bring her son for treatment because his school had called her in repeatedly for conferences about his behavior. The punishments he received from both the school and his mother had not changed his behavior, and the school was intending to expel him. Ms. Green had staved off the expulsion by promising to bring him to therapy. I agreed to see him to evaluate whether I could help. I asked Ms. Green if she wanted me to help the school, her, or her son. She thought that was a funny question but agreed to try to think about whether all of their agendas could fit with the others. I also asked whether I could talk to the school guidance counselor. Ms. Green agreed, after she asked if she was going to be charged for that call. I said I would include the conference in the fee we had already set for the consultation.

When I asked to meet with Jack's teacher, I was referred to the guidance counselor, who set up a meeting with the principal, the teacher, and herself, as well as the school nurse. The meeting at the school did not go as well as I hoped. I was not happy to hear that they were at their wits' end. They had stretched their resources to deal with Jack. They had him tested but found no evidence of an attention deficit disorder, no learning disabilities, no reason for his bad conduct. They were out of patience for him. They really believed that he was a bad influence on the other students. Despite the attention they had given to his emotional needs, he was still unable to pay attention in class long enough to learn. He still left class for hours at a time with the excuse that he needed to use the bathroom, he still played practical jokes on the teacher, he still copied from other students, and he still disrupted class by talking to other children. I was glad to learn that they did not believe that he was inherently bad; they thought that Jack was acting out problems that came from home.

I thought the school team blamed Ms. Green and seemed to want me to want to protect Jack from her. At this point in the evaluation, it seemed that Jack's mother wanted me to protect her from them, they wanted me to protect Jack from her, and Jack just wanted out. I met with him the following week.

I greeted Jack by saying that I was glad to see him but that I couldn't blame him if he wasn't so eager to see me because I realized that I was his newest punishment. He thought that was funny. He laughed with relief and seemed to relax his rigid posture. Jack told me a lot about the school and his complaints about it. He said everything was fine at home. He liked his mother's new boyfriend, and he got along fine with his father. He was glad that he was an only child because all the grownups wanted him to be with them. He had every other weekend with his father and the alternate weekends with his mother and her boyfriend. Lots of times he went with his mother's boyfriend to his golf club in Florida, and he was learning to play. He liked that a lot. I wondered—but did not ask—where his mother was on those weekends. I also wondered about his calling the man "his mother's boyfriend" rather than by his name or some name that would reflect his own experience of their relationship. I thought he was keeping his distance from this man and wondered whether the mother's boyfriend may have been too interested in the boy, whether sexually or, perhaps, out of longing for this child to be his own son.

Jack was interested in playing card games as we talked. He had been to casino nights at the golf club in Florida and was very sophisticated about odds, length of play, and especially the interpersonal aspects of "faking" and "faking out." Over many sessions and discussions, he began to tell me about how he had lost trust in his world. He enjoyed my bluntness and what he said was my "no flirting." I linked flirting with faking as different ways of fooling the other person. He was impressed that I did not wear makeup or color my hair. I was different from the women he knew in these ways. We talked about how I was like a grandmother.

At this juncture, his mother came in for another session. She told me that she had been afraid to have a child and had only become pregnant with Jack "by accident." Her marriage ended over the issue of whether to have another child. Her husband had insisted that he did not want Jack to be an only child, as both he and Ms. Green were. He thought the experience was too intense, the expectations too high, and there was too much loneliness in the life of an only child. She said that she had insisted that she did not have the energy or interest in babies that she would need if they were to have another child. She did not think it would be fair to the child. He called her a "selfish bitch," and they had arguments that turned into violent fights. The marriage ended, she told me, in terrible loss on all sides.

I asked her how much Jack knew about this. I was thinking that children almost always blame themselves for the failure of their parents' marriages. She said that he must have heard the arguments and certainly noticed the bruises and broken dishes that resulted from their fights. But she did not think he knew what they were fighting about. Besides, she said, divorce was normal in their social set. After all, people could not help growing apart as their lives went on, and choosing someone you could live with forever was something that only happened in the movies or on TV. I said that was a kind of fake ideal world. She said that she felt much better after seeing it like that. The theme of believing that everything good is fake was a precursor to Jack's belief.

Some months later, Jack drew a picture for me to add to the ones I had tacked up on the inside of the door to my toy closet. He drew a pirate and a wrecked ship on a tropical island with one palm tree. A large brown bag with a string around its neck sat in front of the ship. I asked him what was in the bag, and he said: "That's the treasure." At a later meeting with both parents, I showed them the picture. They both smiled knowingly but did not comment. I said that often there were discussions about money in divorcing families. They said that was true for them, but they did not elaborate. I thought there must be some secret they were unwilling to confront. At a still later session, Ms. Green told me that her family money was lost to her in the process of her divorce. Her parents disapproved of her decision not to have another child and violently disapproved of her getting a divorce. As a result, they disinherited her. I said that it was not as rare as one might hope that parents manipulate adult children through money. She laughed, bitterly.

Two years into the treatment, Jack was doing better in school. He turned the math skills he had developed by playing cards and dice games into an academic strength. Math became his best subject, and he was proud of it. His interest in money evolved into an interest in business. He answered an ad in a magazine for a line of greeting cards he could sell to friends and neighbors. He soon began going door to door in his apartment house and then set up a folding table to display the cards outside a park entrance. His business thrived. I bought a set of business cards from him, which he would have engraved. I had almost forgotten our transaction when he delivered them to me one day. Treatment continued, with our talking about how good it felt to make his own money. He enjoyed saving it, and I called it "Jack's treasure." While I did not hear it that way at the time, he must have been hearing his mother complain about her lack of money.

The next time Ms. Green came in, she announced that she could no longer afford his treatment. She said that he was so much better anyway and that she was grateful to me for all I had done for her son. He was now in middle school and doing so well. She admired the cards I showed her. She remarked that she didn't think he had delivered on his orders. She said he just kept the money and did not send in the order or the deposit to the company. "He must really like you," she said. I said that I was worried about this behavior and thought we had more work to do in therapy. She cried, "You don't believe me. You think I am lying about not having the money."

I think now that I missed the earlier, parallel trauma that occurred when she told her husband that she did not have the resources for another child. Now she was telling me that she did not have the resources for Jack. But at the time, I only thought that she could not bear for him to be so attached to me. I suspected that she was so jealous of his having another important relationship in his life that she had to break it up. I assured her that she had been and was a good mother to Jack. I said that she would always be his mother, while I was just a friend in passing for whom he would outgrow his need. She responded, "I never told you. Jack doesn't know. My mother had a child before me. She put that baby into a bath of too hot water by mistake. It died."

As shocked as if I too had been put into overly hot water, I empathized with how painful this must have been. I offered to refer Ms. Green to a therapist to talk about the terrible effect this must have had on the whole family and on her in particular. She refused. She repeated angrily that I did not believe her about not having enough money for Jack's treatment. If she could not afford to pay for Jack's therapy, how could she have money for treatment of her own? She hated that I was teasing her. I talked about clinics. I offered to help her find a low-cost analysis. Nothing helped. I asked to see Jack one more time to say goodbye. She said that was not necessary. She had already told him that the treatment was over, that I only saw him for the money she paid me, and that he did not have to care about me because I did not really care about him.

After she left, I was devastated. I felt completely defeated and useless. I could not see any way in which I had been effective. The whole treatment must have seemed like a tease (or a fake) to him. He had to believe his mother. She was the source of stability in his world. But, as she herself had told me in that terrible last session, she did not have the resources for him. I thought I had included her enough in my work with him so that she would not have to pull him out of treatment before he was ready to be on his own. Like all child therapists, I had had similar experiences with other children. I consoled myself that at least he had had those two years of mutual trust and respect. That had to be better than nothing. I paid more attention to my own family. I cried. I got angry with the parents. I got angry with the colleague who had referred him to me. I got angry with the school. I blamed myself for not seeing it coming. And I went on to other things.

A year later, I saw a story in the newspaper about a boy who had been killed in a video arcade. A young teen had bashed another boy over the head with a baseball bat, smashing in his skull. The dead boy was my former patient. The story said that he had been losing money gambling on the outcome of games but was not paying his debts. This was an eerie reminder of his mother's concern that Jack was accepting money for greeting-card orders that he was not filling. Since he looked like a rich kid, the other boy was sure that he was holding out on him. He had threatened that if Jack did not come up with the money, the other boy would kill him. And he did.

I mourned the failure of the end of our treatment. I cried. I contributed to a charity for children. I mourned the loss of the man he could have become, the loss for his parents, especially his mother. I talked with the colleague at his school who had referred him to me in the first place. None of the mourning work was completely successful. In the end, I decided to stop accepting child referrals. All I could do was protect myself by not taking on any more child cases.

If grief is the internal work that unfolds after a loss, then mourning is the exterior expression of grief. The process of mourning gradually alleviates unbearable grief. It is made bearable by sharing it with others. When Jack died, I could not bear my grief, because I could not really share it. Earlier, when his mother pulled him out of treatment and out of my life, I lost Jack and had no way to mourn. There was no wake for me to attend, no shiva call I could make, no funeral or community meeting, no memorial service. A year later, when he died, once again I could not find any of those ways to mourn. I thought then and still think that I would have been an unwelcome intruder on the family's mourning. I would only be a reminder to them of how they had not protected him. His mother might well think that I had been right, that he had needed more treatment, that his honesty with me was the beginning of wanting to be honest with other people. Perhaps she might have thought that had she allowed the therapy to continue, he might never have gotten into the situation that led to his death. And my own guilt in not having tried harder to preserve the treatment haunted me. I could have pushed her to accept a very low fee or no fee at all, but this would have been complicated for me, given that they lived in a very posh style.

DEFENSES AGAINST MOURNING

That story resonated, perhaps too strongly, with a portion of my own history. I too had siblings who died. To imagine that this was because of my mother's failure to protect her babies was too awful, and I could not mourn. Similarly, I could not mourn my little patient because it brought back the unbearable earlier memories of those babies lost when I was very young. Only when the editors of this book asked me to write about death and therapy could I tolerate truly mourning both the patient and my siblings.

The death of a child seems impossible to mourn, largely because it ends our dreams of immortality. Some believe that immortality can be achieved through their progeny; some believe that it can be attained through religious rebirth, some through art, some through plastic surgery, proper diet, or exercise, some through love. But everyone wants to believe that "death shall have no dominion" (Thomas 1936). No one wants to acknowledge that it is inevitable and natural—an acceptable price for living.

In the process of writing this paper and beginning to mourn more fully the loss of Jack and its connection to other losses, I began to reflect on the various defenses against awareness of the finality of death. I believe that this is what I can add to our psychoanalytic understanding of mourning. At least, it is what I have learned in the process of thinking about the issues raised by my patient's death and the inhibition of my own functioning as a reaction to that loss. These defenses are wide ranging and can include denial of death, preoccupation with gambling, asserting youth and health, love, resurrection fantasies, and immersing oneself in fantastical stories of death, such as murder mysteries and related fiction. All of these defenses have the capacity to occupy the mind to such an extent that they crowd out an awareness of loss. Authentic mourning can occur when the mind is not preoccupied with defensive thoughts. Then it can proceed at a tolerable pace, without devastating the mourner with overwhelming grief that could interfere with functioning. Rather than viewing mourning as a process of moving through the defined stages of denial, rage, sadness, and acceptance, all of these emotions are experienced in doses, separated by periods of functioning in the world. When any of these emotions are too intense or last too long, they exhaust the mourner and give way to another emotion. How do these defenses work? In the following sections, I will examine each of these defenses and how they illuminate our understanding of the ways we protect ourselves from confronting death.

DENIAL OF DEATH

Prayer and belief in an immortal soul are concepts that help some cope with the notion of death (Goldberg 2010). Anger, bargaining, depression, and acceptance of loss are the secular alternatives to the religious denial of death. Belief in the perfection of the loved and lost person subverts the possibility of moving on to find another person to fill the place of the lost one in the griever's internal world. While denial of death seems like a failure of reality testing, it seemed useful to me in that I allowed myself to accept gradually the death of my young patient rather than be swamped by the irrevocableness of it and my own feelings of guilt in not having been able to prevent it. Denial also protected me from feeling shame at being unable to stop his mother from taking him out of treatment. A colleague suggested that I felt enraged and abandoned by Jack when his mother pulled him out of treatment. Such rage may have contributed to my guilt when he was murdered.

GAMBLING

My little patient was a gambler. Every time he took money for something and failed to deliver that something, he was gambling that the person he had swindled would not take revenge. Most of the time, that worked. The one time his system failed, he paid with his life. Thinking about it now, I am reminded of Jack's mother telling me about the death of her infant sibling, the one her own mother failed to protect. She could not help but fear that her mother was the murderer and that she might be one too. She may well have thought that she had inherited her mother's inability to protect her child and thus tempted fate by gambling with his life. For example, pulling him out of treatment may be understood as a failure to protect him. Similarly, Jack tempted fate. I wonder if Jack knew, consciously or unconsciously, of the infant's death and so feared meeting a similar fate that he felt compelled to test it out again and again.

Gambling can be thought of as a way of investing hope in the future (Richards and Richards 1997). By living in the moment of uncertainty of outcome, the gambler provides him- or herself with a buffer against the pain of knowing loss. This aspect of the process of mourning has been attested to by Dostoyevsky (1866), Barthelme and Barthelme (2002), and Mezrich (2002). Freud posits in "Mourning and Melancholia" (1917) that normal mourning and melancholia share a process of detaching from the lost person and relapsing into an unconscious thinking, as if the loss had not happened. Upon awakening, mourners often report surprise that the dead person is still dead or, similarly, that they could not get rid of the dead person's slippers because he might still need them, even knowing full well that the dead do not wear slippers (Didion 2005). This alternating state of awareness seems to allow time for the realignment of brain patterns so that the new mental world in which the lost person is not there replaces the one in which contacts and interactions took place. The awareness is accompanied by pain; focusing on something other than the loss defends against moments of pain.

Gambling seems to have the compelling quality that allows mourning to be backgrounded long enough so that the mourner can recover a bit before experiencing the pain again. Perhaps it worked that way for Jack in his task of mourning our relationship. I think gambling can prevent the work of mourning; maybe it worked that way for him. I was unable to use that defense, so I had to find other ways.

The Barthelme brothers' book *Double Down: Reflections on Gambling and Loss* (1999) delineates just such a situation, one that is closer to melancholia than to ordinary mourning. The brothers describe how their parents deprived themselves and their children in order to accumulate money. When the parents died, the brothers began to gamble away their inheritance. By choosing to gamble in casinos, the brothers knew they were going to lose. In this way, they demonstrated that they did not want their parents' money yet resented their parents' choice to not give them the money while they were still alive and that they intended to get revenge. In an effort to overcome their rage at their depriving parents, they needed to keep enacting it by gambling. Paradoxically, their compulsive gambling interfered with their ability to fully mourn their parents' deaths. As Freud posited about melancholia, the hateful interactions with the lost parents were the most compelling ones. These had to be enacted again and again in the service of expressing their grief and anger. Only when they had finished divesting themselves of every penny of their parents' money could they stop gambling. And thus their melancholia is resolved by revisiting the lost relationship bit by bit until, like the money, it is completely gone.

LOVE AND YOUTH

The modern American aversion to death and the tendency to treat it as a form of illness is brilliantly caricatured in Gary Shteyngart's novel *Super Sad True Love Story* (2010). The story opens with a diary entry. The hero writes: "Today I've made a major decision: I am never going to die." This hero believes he can escape death through love. He earns his livelihood selling "escape from death" through a chemical reversal of genetic aging. Desperate to avoid death, he must evade old age, the stage that leads to death. Then of course he must avoid middle age, which leads to old age. Only youth is safe. He falls in love with a young girl; being with her and having her love will make him feel young. In the end, he grows old alone because his love was not enough to keep his beloved faithful. Antiaging, death-reversing treatments do not work: plastic surgery and hormone therapy are all his company can peddle. This hero ultimately accepts the inevitability of death by enjoying all the days of his life. Similarly, the capacity to engage fully in one's life is what allows one to be able truly to mourn.

The mystery of death, so often explored in fiction, is central to the story of Orpheus and Eurydice. The story centers on Orpheus's refusal to accept the death of his beloved and his subsequent search to revive or resurrect her. As Orpheus looks back at Eurydice's shade, she returns to the dead, and he must go back to the living. In the series of lyric poems that Gregory Orr collected in *Orpheus and Eurydice*, the shade of Eurydice secretly rejoices in her own death, likening it to shedding a binding. Orpheus himself refuses to satisfy his fans, the Maenads, when they beg him to choose one among them as the most beautiful now that Eurydice is gone. To choose would be to acknowledge her death. Not to choose was to court death by being torn apart. He chose death, just as anyone who refuses to accept the death of a loved one chooses to make at least some part of him dead.

RESURRECTION FANTASIES

According to the *New York Times* (August 28, 2010), a number of well-respected psychiatrists offer a form of therapy that promotes the recovery of past-life memories and the promise of more lives in the future. Stephen Prothero, a professor of religion at Boston University, wrote: "Reincarnation means never having to say you're dead." Many cultures use rituals that imply or overtly promise reincarnation as a way to counter death. Many different cultures employ pyramids, burial cairns, or grave sites stocked with food, furniture, clothes, jewels, weapons, and even servants to keep the dead happy when they come back to life. Such places attest to the strength of the wish to believe that death is not permanent. Even Christianity promises eternal life after death and uses stories of resurrection to comfort the mourner. The idea that anyone can come back to life allows one to hope for the possible return of the loved one. The concept of heaven, present in many religions, offers a more abstract version of reincarnation.

While I did not hold the belief that Jack would return, I did find myself crying when I passed the building where he had lived. I realized that I was as disappointed as if I had expected him to still be there, alive and well. Thus, even though my conscious mind rejected the idea of resurrection, I nonetheless held onto the fantasy of his ongoing existence. This fantasy served both a protective and defensive function, as it may for those who consciously believe in reincarnation or resurrection.

READING MYSTERY FICTION

The enormous popularity of detective, war, and spy fiction and especially science fiction and tales of the supernatural points to the universal fascination with death—particularly, what brings it about. We enjoy thinking out puzzles of who killed the victim, how the murder was done, and especially how it was solved. In all of these ideas is the assumption that death is not natural. Rarely does a mystery turn on an accidental death. We want to know "whodunnit." We want a villain to blame. The pleasure in a detective story is the satisfaction of our curiosity but also the unconscious assurance that death is only the result of a malicious act on the part of another person.

In most mysteries, murder is committed in retaliation for some real or imagined harm done to the murderer. Those mystery stories that do not explore the psychology of the murderer's mind are unsatisfying. If there is no motive, there is no solution to the mystery. In the universe of a thriller or "whodunnit" movie, the mystery of death is solved in an apparently rational way, one that renders death explainable to the viewer. In other words, we need not worry about death if we have not enraged someone enough to be killed for it.

For my little patient, courting rage was a way of life. He constantly provoked people at school. He cheated the people who ordered stationery from him. Finally, his cheating enraged another boy sufficiently that the boy killed him in an act of revenge. Was he aware that he was courting death? I doubt that. But, perhaps, his unconscious wish to tempt fate was in response to his fear that what had happened to his mother's sibling—his mother's terrible secret— might also happen to him. Understanding what happened in this way helped me mourn both the incompleteness of our treatment and my inability to save him. But it left me too angry with his mother, the school, and especially myself to be able to take on the risk of treating another child. At the time, I was not aware of the sequence of feelings and thoughts that led to my decision. But even now, looking back on the decades since, I think I made the right choice.

STOPPING THE DEFENSE: GRIEF AND MOURNING

When a person gives up the fantasy of being able to stave off death, what emerges is the hope of becoming strong enough to maintain optimism and faith in life. Connections with family, colleagues, friends, and neighbors, as well as with organizations, bring the mourner back to thoughts of life. It is precisely these connections that are so difficult when mourning is missed or incomplete, as it was with my patient. His mother's impossible mourning for her sibling, who died before she was born, left her with a shadow of fear. Her fantasy that she could kill a baby resonated with Jack's perpetual flirting with exclusion from school and, ultimately, with death. My own refusal to continue treating children resonated with her refusal to bear any more children. Both her refusal and mine were self-protective but also protective of the children whom we believed we feared we were unable to protect. Understanding what happened in this way enabled me to stop blaming his mother for pulling him out of treatment as soon as he stopped acting out her fantasy. I even managed to forgive her for having rejected her own treatment. I now saw this rejection as an outcome of her feeling that she was too hopelessly evil to deserve treatment.

Treatment aimed at facilitating the mourning process can draw on the fantasy of others (Bacal 1998) as well as on the fantasy of ambitions (Kaufmann 2008). Such fantasies serve as temporary comforts for a patient struggling with the loss of self-esteem associated with the death of a beloved person. Referring to both the aspirations for enhanced self-esteem and the disappointments and losses that damaged the person's self-esteem in the first place, Kauffman balances resignation at the experience of loss with the possibility of repair that is embedded in hope for the future. I believe my mourning process was enhanced by my own hope that this paper and the work of reading, thinking, listening, and writing that it entailed would allow something worthwhile to emerge out of my grief.

Since mourning Jack's death, I have not retuned to treating children, but I do feel freer to treat young adults whose parents pay for their treatment and thus could still end it by refusing to pay. I now know that I could find satisfaction in having done as much as I could, even if the treatment were interrupted and the patient's growth suspended or even reversed. At least Jack had one experience of mutual respect and was honest and fair with me. That was something for both of us.

I am grateful to the editors of this book for the opportunity to revisit my feelings about Jack and to mourn his loss through premature termination of the treatment and his death. Had I not been writing this paper, I might never have gotten as far in my struggle to understand loss, death, grief, and mourning.

NOTE

The case discussed here is disguised so that the privacy of the people involved is assured.

REFERENCES

Bacal, H. 1998. "Optimal Responsiveness and the Therapeutic Process." In *Optimal Responsiveness: How Therapists Heal Their Patients*, 3–34. Newark, N.J.: Jason Aronson.

Barthelme, F., and S. Barthelme. 1999. *Double Down: Reflections on Gambling and Loss.* New York: Harcourt.

Didion, J. 2005. *The Year of Magical Thinking.* New York: Knopf.

Dostoyevsky, F. 1866. *The Gambler.* Trans. C. Garnett, ed. G. S. Morson. New York: Modern Library, 2003.

Freud, S. 1912. "The Theme of the Three Caskets." In *The Standard Edition of the Complete Psychological Works of Sigmund Freud [SE]*, ed. J. Strachey, 12:289–301. London: Hogarth.

——. 1917. "Mourning and Melancholia." *SE* 14:237–258.

——. 1920. *Beyond the Pleasure Principle. SE* 18:1–64.

Kaufmann, P. 2008. "The Reparative Quest and the Integration of the Traumatic Past." Paper presented at the International Federation of Psychoanalytic Educators conference, Seattle, Wash.

Mezrich, B. 2002. *Bringing Down the House.* New York: The Free Press.

Orr, G. 2001. *Orpheus and Eurydice.* Port Townsend, Wash.: Copper Canyon.

Richards, A. K., and A. D. Richards. 1997. "Gambling, Death, and Violence: Hollywood Looks at Las Vegas." *Psychoanalytic Review* 84: 769–788.

Shteyngart, G. 2010. *Super Sad True Love Story.* New York: Random House.

Thomas, D. 1936. *Twenty-Five Poems.* London: Dent.

CHAPTER 6

WHEN A PATIENT DIES

Reflections on the Death of Three Patients

SYBIL HOULDING

OUR PROFESSION elevates the status of what we—somewhat brutally—designate the "termination phase" of analysis. A terminated case—one in which both parties agree to conclude their relationship at some specified date in the future—is often a requirement for graduation. We recognize the demands on both analysand and analyst during this anticipated ending of a long and intense relationship. The unexpected death of a patient short-circuits this process for the analyst and highlights the special difficulties of mourning this unique relationship.

Within a five-year period, three patients in three different forms of treatment with me died unexpectedly. The differences among the three situations—the timing within the treatment, the transference/countertransference matrix at the time, and events in my own life—all profoundly influenced my response to each death. They led me, in retrospect, to consider the developmental aspects of this unexpected event in the life of a working analyst. By development, I mean all aspects of a structure-building process that unfolds over time from a recognized starting point and moves to an anticipated endpoint. It is a situation that is not addressed in our training, and it is one for which we are quite unprepared. A patient's death leaves the analyst struggling to find her way, usually alone.

I was not eager to write this chapter. I did not want to revisit the losses that had caused so much disruption in my internal life and that were now sealed over and behind me. But, after considering how much a book such as the editors were proposing would have helped me to locate myself at the time of these deaths, I realized that this would be a unique opportunity to think more carefully and, perhaps, to a larger purpose than my own recovery.

JULIE

Julie was in analysis—first at four and later at five times per week—from May 2003 through August 2004. In her early fifties, Julie was petite, lively, and attractive, a married mother of three. She had been in several relatively brief treatments with a colleague who had seen her in weekly sessions for depression. It was after this final episode of treatment for depression that my colleague recommended analysis and referred Julie to me. Julie seemed eager to understand and change her chronic unhappiness but also reluctant to acknowledge the seriousness of her difficulties. Although often filled with despair, Julie tried to present a happy and successful face to the world. "All my life I've been a really good girl," she reported in our first interview.

Julie was raised in a wealthy family, surrounded by a successful brother and many wealthy and accomplished cousins. Julie's mother was a narcissistic and mentally ill woman. Her primary mode of relating to the world was to maintain a privileged social position and to look good. These were the values she instilled in Julie, without providing her with the means to succeed.

Julie continued to be preoccupied with trying to emulate and please her mother while also rejecting what she perceived as superficial and unattainable. Her brother was the recipient of the family's largesse. It was he who was given the opportunity for private schooling and the financial means for social success. When Julie met her first husband at the age of twenty, she felt she had found a place for herself. But after a year of marriage, her husband committed suicide. Her husband's parents were nurturing—that perhaps had been part of her attraction to him—and continued to be so after their son's death. After her husband's suicide, her brother wrote, "Don't come back [to their family home]—there's nothing for you here."

Her second marriage, to Jack, her modest, intelligent, gentle husband, was a safe haven for her, and motherhood provided satisfaction. At the time that we began our treatment, Julie's children were in college, and she was working at a job well below her abilities, but one in which she still felt inadequate. She was envious of the people with whom she worked who had more education, confidence, and success. Julie's pattern had been to flee treatment when she began to feel better; part of her motivation for analysis was her worry that with her children launched, she could not live without her husband if he died. Jack was older than Julie and had had a serious illness several years before she began the analysis. Julie realized that she needed to become more internally self-sufficient.

An early note from the analysis reads, "*Activity, frantic activity, has been her defense against chronic sad feelings but in the analysis J. has begun to be able to tolerate them. Central themes are her feeling of estrangement, chronic feelings of outsider status, envy of others who have close family bonds, and constant preoccupation with social status.*"

I liked Julie and responded to her eagerness, her capacity for hope. She had an entertaining way of presenting herself. But after a few months, she allowed herself to show me the envy, rage, and deep despair hidden beneath her bright surface.

About one year after we began our work, Julie and I had reached a new phase of treatment. In the transference, I became the close female confidant she longed for. "You remember Jan," she would say, telling me the latest installation in her complicated relationship with a friend. Or, "my mother called again . . ." The comfort of our relationship in the transference allowed her to make tentative contact with the more disturbed parts of her inner world. This new feeling of connection was also used to disguise and avoid her growing dependence on me, one that felt deeply threatening to Julie's conscious ideal of complete self-sufficiency. I was able to interpret her difficulty with our weekend interruptions and her difficulty letting herself acknowledge this. She then accepted my recommendation that she come five times a week.

This period of the analysis also coincided with intermittent comments from Julie about difficulty swallowing and pain in her esophagus while eating. On some level, Julie welcomed this symptom. It helped her to control her appetite and maintain her ideal of slimness, and this supported her fantasy that she was without need—of food or nurturance. But as the discomfort persisted, she did call her doctor, who suggested an over-the-counter remedy for gastric reflux. When this did not alleviate her distress, tests were ordered. Ultimately, a full workup led to the shocking diagnosis of esophageal cancer.

"I did this to myself," Julie wept as she lay on my couch. Julie now threw herself into getting well with all the ferocity she had previously brought to other important challenges. For example, she had become a marathon runner and had pushed herself to learn to ski, despite her terror, because it was important to her husband. Her treatment involved chemotherapy and radiation, to be followed by surgery—but first she needed to gain weight. This required her to have a feeding tube inserted directly into her stomach, a daily procedure that lasted for a month.

A note from this period reads, "*I have been working supportively with J. by phone these last two weeks after an interruption for chemo and radiation . . . slowly I see a glimmer of a fuller analytic process.*" I look back on this note with amazement at my capacity for denial, my wish to preserve the analytic process in the face of such a serious, life-threatening situation. Julie, too, needed the idea that she was "in analysis" and that the surgery would lead to recovery and a resumption of our former relationship. A feeding tube to the stomach is a metaphor for an umbilical cord. So, too, a telephone line. Julie's deep regressive wishes were being met in the context of a life-threatening illness, one that also served her need for punishment for her rageful and envious feelings. While these thoughts are available to me now, they are useless. At the time, I felt like her lifeline.

Julie's surgery was scheduled for early August and coincided with my planned three-week break. "Oh good!" she said. "I'll be out of the hospital and ready to see you right when you return!" Those were her last words to me.

I thought about Julie during my time off. I returned to the office on the day of Julie's first appointment with great anticipation. When she did not show up or call, I became alarmed. I called her home and left a message, which was not returned. I want to write "weeks went by," but probably it was only days. This time is still a blur in my mind. I called the hospital, but they would tell me nothing except that she was still a patient. When Jack did call, he informed me that the surgery had been successful but that Julie's lungs had collapsed afterward and that she was being kept alive by an artificial respirator.

After a number of agonizing weeks, Julie died. I remember those weeks as a time of waiting with very little access to news about Julie's situation. I don't remember whether it was Jack or a member of his office staff who called me. And there is no one to ask, no family or friend to whom I can turn and ask, "How do *you* remember this?" Bereft, lonely, isolated, I searched the literature on PEP-Web for reports of others who had endured this experience, but I found nothing.

I went to Julie's memorial service with two colleagues who knew her husband and thus, tangentially, knew Julie. They were caring and aware of my situation, but they were not grieving as I was grieving. Sitting at the service, I struggled with the feeling that most analysands express at some point in treatment: *who am I—really—to you?*

Listening to Julie's children, her friends, her husband, I thought, *oh, I know you!* This helped me feel connected to Julie, as if later—*after it was over*—we could discuss it. As her community mourned Julie, I was invisible. I knew Julie as no one there knew her, but only she and I knew that. I was in that strange state where the mourner both knows her object has died but has not fully accepted this knowledge. Julie had often talked of feeling outside the bonds of the human community, very much alone. I felt outside the bonds of the mourning community, unable to participate in the comforting ritual of talk with others who knew and loved her. It was clear to me that as important as I was to Julie, I was totally irrelevant to her family. Several months later, I did receive a kind letter from Jack, when he paid the final bill, telling me how grateful he was for the work with Julie and how much it meant to her. The letter was meaningful to me in part because I felt acknowledged as someone who had sustained a loss.

For months, I walked around with Julie in my mind, hearing her chattering voice, imagining what story she might bring to a session, thinking of all the promise this analysis had held.

There were two important factors in my own life that had special resonance for me and made this loss unusually powerful. Nine years earlier, my mother had also died in August, also of cancer, also unexpectedly, during a reunion after a long and difficult estrangement, which left me hopeful that we were on the verge of a new and different relationship. The wound was not fresh. Analysis had helped me to mourn her. There was a powerful resonance about lost opportunities when Julie died. The loss of a compelling patient in a shocking way at a time of hope was very difficult, but in time I experienced this loss as part of my professional identity, something I understood and had integrated, rather than as a personal loss.

RALPH

Ralph and Lucy were referred to me by Dr. Jones, a clinician in the community who I knew by name and reputation. I met with the couple for seven sessions over the course of several months. Ralph was a highly successful professional; Lucy had decided to stay home with their two children after the birth of her second child. Much of the tension in the marriage revolved around Ralph's parents' opposition to his marriage to Lucy. The second source of tension was Ralph's obsession with work and his unavailability to Lucy and his children. Lucy had filed for divorce the previous year but agreed to reconcile after three months.

During the period after Lucy had filed for divorce, Ralph moved into the garage, drinking heavily and threatening suicide if Lucy went through with her plan. Lucy withdrew her motion for divorce. Suicide was thus in the air from the first session.

Ralph was a large, aggressive man. It was clear that his only reason for participating in the sessions was to persuade Lucy to stay in the marriage. Alternately pleading and bullying, Ralph was unreachable. While he continued to insist that suicide would be his response to a separation or divorce, he was equally convincing that he could not be committed because he knew what to say to avoid this outcome.

Ralph rejected any interpretation I attempted to make about his extreme reaction to the possibility of separation; Lucy wavered between trying to persuade Ralph that she was no longer attracted to him and wanted to separate, while still wanting to maintain a good working relationship with him on behalf of the children. She hoped I could help them find a way to stay together for the sake of the children.

I too felt alternately hopeful—when Lucy suggested she might want to stay—and despairing and trapped by Ralph's intransigence, when Lucy expressed her wish to leave. The sessions were often stormy, and I worried about Ralph's stability. He categorically refused any suggestion of treatment for himself.

My note for our last session reads as follows: "*During this session spelled out rationale for continued therapy: to work out a companionate marriage on behalf of children.*" This was the couple's new goal, and I felt some relief that we had seemed to settle on a plan, one that I could help them with. I was to be away from the office for a week, and we were to resume when I returned. While I wasn't sure my feeling of relief would last for long, I imagined it would last at least until we met again the following Wednesday. On Tuesday, I received a telephone message from Lucy. In it, she told me that on the prior Sunday she had requested a divorce and that Ralph had agreed. He went to work the next day but that night completed his suicide. In this message, Lucy also indicated that her individual therapist had "told" her she must tell Ralph she wanted a divorce. Yet it is hard to believe that Lucy really conveyed such a significant piece of information to me over the telephone. But such is the nature of shock. I just can't recall.

Shortly after I heard the news, I ran into a senior colleague on the street, a friend who saw that I was distraught. We retreated to his office, where he listened, empathized, and helped me to regain my balance. He was pointed in his comments about the therapist who had encouraged Lucy to confront Ralph in my absence. I worried that if I had not been actively complicit in this *folie a deux*, I had, at the very least, been incompetent. I felt angry with Lucy for her timing and angry with Ralph for his belligerence and hate. I felt sorrow for the tragic outcome. I felt grief only in the grand sense: that the human condition is ultimately tragic. I felt profound concern for the children. But personal grief requires personal connection.

In the aftermath, I received a call from Dr. Jones, who wanted to talk about what had happened, and we found solace in our conversations. We were comrades in arms in a battle we had lost. I learned that Lucy had terminated her treatment with Dr. Jones shortly after the couple had begun to see me and had begun to see a different therapist, the woman who (perhaps) had encouraged her to leave Ralph. I felt like I had been dealt a bad hand from an incomplete deck of cards. I had a final session with Lucy several weeks later. My memories of what we talked about are vague and blurry. Lucy was still in shock, and probably I was too. I have no notes from that session. I was grateful to learn that clinical interventions had been initiated on behalf of the children and Lucy.

This death was very disturbing in a way markedly different from the death of Julie. In the immediate aftermath, I felt manipulated and used by this couple, an unwilling witness to their game of Russian roulette. This characterization is harsh—they were in pain, floundering. I felt the assault on my competence, and it stung. I had consciously felt that the only way for this couple to separate would be through death—Ralph's suicide—but I had also hoped, perhaps expected, that I could help prevent this. I think about this couple from time to time, mostly trying to find the intervention that could have changed things.

Another significant difference was that I now had a context in my mind: a category marked "when a patient dies." I had moved—without my consent—from innocence to experience, and I knew that, however disturbed I felt, I would recover. With Julie, I did not have to question my implication in her death. With Ralph and Lucy, I felt different things.

PETER

Peter too died in August, also during my summer break. At the time, I had been experiencing some medical worries. I left the doctor's office with good news, feeling elated. Sitting in my car in the warm sunshine, I was relaxed and happy. I picked up my cell phone to check my messages and found one from a former patient who had referred Peter, asking me to call her. Alarmed, I phoned her and learned that Peter had died that week. While on vacation, he had fallen down a flight of stairs. My mood also plummeted. The transition from elation to shock and horror was swift and in itself disorganizing. Slowly, I absorbed the few details that my former patient knew. I called the psychiatrist who had been medicating Peter, and she was able to gather more details. We learned that he had fallen, hit his head, and died instantly. As it turned out, the stairs in his rented house were not up to code. Somehow this tiny nugget of information provided solace of a kind, perhaps a *cause.*

I had been seeing Peter for about fifteen months in weekly psychotherapy. In his first session, he announced he had become depressed when he received the papers from his second wife, who was suing for divorce. Although the couple had been separated, and in fact it was Peter who had moved out, he was still troubled enough for his friend, my former patient, to refer him for treatment. Usually, although I take notes after an initial session, I have no trouble remembering what was said when the patient returns for the second session. But with Peter, I found myself struggling to remember him more clearly, and I checked my notes, which still did not bring him into focus. When he arrived for his second session with a large bandage on his head, he said, "Now let me tell you why I'm really here." Peter had struggled with alcoholism in the past, but after a long period of being sober, he found himself drinking heavily during this separation, even prior to receiving the divorce papers. The bandage covered a wound incurred when he fell and hit his head on a coffee table in the living room, after having drunk an entire bottle of scotch.

The beginning of treatment was marked by a detoxification program, followed by Peter's voluntary participation in AA and in an outpatient treatment program for substance abuse. He also accepted my referral for a medication consultation. Peter was a talented and valued teacher, and the university where he taught gave him time off to recover. He was also a successful artist and a musician who had toured Europe after college, supporting himself playing music. He had been married to his first wife for twenty years and had been very involved in raising his daughter. Even with all these talents, however, he was a very lonely man. Peter had sought therapy once in the past for help with his drinking, which had led to the twelve-year period of sobriety prior to his current lapse. His working-class background and his deep identification with his family left him feeling shame at the prospect of needing therapeutic help. Like Julie, he presented a happy face to the world, and although his inner world was richer, deeper, he often felt very alone. Slowly, over the course of the year, Peter began to open himself to the process, and I was more aware of his dependent longings. He recognized that our relationship was becoming much more important to him.

In the weeks before the August break, Peter was in good spirits. He was going to a place he loved, the island to which he returned each summer, and he was feeling hopeful about a new relationship. He appeared healthy and sober. I was feeling much more deeply involved in the treatment—a very different state of mind from my initial difficulty forming an image of Peter. I was looking forward to continuing our work together after the August interruption.

I went to the memorial service with my colleague and friend who had been medicating Peter, and we cried quietly together. It was a small gathering, but the eulogies were eloquent and heartfelt. Peter had touched people very deeply. There was an image of him on the podium, smiling and radiant.

In addition to my grief about Peter, I was struggling with the parallels with Julie: August, vacation, a time of hope followed by death. This was the third time in five years that I had experienced the death of a patient, and I wondered if I had the psychic energy to do the work of mourning. But what choice did I have? I felt tired and on some level resentful that this had happened again. I was also in a vulnerable place because of the recent concern about my own health. Looking back, I think that in addition to the real grief over the loss of someone I had come to care deeply about, I also knew about the toll and trajectory of mourning a patient one has lost to death.

CONCLUSION

The termination phase of an analysis will revive, for the analyst and her patient, previous experiences of loss and mourning. These feelings will be encountered within the frame that the analytic pair has agreed upon, in the service of the analysand's development.

The death of the patient—a person with whom one has been involved at the complicated intersection of professional obligation fueled by personal involvement—truncates the development of the treatment and deprives the analyst of the opportunity to anticipate and process the ending to an important relationship, one in which the sadness of the ending is accompanied by feelings of accomplishment and satisfaction.

The sudden and unexpected deaths of my three patients suggest to me that how one experiences the death of the patient is closely linked to a number of factors. These include the timing of the death in relation to the development of the treatment and the particular moment when the death occurs in relation to the analyst's personal and professional life. When Julie died, I was three years post graduation. Five years later, Peter died. Ralph's death occurred in the interim. I suspect that these deaths affected my analytic identity in ways that I cannot articulate, although I now have a hard-won inner knowledge of this particular terrain.

My experience of Julie's death was heightened by the revived memory of my mother's death and the long mourning it initiated. I felt much more keenly the loneliness and isolation that accompanies mourning a significant loss without a context or community. The intensity of my involvement with Julie, which was invisible to people who mourned her, coupled with the newness of the experience, made this death particularly difficult.

Ralph's death was disturbing in a very different way. While I was deeply upset about his tragic suicide, my grief was mixed with anger. The feelings were more short-lived and less painful. After Peter's death, I grieved for him and our process, but with an element of fatigue. I deeply regretted that a vital life and process had been cut short. But I was also somewhat preoccupied with my own resolving health crisis. Mourning was something to be endured, and I was weary. And while I was emotionally involved with Peter, the rhythm of psychotherapy is necessarily different from an analysis conducted five times per week and the involvement less intense.

The cumulative but varied experience of these three deaths led me to consider developmental aspects of the unwanted experience of the sudden death of a patient. The phase of the treatment, the state of the transference, the status of the analyst's professional development at the time the patient dies, as well as the proximity—both in timing and content—to resonant issues in the analyst's psyche at the time of a patient's sudden death will have a profound effect on her experience. As our field becomes more prepared to discuss this aspect of our professional work, perhaps these reflections will help to chart the territory.

CHAPTER 7

WHEN WHAT WE HAVE TO OFFER ISN'T ENOUGH

Suicide in Clinical Practice

CATHERINE L. ANDERSON

LIKE MANY psychically powerful pursuits, my struggle to make sense of the ways in which a patient's suicide affects the therapist stems from my experiences with patient suicide. These painful events propelled me to examine the process by which we work through a patient's suicide in light of the specific developmental and professional context within which it occurred. In order to give form to this discussion, I provide three clinical examples of suicides that occurred during distinct phases in my career, each of which contributed to a deeper understanding about what had happened and the eventual meaning that each suicide came to hold for me.[1]

EARLY IN MY CAREER

My first experience with the loss of a patient to suicide occurred when I was just a couple of years into my career, a newly minted and very young therapist working in a regional community mental health center. This was community mental health as it was originally envisioned, with excellent patient treatment of whatever length was deemed clinically appropriate. The professionals with whom I worked represented various disciplines and theoretical orientations, and it was an environment in which I soon thrived. Although I was, by far, the least experienced member of the clinical team, there was excellent and abundant supervision and a strongly held ethic of group consultation and support. My supervisor's expectation that I would develop a deeper understanding of my self, my patient, and the work that transpired between us became my first meaningful exposure to psychodynamic thinking.

At such an early stage in my professional development, this "holding environment" provided the all-important framework within which to begin to metabolize the devastating experience of my first patient suicide—that of an adolescent boy who had been court-ordered into individual and group therapy with me and who, about a year into treatment, went into the woods behind his home and shot himself. This suicide, and the one that followed a couple of weeks later—the surprising death of a popular and accomplished high-school girl whose father had died of a debilitating illness the year before—was devastating for me and my other patients. In the months that followed, what initially appeared to be two isolated suicides became linked to others in our community. It was only because I experienced such deliberate, thoughtful supervisory reflection that I began to develop the cognitive and affective scaffolding within which to take in the enormity of what had happened (Tinsley and Lebak 2009). Through this process, I began to understand the multiple intense emotions that I experienced.

My clinical work at that time was with a very vulnerable population of adolescents and young adults, most of whom abused drugs and alcohol and had some involvement with social services or the local courts. They typically came from families with multigenerational patterns of profound abuse and neglect. By and large, the patients with whom I worked also had severe mood disorders and significant difficulty with emotional regulation: several had prior suicide attempts. In other words, they were a classically "at-risk" population, and I quickly found myself at the epicenter of a growing crisis within the community.

In a perverse variant of a sociogram, over the next year I found myself linked to an increasing number of patients who were scattered across the beginning, middle, and end of an epidemiological suicide cluster. A number were completed suicides—mostly by gun—and even more adolescents and young adults made serious suicide attempts. I had come to know these patients through varied therapeutic roles, including those of group therapist, individual therapist, and forensic evaluator. With some, I had a current relationship; with others, I did not. Most of the deaths occurred with no forewarning, so that I soon came to brace myself whenever a patient wouldn't show up for a session. On three occasions, this was how I initially discovered that another of my patients had died.

It was within this professional environment that I first experienced the transformative power of supervision, consultation, and institutional support to help young therapists work through otherwise overwhelming and unarticulated events. In the absence of such support, how does one develop the ability to make sense of events, especially those that seem so horrifically random? These deaths defied comprehension; they seemed to occur without rhyme or reason. Fortunately, the repeated telling and retelling that constitutes, at least in part, the "working through" of trauma allowed me to use supervision and peer support to piece together slowly my experiences into a more coherent narrative. It was during this time that I first began to understand how, despite my fantasy that I should be able to prevent patients from killing themselves, I could not.

Of equal importance, I also came to comprehend that knowing this reality did not leave me powerless. Instead, I was repeatedly encouraged to bring to my patients the same "holding environment" that I experienced in that work environment—a collaborative model that could develop out of the therapeutic relationship, within the context of my patients' available support systems and my own. By relying on the supports that were readily available to me in that setting—including therapy, supervision, support from my peers, and ongoing training—my patients and I were increasingly able to find words for these terrifying fears and powerful urges toward annihilation and work them through. Within this milieu, I eventually came to appreciate the value of repeatedly turning my attention to how the patient and I could work together within our shared therapeutic space so that we could contain the storm that confronted us both.

A FEW YEARS LATER

A few years into my career, I moved to a large urban setting. There I opened a small private practice to supplement my income while I continued to work in community mental health. After a few months, I began a consultation with a woman in her mid-thirties. Her concerns were familiar ones. She was afraid that her husband no longer loved her and that he was preparing to leave the marriage. Although she was anxious, with some rumination and difficulty sleeping, nothing about her presentation seemed outside the familiar, predictable distress that people often show when they are threatened with the loss of an intimate relationship.

At the end of this first session, we agreed to meet again in three days, but that was not to be. Instead, two nights later, her husband came back from his travels and told her that he wanted a divorce. A few hours later, as he slept on the couch, she took an overdose, went to sleep, and never woke up. Her husband found her the next morning when I called to follow up on the missed appointment. That moment of discovery, transmitted across the phone lines, is indelibly etched in my memory.

It would be one thing if I could say that my inability to remember her clearly was the result of the many intervening years since we had so briefly met. That would be readily understandable. If I am honest, however, I have to admit that, almost from the time of our meeting, she left only an ephemeral trace in my memory. I now think that the lack of lasting memory is largely because I never really allowed her to inhabit my mind in any meaningful way.

If we could look back at the session as observers, however, there would be no hint of anything that was amiss in the relationship between us. I was attentive and engaged and asked the sorts of questions that we all ask in our initial meetings with patients. She answered my queries in a similarly thoughtful, although distressed, manner and was willing and able to engage with me. If we had a transcript of the session, it would appear that the important therapeutic issues all had been addressed. Yet, somehow, ours did not constitute an authentic, albeit nascent, connection. I now know that while I was willing to take in the details of her story, I did not let myself fully encounter her. Much like Frankenstein's monster, all the component parts were there, alive but isolated and unnamed.

I do not know—in fact, I cannot know—if her story would have ended differently had I listened to her on that day with what Reik (1948) referred to as the "third ear" of the analyst's unconscious. What I can know, however, is that on this occasion I did not. Such attuned and potentially transformative listening involves the therapist's willingness to "learn how one mind speaks to another beyond words and in silence" (144). On that particular day, however, for reasons both mundane and unique to my intrapsychic makeup, I was not able to listen from within the spaces that existed between the words—that place where deeper psychic meanings are first encountered.

In the years since, I have struggled to make sense of my patient's wish to reach out for help and of my inability—or, maybe if I am completely honest, it was an unwillingness—to meet her fully in that place of neediness and despair. One of the ways that I now understand that subtle yet potentially devastating therapeutic impasse is through the lens of the Jewish philosopher Martin Buber (1923). He framed such moments of meaningful dialogical encounter—those that we attempt to elicit in the intimacy of our shared therapeutic spaces—as "I-Thou" moments. According to Buber, in the absence of these meaningful dialogues, we may believe we are communicating with another individual in an essential and attuned manner, yet that person will somehow remain outside of us. According to Buber, in such moments, we may instead seek refuge in our habitual self-absorption and not risk establishing an authentic contact with the other.

Buber theorized that it is only when we filter out these distractions that the other person becomes a "Thou" with whom we are directly and meaningfully confronted. Buber maintained that such encounters were rare and transformative moments for both parties. This capacity for an I-Thou connection came to be understood as an embodiment of the importance that Buber placed on trying to "know the questions" held in the mind of the other before they had even been formulated (Hodes 1969).

Buber's writings describe how he came to understand the importance of "knowing the mind of the other" following an encounter—much like my encounter with my patient—with an unknown young man who sought him out to talk. During this interaction, Buber stated that he remained absorbed in his spiritual pursuits, describing himself as friendly but not really there in spirit.

> I did not treat him any more remissly than all his contemporaries . . . I conversed attentively and openly with him—only I omitted to guess the questions that he did not put. Later . . . I learned he had come to me not casually, but borne by destiny, not for a chat but for a decision. He had come to me, he had come in this hour. What do we expect when we are in despair and yet go to a man? Surely a presence by means of which we are told that nevertheless there is meaning.

> (Hodes 1969, 242)

Following his meeting with Buber, the young man killed himself. Buber contended that this encounter with the despairing young man ultimately forced him to confront how the mere exchange of words and ideas is not sufficient for meaningful communication to occur, unless we are similarly willing to listen for the "unspoken question" that is held by the other. Similar to Buber's epiphany, such capacity for deep listening is central to the ideals shared by all of the various psychoanalytically oriented psychotherapies.

Of course, such transformative moments are largely aspirational and cannot be simply created. The conditions under which they may occur, however, can be cultivated in the interpersonal relationships in which we work. In reality, of course, our typical days are ones in which we markedly fluctuate in our capacity to listen and our willingness to be present with our patients. Like Winnicott's "good-enough" mother, we similarly strive to be good-enough therapists so that a space is created within the relationship from which both patient and therapist can interpret and understand the various intrapsychic conflicts that play out in the room. From that base of "good-enough" therapy, we are challenged to attune ourselves again and again to the hidden meanings of the deeper exchanges occurring between us. In our psychoanalytic world, these hidden meanings form the unspoken questions that exist within the relationship between patient and therapist.

IN MORE RECENT YEARS

Several years ago, I was the clinical supervisor for a young postdoctoral therapist; we both worked in an inpatient setting with very vulnerable and chronically suicidal patients. All of these patients had, by virtue of their admission to the program, reported histories of severe interpersonal trauma often dating back to childhood. Although she was well liked and well trained, this young therapist was quite reserved, and I struggled to find a way to be useful in my role as her supervisor. She readily engaged around technical issues in the treatment, but I had little success in helping her to look at her countertransferences with these difficult and demanding patients. It was as if, although I tried, I could never really find "her" within our supervisory relationship. Despite my vague uneasiness, however, I soon attributed this distancing to the profound ethnic and cultural differences that existed between us. My discomfort with these differences and my inability to find a way to talk about them productively led to important areas in the transference and countertransference that remained largely unexamined. As a result of my reticence, the supervisory space between us remained unbridged.

Almost a year after she began supervision with me, I was informed that this young therapist's husband had unexpectedly and violently killed himself the night before. Following the funeral—one of the most painful I have ever attended—she requested an extended leave. She was clearly devastated. Many of the staff members with whom she worked generously donated their leave. While she was on extended medical leave, we met on several occasions to consider her private and professional options. She began the painful process of rebuilding her life.

A few months into her bereavement leave, however, I received a weekend phone call from the medical director of the unit on which I worked, telling me that the husband's suicide had occurred after he had discovered that my supervisee was sexually involved with one of the traumatized and acutely suicidal patients who had been treated on the unit. My supervisee had been assigned as this patient's individual therapist, and I had been the clinical supervisor. Unbeknownst to any of the staff, shortly after the therapist's husband killed himself, my supervisee had encouraged this patient to move into her home. A few months later, the relationship abruptly imploded, and the patient filed a formal complaint against the therapist, precipitating the weekend phone call. The patient's accusations were soon substantiated, and criminal proceedings were successfully brought against the therapist.

It is hard to adequately describe the range of feelings that I experienced during those initial weeks and months. While simultaneously dealing with my intense feelings of betrayal, rage, and helplessness, I needed to support and contain the patients and clinical staff (several of whom I also supervised) and help manage the ongoing inpatient program. For several months, it was unclear whether I, as the clinical supervisor, would also be named as a party in the legal proceedings. Anxiety became my constant companion. The stress was further exacerbated because the legal constraints in this case prevented me from utilizing my usual well-established supports from peer consultation and clinical supervision.

An unanticipated consequence of this threatened legal involvement was that, out of a pervasive sense of shame and fear, I became increasingly withdrawn and isolated. My anxiety further escalated when my malpractice insurer informed me that I would not be covered if I was named in a civil or criminal case or an ethics hearing before my licensing board, since this was a case of sexual misconduct and thus excluded from coverage. My protests that this was about the actions of my supervisee and not about my behavior as a supervisor were to no avail. I felt alone, afraid, and powerless. The lines between what was my responsibility and what was not were fundamentally blurred. According to the lawyers, I was to talk about this only with the other professionals directly involved in the case, each of whom was equally overwhelmed and traumatized. My shame followed me around like a shadow, casting a pall on all of my subsequent interactions.

Over time, I came to understand that the relationship with my supervisee had created an enactment in which projective identifications unfolded both before and after the suicide. I now believe that both my supervisee and I became initially immersed and subsequently entangled in a parallel process of projective identification within the supervisory relationship. This supervisory experience is similar to those in which I have treated someone in the field who brings their own experience of a patient suicide into the treatment. In each situation, powerlessness is a dominant emotion.

The supervisory relationship with this therapist was far removed from my experiences with suicide earlier in my career. Then I had to contend with the failure of relationship and insight—both mainstays of our psychoanalytically oriented work—to hold adequately my suicidal patients. In contrast, within the "once-removed" situation that characterizes supervision—one in which the supervisor is both observer and participant—a potent process of projective identification may occur. Such unconscious processes are understood to occur as a reaction to the supervisee's feelings of strong, often overwhelming emotions arising from his or her work with a patient who is experiencing powerful primitive urges toward self-destruction. These same feelings can become similarly and powerfully activated within the supervisory dyad. At such times, the supervisor risks responding—as does the supervisee with her patient—with what Shapiro (1982) described as "pathological certainty," in which curiosity is replaced by an inability to tolerate the anxiety inherent in uncertainty and helplessness. In such moments, the potential relationship becomes impenetrable, and the unconscious pull toward concrete thought or acting out is heightened.

Furthermore, my response to the filing of the complaint formed yet another parallel enactment of the isolation, fear, and shame that both my supervisee and her traumatized patient likely experienced. In my attempt to master my anxiety through the illusion of control, which is a hallmark of projective identification, I ritualistically attended many ethics trainings over the next couple of years. My motivations alternated between a desperate need to understand what had happened and a magical wish to protect myself against any future vulnerability. Simultaneously, this stance also allowed me to punish myself for the betrayal that had transpired under my supervision. It was not until I began to break this shame-based pattern of enacting isolation and fear that my curiosity and capacity to think—the ability to construct meaning out of these events—returned. Only then was I able to struggle with both the current and future meanings of the betrayal and allow myself finally to move beyond them. Emerging from this struggle marked the turning point where I could fully reenter my professional and personal relationships from a position no longer dominated by shame and fear.

I now believe that my failure to maintain curiosity about our mutual unwillingness to speak honestly in supervision about these important yet unformulated issues was an outgrowth of my own uncertainty and helplessness, feelings that too closely mirrored her own. At a minimum, in addition to the ethnic and cultural differences that existed between us, my supervisee also experienced marital and sexual identity issues of which I was unaware. When these unacknowledged issues became activated within this inpatient setting—issues that were repeatedly and powerfully woven together with our patients' primitive urges toward self-destruction—our mutual failure to find a way to "speak the unspeakable" resulted in catastrophic consequences.

DISCUSSION

Within the framework of these three episodes, I slowly deepened my understanding of the powerful and often unconscious forces that suicide and loss create within the psychotherapist, as well as the future effect of that loss on our personal and professional identity. When we encounter a patient who, despite our efforts, actively chooses to turn away from us through death, we are profoundly and inevitably unsettled. Such an irrevocable choice severs both the existing relationship as well as any potential it possessed. Instead we are abandoned, left to encounter our own impotence.

At its most basic, the act of suicide represents a powerful proclamation that all hope for a satisfactory rapprochement between patient and therapist has been annihilated. How we recover from this loss, however, depends on several factors: our intrapsychic understanding of the event and of ourselves, the stage of our professional development at the time of our patient's suicide, and the professional and personal context within which we experience and begin to work through the loss. My experiences provided me with valuable insights into the various facets of grief and self-doubt that clinicians may confront after a suicide. At a personal level, during the immediate and longer-term aftermath of each death, I was forced to confront my own fantasies and unresolved conflicts that were activated by the experience of loss. It was only then that I could begin to work through the distress and painful narcissistic wounds that inevitably resulted.

Allowing one's self to be deeply unsettled by the countertransference anxieties that arise during such times has the potential to produce profound, even transformative change in the therapist. However, to work through the anxieties in such a way that we ultimately metabolize these hard-won insights, we must somehow tolerate the destabilization that occurs at the very point in time when we are at our most emotionally vulnerable. This is no small undertaking. As Gabbard (2006, 184) aptly noted in his article about ethical pitfalls with suicidal patients, "Those patients who hate us, defeat us, mock us and torment us also penetrate us in a way that lays bare our vulnerabilities. They make us face the complexity of our motives in choosing our impossible profession."

While such words would ring true in our work with any chronically hopeless/suicidal patient, we encounter these feelings most powerfully at the point where we are confronted by our patient's deliberate choice of death over life. Following a patient suicide, we are forced to confront the reality that this act carries with it the unambiguous rejection of the therapeutic relationship we were attempting to create together. Such a stark decision denies the grieving therapist access to the wide array of possibilities for change and healing that are otherwise contained, at least in embryonic form, within the latent capacity of even the most difficult therapeutic relationships. The suicide thus marks the death not just of the patient but also of the possibility that existed within the dyad for the eventual construction of shared therapeutic meaning.

Thus, all hopes of eventual relational repair are thwarted; there is no possibility to resolve any treatment errors and failings that we may later painfully identify. As a result, we are caught between the simultaneous experience of knowing the facts of the death yet still not truly comprehending what transpired within the relationship or within each of us. We are suspended in a fundamental state of confusion. The narrative remains unformed.

Among therapists, there is a powerful wish to deny the reality that a suicide may occur in our clinical practice. The belief in our professional immunity— a belief that is, unfortunately, infused with magical thinking— is in stark contrast to the statistics demonstrating the "very real occupational hazard" of patient suicide among mental health practitioners. Although we typically persuade ourselves that such an event could not happen with our patients, the research paints a bleaker picture (Courtenay and Stephens 2001, Dewar et al. 2000, McAdams and Foster 2000). Yet a central aspect of our "impossible profession" requires us to be willing to encounter fully and thereby bear the pain, hopelessness, and rage of our patients. A similar defensive retreat into institutional denial undermines both the training that we provide young therapists and our ongoing work with individual patients. Especially in the current climate of the "widening scope" of psychoanalytic treatment, we are now more likely than ever to encounter at-risk patients within the relative isolation of our treatment rooms. Tendencies toward such institutional avoidance can result in disastrous consequences for the young therapist, since negative personal and professional outcomes are disproportionately noted among those therapists and psychiatrists who experienced a patient suicide during an early stage of their career (Chemtob et al. 1988). Thus, as we acknowledge the very real possibility that a patient of ours could suicide, we must also find a way to tolerate the inescapable anxiety that such awareness produces. In this process we create the necessary relational and intrapsychic space to function adequately in our familiar psychotherapeutic roles.

A personal and institutional overreliance on denial has grave consequences for our treatment of despairing patients. By adopting a stance of professional invulnerability, we deny the distress that is inherent in the work and run the risk of responding in ways that are clinically foreign to us. In addition, such a defensive stance may cause us to respond in ways that render us unrecognizable to our patients or ourselves. During such moments, we may find ourselves taking refuge in a flight into action, where we replace our familiar analytic curiosity with an overreliance on concrete thought and primitive defenses.

In an attempt to master our collective anxiety, our profession instead relies on magical rituals like the use of patient suicide/no-harm contracts or diagnostic checklists—despite the flimsy scientific evidence that these actually are successful in preventing suicide (Rudd, Mandrusiak, and Joiner 2006)—to provide powerful talismans against our own helplessness and any feared legal repercussions. Both in the privacy of our clinical offices and in our training institutions, we struggle with the fantasy that the loss of a patient to suicide is always, temptingly, "someone else's issue." The powerful, often unconscious conflict between this pull toward an inflexibility of theory and practice and a simultaneous incompatible belief in the importance of the holding environment provides us with a crucible that is central to the development of our psychoanalytic identity. Such rigidity is in conflict with the fact that we are taught—through our literature, our supervisions, and our own analyses—that the transformation of such affects comes, in large measure, from our ability to be a "good-enough" object with our patients.

Allowing ourselves to encounter our vulnerability during clinical crises is potentially dangerous for the patient and therapist, since any such encounter is fraught with the painful reality of our inevitable limitations, yet if this vulnerability is not acknowledged, the therapist's anxiety may become overwhelming, leading to poor treatment. Similarly, in response to the onslaught of the patient's destructive urges, the therapist may rely on manic defenses. These may take the form of a desperate, poorly directed attempt to "save the patient," thus masking an awareness of unconscious anger and powerlessness and simultaneously providing the therapist with the illusion of control.

In the midst of this crisis, the therapist is more likely to operate out of what Gabbard and Lester (1995) describe as a "deficit model." This rescue paradigm becomes activated when there is a countertransference collapse of the space within which the therapist and patient can think together. The psychotherapist then becomes convinced that, in a desperate attempt to save the patient's life, she must somehow compensate for what the patient is missing. A parallel dynamic can be observed when the supervisor is powerfully pulled to over-function or to break the frame with the supervisee in an uncharacteristic way when confronted with the supervisee's patient's intransigent suicidality.

During such times, we may "forget" that the most valuable contribution we can offer our patients and supervisees is our therapeutic stance. During these countertransference assaults, the primary danger occurs when we do not rely on our training (e.g., the use of careful assessment, a collaborative and thoughtful interaction with the patient or family, consultation, review of the "best practices" in the field, and, if necessary, voluntary or involuntary hospitalizations) but, instead, choose an impulsive, secretive, or unsymbolized/unthought approach. Whenever we are under such a profound attack on our thinking, we are at heightened risk of either a retreat into cognitive rigidity or toward engaging in boundary violations. For example, I now believe that a retreat to manic defenses, to fend off the awareness of her fear, anger, and powerlessness, may have been present in the initial boundary violations by my supervisee toward her patient.

In contrast to this countertransferential retreat to action, we are instead best served in our role as psychoanalytically oriented clinicians when, as Richard Almond (2003, 150) eloquently stated, we rely on the "holding function of theory" to navigate our way through the complexities of the clinical situation. He maintained that "the availability of such models . . . gives us, as we live in the analytic moment, additional reference points—helpful analytic thirds reassuring, informing, critiquing, and guiding us in the midst of the inchoate experience of one of life's more frightening situations." In such situations, theory provides the flexible holding that allows us to think in the midst of the storm and to provide this same analytic space for our patients.

Similar to the anxious, often dread-filled responses of my supervisees or patient-clinicians, these crises were ones in which my anxiety became markedly heightened as the intensity of the patient's suicidal ideation or attempts increased. My anxiety and dread created an impulse to respond in ways that were not typical for me and that would have, if acted upon, shifted the familiar, safe boundaries of the session by pulling me to over-function rather than to retain my clearly delineated role as supervisor or therapist.

This seductive pull toward action thus provided me with an illusory "siren song" of comfort and control by allowing me to substitute action for understanding. This served to facilitate an almost irresistible denial of my own powerlessness and anger, as well the powerlessness and rage of my patients and my supervisee, in the face of overwhelmingly potent, destructive impulses. Thus, the dynamic within these dyads had the potential to create what Gabbard (2006, 195) compellingly labeled a therapeutic impasse, in which there is a "failure of mentalization and collapse of analytic space." Within such a bleak internal landscape, the therapist suddenly lacks the capacity to think clearly and is, instead, pulled toward some form of unsymbolized action.

Gabbard wrote about such countertransferences within the context of serious professional boundary violations with very disturbed patients. What he said also applies to what happens in the "once-removed" space of supervision. In the supervisory experience that I described in this paper, I found myself unable to think with clarity and coherence about what was happening in the space between us. I would suddenly find myself becoming narcissistically invested in my capacity to save my supervisee or my patient from his or her perceived helplessness. Whenever we discover that we are adopting such a dangerous stance, we must seek to reestablish our curiosity and once again find a way to talk openly and honestly about it with each other.

CONCLUSION

The suicide of a patient is a fundamentally destabilizing and overwhelming event. We likely search, often obsessively, for any signs that we may have missed. Perhaps we feel numb or else rage against our helplessness—as well as the patient who caused it—and feel deep, isolating professional and personal shame. At least, those are feelings that are familiar to me.

How the situation unfolds depends on a number of important yet often idiosyncratic issues: the therapist's unique history and psychic structure, conflicts, and fantasies; what developmental stage the therapist's career is in; the availability and capacity of the professional and personal support systems that the therapist can access; and the previous relationship that existed between the patient and the therapist. These factors exert their influence—to greater or lesser degrees—during the therapist's subsequent attempts to form a coherent narrative around the loss. Without such a narrative, the coda of loss and grief remains unfinished. In this way, the grieving process is circumvented, and the bereft therapist is left without the capacity to name and, thus, fully mourn the multiple losses incurred by the suicide of a patient.

NOTE

1. The clinical vignettes used in this chapter span over thirty years of clinical practice and occurred in different regions of the country. Details that were not central to the clinical material being presented or were not part of the public record were disguised.

REFERENCES

Almond, R. 2003. "The Holding Function of Theory." *Journal of the American Psychoanalytic Association* 51: 131–153.

Buber, M. 1923. *I and Thou*. London: Continuum Impacts, 2004.

Chemtob, C., R. Hamada, G. Bauer, R. Y. Torigoe, and B. Kinney. 1988. "Patient Suicides: Frequency and Impact on Psychologists." *Professional Psychology: Research and Practice* 19, no. 4: 416–420.

Courtenay, K., and J. Stephens. 2001. "The Experience of Patient Suicide Among Trainees in Psychiatry." *Psychiatrist* 25: 15–52.

Dewar, I., J. Eagles, S. Klein, N. Gray, and D. Alexander. 2000. "Psychiatric Trainees' Experiences of, and Reactions to, Patient Suicide." *Psychiatric Bulletin* 24, no. 1: 20–23.

Gabbard, G. O. 2006. "Miscarriages of Psychoanalytic Treatment with Suicidal Patients." In *Contemporary Psychoanalysis in America: Leading Analysts Present Their Work*, ed. A. Cooper, 187–204. Washington, D.C.: American Psychiatric Press.

Gabbard, G. O., and E. P. Lester. *Boundaries and Boundary Violations in Psychoanalysis.* New York: Basic Books.

Hodes, A. 1971. *Martin Buber: An Intimate Portrait.* New York: Viking.

McAdams, C., and V. Foster. 2000. "Client Suicide: Its Frequency and Impact on Counselors." *Journal of Mental Health Counseling* 22, no. 2: 107–121.

Reik, T. 1948. *Listening With the Third Ear: The Inner Experience of a Psychoanalyst.* New York: Grove.

Rudd, D. M., M. Mandrusiak, and T. Joiner. 2006. "The Case Against No-Suicide Contracts: The Commitment to Treatment Statement as a Practice Alternative." *Journal of Clinical Psychology* 62: 243–251.

Shapiro, E. R. 1982. "On Curiosity: Intrapsychic and Interpersonal Boundary Formation in Family Life." *International Journal of Family Psychiatry* 3: 69–89.

Tinsley, R., and K. Lebak. 2009. "Expanding the Zone of Reflective Capacity: Taking Separate Journeys Together." *Networks* 11, no. 2: 1–11.

PART III

AT THE CROSSROADS OF THE THERAPIST'S PERSONAL AND PROFESSIONAL WORLDS

When we recover,
what have we mastered—
our love or our grief?

—Jody Bolz

IN THIS section, we examine the clinicians' experience of coping with personal changes and loss, which can profoundly affect one's sense of self as a therapist. When the frame of our work is shaken—whether by illness, old age, institutional changes, or the everyday losses we encounter in our practice—our identity as therapists is challenged. Such changes can land us in the realm of the middle-distance, where we may lose our perspective. Here, each of our authors examines the consequences of such shifts and highlights the inevitably of the denial and disavowal that we encounter in the middle-distance. These authors describe their efforts to be mindful of these pitfalls, even as their vision is partially obscured.

In her chapter, Jenifer Nields considers the question: how does illness in the therapist affect the frame of the treatment? She describes the onset of a debilitating and mysterious illness that interfered with her work as a psychiatrist, both as a therapist and as a supervisor. It took many long months to receive a diagnosis, during which time she experienced fear, isolation, and confusion. With neither a diagnosis nor a road map to plan the future, she too was trapped in the middle-distance. She relates a disruption in her sense of personal and professional identity, one that profoundly derailed her long-anticipated professional trajectory. Suddenly, she felt she no longer knew what her future would hold.

As with many of our authors, Nields describes the magical omnipotent wish that she could preserve and protect both her patients and her supervisee from the pain of uncertainty and loss. While her illness is invisible to others, its presence leaves an indelible trace. In the countertransference, she becomes aware of holding on to the idea that her recovery is just around the corner, which keeps despair at bay but at the same time keeps her patients on hold too long, with diminished therapeutic benefit. Importantly, she points out that "crisis also breeds intensity of attachment: those who are nearby and empathic at a time of tragedy in one's life become especially important to us." This observation also sheds light on the many ways in which therapists may find themselves holding on to patients too long.

Richard Waugaman's chapter, "The Loss of an Institution: Mourning Chestnut Lodge," expands the scope of our lens. For Waugaman, the closing of Chestnut Lodge required that he take his leave not only from each and every patient but also from his cherished hospital and the professional identity he had developed there over the course of many years. Through his correspondence with Harold Searles, which evolved toward the end of their decades-long relationship as student, mentee, and colleague, we get a glimpse of how both men—one still in the prime of his career, the other already retired—coped with the closing of the hospital. Waugaman writes, " 'Bereft' ultimately comes from a word that means 'rob,' and we certainly felt robbed of our beloved hospital."

As therapists, we are all shaped in by our connections with colleagues, supervisors, and the institutions where we trained and with which we are affiliated. Our professional identity is also rooted, in part, in our identification with the professional world of which we are members. Many of us feel that the institutions where we trained, worked, honed our skills, and developed our voices as clinicians become, in a sense, our professional homes. Our colleagues can be like family—at times we support one another, at other times we squabble, but still, we speak a shared language. Waugaman provides a moving eulogy for Chestnut Lodge and for a long-ago era of intensive inpatient care, where patients' dignity and selfhood were in the foreground.

Robert Galatzer-Levy addresses the issue of the analyst's difficulty in assessing when illness or old age interferes with the capacity to work. He wonders: how are we to judge when we can and when we cannot continue to work effectively? Like Nields, he highlights the various ways that analysts may "need" their patients and their work even more when they are ill or dying.

Galatzer-Levy points out that there is an additional layer of communal and institutional disavowal that heightens the risk of ethical violations under such circumstances. He discusses the tendency, even within our "impaired analyst committees," to replace what might be effective and useful oversight with perceived kindness and leniency, in the hope of "protecting" the reputation and the well-being of the impaired analyst. He argues that the analytic community fails to address productively this issue in part because it brings our own mortality to the forefront and gives rise to primitive fantasies and defenses. He writes, "The fantasy that 'we could all be in his shoes' hides the reality that we all are already in his shoes. . . . Every confrontation with a colleague's death is a confrontation with our own mortality and thus is experienced as a hostile attack."

Barbara Stimmel also addresses the question: how is the patient most effectively helped at the moment when the analyst is ill or dying? In contrast to Galatzer-Levy, she suggests that valuable and important therapeutic work can be achieved in the face of the analyst's illness or impending death. In her discussion, she suggests that ultimately there is no one right way. Each dyad must struggle with complex decisions. For example, how much does one reveal to the patient about the details of one's illness? For each therapist, the choice is partly informed by theoretical underpinnings and also by the idiosyncrasies of the therapist. Stimmel suggests that the outcomes of any such decisions are also specific to that particular patient-therapist pair.

Multiple fantasies and fears exist alongside the reality of an illness or impairment. Therefore, how can we know for sure when the decisions we make—for example, when to tell a patient the details of our illness—are based on the best interest of the patient or, instead, on our own needs? Stimmel makes the point that, with the dying analyst, as with any other aspect of the therapeutic encounter, both sides inevitably exert their influence. "The hope is," she writes, "that each of the two can play his or her part, helping one another with dignity, respect, and intelligence, until the time to stop is clear. And then mourning can fully begin."

As therapists we strive to hold simultaneously in mind multiple perspectives and to be aware of how internal and external forces affect the therapy and the therapeutic dyad. However, as we come to understand in this section, we are all in the sway of unconscious factors that we can never fully know and longings that can never be fully quelled.

CHAPTER 8

WHEN THE FRAME SHIFTS

A Multilayered Perspective on Illness in the Therapist

JENIFER NIELDS

> Those who know ghosts tell us that they long to be released from their ghost
> life and led to rest as ancestors. . . . In analysis, ghosts of the unconscious,
> imprisoned by defenses but haunting the patient in the dark of his defenses
> and symptoms, are allowed to taste blood, are let loose.

—Hans Loewald, "On the Therapeutic Action of Psychoanalysis" (1960)

INTRODUCTION: CRACKS IN THE FRAME

ONE'S PHYSICAL experience makes up a "frame" within which psychic action takes place. We don't notice the power of our bodily experience until it
changes. For me, this occurred most dramatically through illness.

What do we notice then? What happens to us psychologically when our
bodily "frame" shifts because of an illness, and we find ourselves functioning under altered conditions, adjusting to new physical sensations, or unable to function at all?

As therapists, how are we to judge when we can and when we cannot
continue to work effectively despite the effects of illness? How are we to
discern when the frame is shifted and when it is broken or too bent and
deformed to contain the treatment effectively? What are the countertransference and transference ramifications of our being ill?

Which aspects of the "field," of the unconscious interplay between patient and therapist, are heightened, enlivened? Which ones are obscured, distorted, or simply become too hot to touch? What "ghosts"—"let loose" by the illness—become once more visible, available to us perhaps to recognize and understand and thereby to enrich our work? Or so haunt us once again that we can't distinguish aspects of our present life from these specters from the past?

The narrative below explores the netherworld of an illness; by virtue of an unlikely conjunction of circumstances, it touches on these questions from several distinct vantage points: that of the patient, the therapist, and the supervisor.[1] My perspectives are informed by a medical illness that I sustained twenty years ago during residency training as well as by the experience of supervising a resident ten years later who fell severely ill with the very same disease. I hope these reminiscences, occurring over the course of two decades, may prove helpful to others who, struggling with illness in themselves or others close to them, may find resonance, illumination, and food for thought.

TWENTY YEARS AGO: RECOLLECTIONS OF AN ILLNESS DURING RESIDENCY TRAINING

During my last year of psychiatry residency training, my body turned traitor. Gradually, I became severely ill. At first I was determined to keep going, to keep my work as a fourth-year resident intact regardless of what assailed me, but eventually the symptoms—most dramatically, those affecting my balance and sensorium—became severe enough that I couldn't. I had no choice but to call in sick.

To live in my body now was to live in a world "through the looking glass," where all the rules had changed. I would be walking along and suddenly have the sensation of the ground dropping out from under me. My visual field would become dotted with sparks of light or would bend and move, as if viewed through rippling glass, and then return to normal. The edges of things seemed abnormally sharp, as if a flower petal could cut my skin. Colors seemed ultrabright. Sounds affected my balance, such that the flow of water from a faucet might topple me over. The sounds of glasses clinking together or of forks on plates, even if I were in the next room, would shoot through me like gunshots. The hum of the refrigerator seemed like the sound of a cement drill. Stabbing pains would startle me out of sleep, which I caught in round-the-clock catnaps never lasting more than an hour or two. For months, no one could explain what was happening. Eventually, via serendipity and my own and my husband's researching, I found my way to a doctor who finally could.

Even after receiving the diagnosis of what at the time was a little known tick-borne disease, it took years of trial-and-error treatments before I was substantially better. But of course I didn't know any of this in advance; the first several months were characterized by a steady and, at the time, inexplicable deterioration. I was in a personal crisis, with a poorly understood and progressive illness.

Meanwhile, the hospital unit where I worked was in its own crisis, being short staffed to begin with and now dealing with both the logistical and the emotional repercussions of losing a staff member. The unit was a long-term, psychodynamically oriented and milieu-based treatment program of a sort that no longer exists. Patients stayed for between six months to two years on the locked unit where I was a resident. Relationships among and between patients and staff members were intense, and the patients were exquisitely sensitive to changes in the setting, disruptions in their schedules, and anxiety in their caregivers. The community was already destabilized by the recent move to a new hospital building. High anxiety and a rash of acting-out behaviors had characterized the months leading up to and following the move. A patient had lost a piece of a finger when he stormed out of a community meeting and slammed it in the door, we'd had a convicted murderer on the unit, and staff members had been injured in multiple daily codes. Fantasies about what had happened to me or, perhaps, what had been done to me must have been rife. And I suspect there were those who were envious that I'd escaped the mess or who thought I must have fabricated the illness *in order* to escape. Adding to the ominous atmosphere was the fact that earlier that same year a senior resident had committed suicide.

As my illness progressed, I called in sick daily and then weekly. Someone on the ward staff ran my ward group; the chief resident took care of medication issues. I was in telephone contact with my therapy patients. After a few weeks, my therapy patients were reassigned to new therapists. This made sense to me, of course, but I experienced it as a loss. For months I had worked intensively with them and thought that any day I might be better and able to return to work. That I was deserting them, perhaps hurting them, and helpless to do anything about it was painful. I remember feeling irrationally betrayed when one of my patients requested a new therapist, and I sensed her withdrawal from me over the phone. Over the course of weekly contact with the director of education, he eventually suggested I take a medical leave. Actually, he formalized that as my status.

In retrospect, I think my disappearance must have been threatening to my fellow residents. A member of my residency group had died of AIDS a month or two previously. He had been ill during most of his residency training and had been in and out of work and in and out of the hospital. We'd been taking turns doing his call; he'd become cognitively impaired and eventually went blind. I imagine this context made my disappearance all the more frightening; it seemed almost like another death. This point was brought home to me years later when my supervisee became ill with the same disease I'd had and mentioned her diagnosis to a nurse at the training site where I'd been working when I got sick. The nurse responded with some alarm and great concern: "We *lost* a resident to that disease ten years ago."

While my workplace was losing me, I was losing my work. I struggled with letting go of each piece of my work life, not knowing when, if ever, I'd be able to reclaim any of it. Each step along the way was a step away from what I'd loved and was losing—my patients, my work, my colleagues, my working self—and toward the prospect of being isolated and unable to function.

One of the hardest aspects of letting go, and the one area where I had to use my own judgment—where the decisions were not made for me—was with my long-term patient, a woman with whom I had worked intensively in outpatient psychodynamic psychotherapy throughout the course of my residency. She and I had arranged to continue therapy even after the completion of my residency training. The work had gone well, and I felt there was a deep attachment on both sides.

When I first got sick, I phoned her the night before our session to cancel, saying what I thought was true, that I had the flu. I phoned her again the night before each subsequent session. After the second week, she asked that I not call her. She said it was too painful to receive that call the night before each session; she would rather wait to hear from me when I was better. When it became clear to me that there was no predicting when I'd be back, I called her and told her that and gave her the option of continuing her treatment with someone else. At that point, she said she felt she was not in crisis, was managing okay, and would rather wait for me. I agreed to phone her monthly to see how she was and to inform her of my status. After a few months, she wrote me a card saying that clearly whatever I had was more than the "flu," wishing me well, and saying she missed me but was okay and looking forward to my return.

It seems odd to me now that, as a trainee, I was nevertheless working in such isolation in relation to this particular patient—one who, by virtue of her being my first long-term patient as well as by virtue of a natural affinity between us, was particularly important to me. The person who supervised me on this patient had been supportive but saw his role as a didactic one, preferring not to be involved in details of patient management. I had not met with him since I'd fallen ill, so there was no one to advise me on this issue. (I shall return to this topic of isolation in the ill therapist later on, but suffice it to say that, ten years later, when I was the supervisor of an ill resident, I wanted to be much more actively involved.)

Even with the support of family and friends, small gestures, even from distant others, held tremendous import: a card from the secretary of the residency program brought me to tears and created, for me, a lasting bond and feeling of gratitude toward her. The one supervisor who continued to reach out to me became, from my perspective, a friend for life. The doctor who finally diagnosed and treated me appeared in my dreams as Luke Skywalker, showing the way and keeping me safe on this strange journey through an unfamiliar universe. Those who helped me seemed larger than life, their significance magnified greatly in my inner world.

When eventually my illness was diagnosed, I had some idea about a timeframe. I called my patient to let her know the diagnosis. I told her that I was embarking on treatment and expected to be better, but not for at least a month or more. I reiterated my concern that although I was hopeful I'd be able to resume work with her in time, there was no certainty, and I did not want her to be left hanging. Once again, I offered to make arrangements for her for treatment with a new therapist. She again opted to wait.

I was afraid I might be damaging my patient by having earned her trust and then disappearing; the words that kept going through my mind were "ripp'd untimely from the womb"—an image I learned from her much later that she had had as well (she had dreamed she'd had an abortion, then realized it was she—and her treatment—who had been aborted), yet, even if I could have overcome the physical obstacles, I knew I couldn't do the work: I was too frightened for myself at that point, my own health too unstable and perplexing, to hear about others' suffering. I imagined wanting to yell: "You think *you've* got problems!" I also knew I could not at this stage bear the inevitable negative feelings toward me that my illness might have occasioned—my own screaming need to feel I could still be a good object was too raw and pressing to enable me to help her process whatever mix of reactions and emotions *she* might be having and to protect her, and the treatment, from the pressure of my own needs. As one of my colleagues framed the therapeutic encounter: "you're the constant, they're the variable." This was so clearly not the case for me at that time.

About five months later, when I called her as usual, she greeted me anxiously and eagerly with the query: "Any news?" She said she desperately hoped this time I'd be calling to say I was returning, because she was starting to feel depressed again and felt she needed to see someone soon. If there would be any way to work with me in the foreseeable future, that would be her first choice, but she felt greater urgency than she had previously. I said I'd look into what arrangements could be made—reassignment to another trainee through the long-term psychotherapy program, another intake at the clinic from which she'd been referred, or, perhaps, some way to work with me—and call her in a week.

I called a former supervisor to discuss how to handle this juncture. I said, "I don't *know* when I'll be better. It could be next week, or . . . it could be months." He said, "That's *your* answer." He argued that it would be in the patient's best interest for me to tell her that at this juncture it was clear I would not be able to treat her and that she should be reassigned. I understood the wisdom in this, but, nonetheless, it was hard for me to hear. I remember my anguished refrain: *how* do you let go of the patient, and *when* do you let go of the patient when you're sick and don't know when the sickness is going to end? Or *whether* it will end?

When I called her the next week, she said she had already taken some action: she had made an appointment for a reevaluation at the clinic from which she'd originally been referred to me, hoping to get into treatment immediately and still have the option of returning to me if and when I was better. Partly I was delighted that she'd taken the situation in hand, and partly I felt kicked in the gut. She had become the strong one, and I was left in the dust.

My longing to be able to work with her again was disproportionately intense; the relationship with her was the one piece of my work life that was still in some way alive. And I loved my work. The image that kept haunting me was of hanging onto a cliff and having my fingers peeled off, one by one. This was the last finger by which I was hanging.

TWENTY YEARS AGO: TURNING TO
THE LITERATURE

Feeling alone as a resident making clinical decisions during my illness, bereft of the role models I was used to having before me, I wondered how other, more experienced therapists, faced with a situation such as mine, might have responded. I combed the literature for articles about illness in the therapist. I wanted to know what others had been through and, especially, how they had gauged their capacity to continue clinical work during their illness and how they had chosen to handle the clinical ramifications of their being ill. I was disappointed to find that most of the articles addressed *acute* illness from which there had been more or less complete recovery: a psychiatrist looking back with some amusement at the denial that had accompanied the onset of his illness (Arlow 1990), questions about what to reveal about one's illness, how and to what degree to preserve anonymity (Dewald 1990, Abend 1982, Lasky 1990). These papers were interesting, but they didn't address what was most pressing for me at the time: the *angst* over losing one's work and perhaps never regaining it, or the difficulty of trying to make clinical decisions when one is feverish, in pain, frightened, and facing a radically uncertain future, wherein the prognosis and even the diagnosis remain unclear.

One paper, however, a book chapter by Abraham Freedman (1990) stood out as an exception, and it bears summarizing here, as it addressed all these topics and more. Freedman tells in unflinching detail the story of the illness and death of a senior psychoanalyst and personal friend, Dr. A. The story makes use of personal conversations with Dr. A before his death, a private journal in which Dr. A had recorded his dreams at the time, and interviews with Dr. A's patients.

Dr. A was initially quite forthright with his patients about his illness. He told them he had been diagnosed with colon cancer and would be undergoing treatment for it. He offered them the chance, with this knowledge, to transfer to another analyst for their ongoing therapy. All of his patients opted to stay in treatment with him. Later, when he suffered a relapse and his prognosis precipitously worsened, he no longer had the presence of mind to reiterate this choice, and none of his patients, despite his visible decline, felt comfortable raising it themselves.

His work with one particular patient, a wheelchair-bound psychiatrist and psychoanalyst whom Dr. A saw in the patient's home, is told in particularly heart-wrenching detail. As Dr. A's condition deteriorated (to the point of his seeming disoriented at times), he continued to visit this patient as before, but their roles subtly reversed to the point where the latter felt he was, in effect, offering supportive treatment to Dr. A while nonetheless continuing to pay him. Thus Dr. A's analytic discernment and professional ethics, at first quite sound, were later "co-opted" by his physical decline and by an attendant urgent need to hold onto his patients, and to his work, as a way of holding onto life itself. This story brought forth, in all its poignancy, the power of some of the pulls I too was feeling. I was an ill physician longing to be able to function again and wanting to hold onto my patients and my work with an urgency that threatened to cloud my clinical judgment. Freedman's chapter has stood for me, ever since, as a sort of cautionary tale.

Freedman states that, while efforts have been made to protect the anonymity of Dr. A and his patients, he cannot rule out the possibility that they might be recognized, and he urges the reader to continue to respect these people and their courage to come forth in such a richly honest way. Freedman recognizes the value of their story for others caught in a similar situation. He hopes, by telling Dr. A's story, to help other analysts devise a more effective way of working in the context of illness, planning termination when the illness is fatal, and caring for the patient whose therapist has died. The present chapter is offered in a similar spirit.

I am fortunate to have gradually recuperated from my illness—an infection that, while treatable, is prone to leaving one with autoimmune or neurological sequelae—but it nonetheless changed me. It changed my career trajectory as well as aspects of the course of my personal and family life, and it has left some lingering symptoms and has affected the way I see things. I am more mindful of the fact of living in a physical—hence mortal—body and of the ever-present reciprocal interplay of physical and emotional states, an awareness that has informed my clinical work.

TEN YEARS AGO: A FRAME WITHIN A FRAME (WITHIN A FRAME)

Ten years later, I was in the midst of supervising a resident—a gifted one and one of whom I was particularly fond—when she developed a severe neurological illness that turned out, to my astonishment, to be the very same illness of which I'd fallen ill during my own residency.

In our initial session, when telling my supervisee about my own work and career path, I mentioned having been ill and that, in addition to my regular psychotherapy practice, I provided consultation to patients and their physicians regarding the neuropsychological and neuropsychiatric effects of medical disease.

A few months later, she mentioned that she had some personal medical questions she wanted to run by me. She had been having some odd physical symptoms, had tested positive for the same infection that had triggered my own illness, and wanted to seek my advice. She was about to embark on treatment under the care of a doctor under her health plan, and I encouraged her to proceed.

When initial treatment proved ineffective, I offered her names of physicians with whom she might consult. Her symptoms continued to multiply and worsen. Her vision was affected; she developed severe visual and auditory hyperacuities, fasciculations, crushing fatigue, and transient cognitive impairment. She was diagnosed, as I had previously been, with a co-infection that further complicated her course of illness. Eventually, she took a medical leave during which she arranged with the residency program to continue to do call, see her long-term patient, and attend supervision with me.

My work with her was both enriched and complicated by the remarkable conjunction between our two experiences; in many ways, it was a most fortuitous conjunction. For her, it may have been lifesaving and instrumental in enabling her to complete her training. For me, it provided deep psychological rewards and was healing in that it gave meaning and purpose, retrospectively, to what had been a lonely and demoralizing experience. I suspect, too, that the supervision, and her work with two patients under my supervision, may have been enriched and enlivened by the ways in which our shared illness experience brought into view and into our discussions a greater range of levels of emotional experience than would have been the case under more ordinary circumstances.

At the same time, I feared the striking parallels between her experience and my own might be blinding me to aspects of the situation that would have been more readily evident to another supervisor who was not so personally involved. There were moments when I felt pulled to fill multiple, often contradictory roles, where my responsibilities toward her, toward her patients, and toward the residency program seemed at odds with one another, and there were moments that felt almost surreal, in that her experience coincided to such a remarkable degree with my own previously solitary memories.

In addition to being concerned about her, I was fond of her and held her in high esteem. I remember thinking, after our second or third meeting: *she is intuitive, gifted with people, gracious, and capable, and the material resonates with her in a deep way. My job will be to foster and not get in the way of this natural giftedness.* She was older than the other residents—closer to my own age than theirs—and had life experience both as a mother and as a teacher that greatly enriched her work. Sometimes I thought: *what tremendous (and, again, almost uncanny) good fortune it is—for her as well as for me—that she was assigned to me*; at other times, I wondered about my capacity to be objective, given the intensity of what the situation stirred up for me.

While my supervisee was on medical leave, I received a message saying she had become suddenly very sick in the night and was in the emergency room. She had been out of town visiting her parents and had left me their phone number. I wasn't sure whether or not she had notified the long-term psychotherapy patient whom she was still seeing or if she had missed any sessions with him. I debated contacting him but felt it would be better, if she felt up to it, for her to contact him herself. When I eventually reached her in the emergency room, she told me what had been going on and let me know that she had indeed reached her patient. She had informed him that she was in the hospital and would be in touch with him some time within the week to let him know when she'd be returning. She also gave him my number to call if he needed to speak with someone in the meantime.

This juncture proved a particularly poignant reliving of the isolation of my own illness. Still quite green as a supervisor, I was at that point the only person in the training program with whom she was in direct contact.

It had been almost uncanny to watch the unfolding, in this resident, of not only the *very same* illness I had had but also some remarkably similar— and quite uncommon—aspects to its presentation: an acute sensitivity to sound, light, and vibration; intense disequilibrium and nausea in response to loud or persistent sound; and confusional states in response to sensory overload. Eerily, it turned out she and I even shared a birthday, having been born exactly one year apart.

My desire to help was huge, motivated by my concern for her and intensified by this déjà vu: the sensation that I was witnessing—and reliving from a new vantage point—something intimate and formative from my own past.

WHEN THE FRAME SHIFTS 147

It seemed, if handled well, that my role could prove crucial not only in helping this resident through her training and in guiding her in the conscientious treatment of her patient but also in her personal life, in the intimate experience of navigating the maze of medical care. I hoped, by sharing what I knew, to spare her the lengthy battle I had waged or, failing that, to help her in coming to terms with an illness that, while not typically life threatening, could leave one with chronic sequelae and hence require a lifelong adjustment. This potential role was a deeply gratifying one in that it gave new meaning to my own experience, a way to make something positive out of it. I was also aware, however, that such strong feelings of personal involvement could lead me to overstep my role as supervisor or read too much of my own experience into what I was observing in the resident.

I tried—with partial success—to offset these dangers by delineating separate roles—"supervisor" versus "advisor"—and by ensuring that there was ongoing communication between the residency director, clinic director, resident, and me. A monthly seminar for supervisors afforded me the opportunity to consult with trusted colleagues regarding my management of the supervision, and I had also a supervisor of my own at the time. Still, much in the situation was unique, and often I had to "fly by the seat of my pants." At my supervisee's request, I gave her referrals for personal psychotherapy and encouraged her to pursue it.

As "advisor," I was hoping to provide guidance and support in the handling of any illness-related work concerns, areas where I had felt rudderless and alone, and to mitigate the potential for wishful thinking and denial. The cautionary tale of Dr. A's work with the wheelchair-bound patient-analyst and the ultimate reversal of their roles loomed large in my mind. I hoped, in the support I gave my supervisee, to help her not lean too heavily on the patient as a source of connection to her working self, of reassurance regarding her clinical competency.

Beginning with the long-distance call from the emergency room, I felt as if I had been entrusted with the responsibility for a life (hers) and a treatment (hers with her patient) for which I lacked both the position and the expertise but that nonetheless seemed to have fallen into my hands. Hence the present challenge—outside the normal confines of the supervisor/supervisee relationship—felt especially daunting, almost larger than life. This larger-than-life quality was shared, partly engendered, by the resident. She said, later on, "I don't believe in angels, but you were my angel."

A week or so following her phone call from the emergency room, my supervisee returned to town and resumed work with her long-term patient. As her "advisor," I set up a weekly time to check in by phone regarding her clinical status and any illness-related work concerns. Our weekly, in-person "supervision" time was devoted, then, to her work with her patient. Sometimes, when something particularly emotional—or an illness-related concern on her part or mine—came up during supervision, I extended the time in order to give her direct emotional support and counsel—all the while aware, concerned, and explicit with her about the fact that this was not the way, under normal circumstances, to model and maintain optimal professional boundaries. I had to make a decision: whether to care for her in a mentoring capacity—and give her the support and medical advice I felt she needed—or whether to keep scrupulously to the boundaries that, under normal circumstances, I would wish to model. I chose the former.

Over the next several months, she gradually recuperated. She and I met together with the residency director to map out a timeframe for resuming her training and returning to full-time work. I talked with her about the importance of her responsibility not just toward her work but toward herself and about how hard it is, especially for physicians whose identity consists of being the one to care for others, to be realistic about one's own vulnerabilities.

As she got better, she confided in me less regarding her personal life. Supervision returned to its more ordinary dimensions and, while this was of course a relief to both of us, I experienced it as a loss reminiscent, perhaps, of the loss of my long-term patient. I was being once more left in the dust, struggling still with the remnants of my own illness, while she had moved on . . . I was no longer needed with the urgency of life-and-death.

I backed off, now, from the "advisor" role. But, seeing that she wasn't fully recovered—she continued to have ups and downs in her clinical status, level of fatigue, and cognitive and organizational skills—I remained concerned about her. I was worried lest denial set in again and perhaps cloud her judgment, yet at the same time, I wanted to respect her resumption of both fuller autonomy and privacy. And, I suppose, I felt shut out.

It was a bit of a tightrope walk. I wanted to give her every opportunity to finish the residency, to realize and develop the clinical giftedness that I knew she possessed. At the same time, I carried a responsibility toward both her patients and the residency program to intervene should her work became compromised by her illness. It was unnerving to know that these mandates might at any point become incompatible.

I dreaded the possibility that I might have to play the role of telling her she was not fit to work, hearkening back to my supervisor, who suggested it was time to refer my own patient to someone else. I did not want to have to rip this embryonic treatment untimely from the womb.

I offer below a vignette—one still-frame from my supervisee's work with her long-term patient—to illustrate some of these tensions and the way in which I chose, for better or for worse, to handle them. The session I shall describe involved a startling enactment, one that worried me at the time but that seemed to occasion a turning point in the therapy.

TEN YEARS AGO: CLINICAL VIGNETTE

My supervisee was in the winter of her fourth year of residency; because she had taken medical leave, she had one more year to go. She was back at work two-thirds time, but her neurological symptoms had recently worsened, and she was undergoing some adjustments in her medical treatment. She was struggling to manage her workload while at the same time taking care of her health.

A few weeks before the session, I had asked her if she had any concerns regarding her competency. She said no. Although she had noticed a few things in herself that concerned her, including that she was a bit emotionally disinhibited at times, once she was in the room with a patient, she could focus fully on the patient and the work at hand. She said, furthermore, "I'm rather tenacious about my patients. I've built relationships with them over the course of the year, and if I can possibly avoid it, I don't want to disrupt any of those treatments." Her "tenaciousness" was strongest with her long-term patient, the young adult man whom she had continued to see while she was on medical leave.

The patient had a history of feeling that primary attachment figures were using him for their own needs rather than attending to his, and hence he was exquisitely sensitive to both abandonment and betrayal. These themes were often reflected in the form of enactments: preemptive abandonments of girlfriends—as well as therapists in the past—and a tendency to miss appointments around vacation breaks. The associated affects remained, for the most part, unspeakable and instead were disavowed, projected, or enacted.

At the time of the session I shall be describing, she had been seeing him twice a week for about two years. She had had to cancel a prior appointment and reschedule this one because of illness.

In an atypical fashion, he began the session by describing situations where he had triumphed over someone else, pulled one over on them, or one-upped them. Alternating with these cocky stories were abrupt changes of affect in which he expressed the fantasied wish that he could get on a train with a conductor whom he could trust to get him to his destination safely.

Bypassing the transference implications of this fantasy, my supervisee began querying whom he could think of who could be that conductor; he could think of no one. She prompted him, finally suggesting his beloved Nanny, the one figure of loving constancy in the inner world he had portrayed. He brightened and said yes, she could, started reminiscing about her, and then, in another abrupt change, said, flatly, "But she's going to die." After a pause, my supervisee said "I'm struck by how you said that . . . with no feeling . . ." She went on, very gently, "Everybody dies eventually; that doesn't mean you don't love them while they're alive and treasure their memory when they're gone, even though it's very painful to lose them . . ." Perhaps to her surprise, certainly to mine, though perhaps she knew he was closer to the feeling than I realized, he started sobbing. She was quiet but noted, with some dismay, that their time was up. Feeling uncomfortable about having to end the session at this particular moment, she said to him, again very gently: "We need to stop . . . we met today at this time because (and she reviewed the circumstances of the rescheduling) . . . but after this we'll meet Fridays at 2, always."

He looked a bit startled and said "Always? But I'm graduating in six months!" And she became even more startled by this quick and charged interchange as well as by her own momentary disorientation. She had known since the beginning of the therapy of his projected graduation date and his subsequent plans to return to his native country. Yet, much to *both* their surprise, she abruptly burst into tears and said, "Oh! Oh no! I forgot," then quickly composed herself. Then he, suddenly more engaged and genuine said, "It's okay . . . I hope you don't think that was unprofessional . . . I hope you're not embarrassed. It wasn't a bad thing that you did. It wasn't a bad thing at all. It was a *good* thing."

The transference implications of the train conductor fantasy were upstaged by this charged interchange, marked both by a momentary forgetting on her part and by her tears. She noted, as I had, that she had seemed as if reacting to a personal and primal abandonment of her own. Indeed it was true that, at the time, she had been fearful of losing her work—hence her "tenaciousness" with her patients—fearful indeed of manifold losses with which her relapse threatened her, and she had been aware of echoes, with this patient in particular, of painful separations from her toddler son when she went off to work in the morning and from her stepsons as they went off to college.

It seemed to both of us that while her "lapse" reflected the kind of illness-related emotional disinhibition to which she had referred earlier, it was also, in part, a product of the therapy relationship at the time. Hence we came to see her tears as, perhaps, a bursting forth of the affect that he'd been dis-avowing, a response to a projective identification on his part that found fer-tile ground in her, rendering affects around attachment and loss very much alive in the "field" at that time. This had the effect of making his own feelings and his experience of her seem vibrantly alive and real to him in a way that had not been the case previously.

At the time, I said to her that this was fascinating; it could be a salutary development, with the potential to propel the treatment forward, deepen it, and enliven it. He *cannot* see her as a phony here, and she is modeling for him the experience of and tolerance for some of the affects that he habitu-ally disavows. But it's also a perilous one, lest he turn it into a seduction, lest he play on her vulnerability and pull her into subsequent enactments, lest he become disorganized and frightened by her vulnerability, lest he come to devalue her, or lest he come to feel exploited, fearful of her using him to fulfill her own needs. I suggested that how it came to be experienced by him would depend very much on how she handled its aftermath over the course of the treatment.

While clearly I had a vested interest in emphasizing the positive aspects of her "lapse," and while I see its effect now as being more complex, this did seem to mark a turning point in the treatment, which was character-ized by greater freedom of emotional expression on his part, a seemingly more genuine engagement with her, and a diminished tendency for pre-emptive cancellations/enactments. With her help he was now able to put into words what had previously been unspeakable. I shall leave for another time a fuller discussion of some of the transference and countertransference ramifications of illness. What strikes me now is the way in which, at the time, both my supervisee and I were reluctant to explore openly, she in the therapy and I in the supervision, the transference implications of his fantasy about the train conductor. I wonder, now, how my "countertransferences" as supervisor—wanting to protect her from shame, from fear of failure—may have blocked me from exploring with her how impaired she might have seemed, at times, to her patient. For instance, in his wishful fantasy of a conductor who could be relied upon, in contrast with her recent cancellations, we get a glimpse of how he may have perceived her illness.

When, years later, I did ask her what her thoughts had been at the time, she said she'd been well aware of the transference implications of his train conductor fantasy but had felt threatened by them and even somewhat angered. Here she was, she thought, having seen this patient through thick and thin, throughout all the vicissitudes of her own health, taking time away from her toddler son, *and he's saying he can't trust me. Why can't he trust me?* She felt an implicit disparagement or reproach but neither articulated it to the patient nor to me. I, too, evaded these implications and thus missed an opportunity, perhaps, to help her explore them as reflections of her own worries and fantasies about herself and/or his fantasies about her. Perhaps he was concerned on her behalf or frightened by how she seemed; perhaps he was gratified by an image of himself as the one up, the strong one, the one who has witnessed the other's shame. Perhaps both. I was reluctant, it seems, to help her find out.

I felt protective of her. Insofar as I identified with her I wanted to see her in a good light, to see her triumph, despite the effects of her illness, not only for her sake but also for my own. I wanted, too, to be a purveyor of goodness and hopefulness in her inner world, identified, thus, with those larger-than-life figures who had helped me through my own illness. Perhaps, were I to do it over, I would handle the situation in much the same way, but I hope I would have felt freer to invite exploration of the patient's fears and fantasies about her, *qua* fantasies, however uncomfortably close to reality or to her own worst fears (or mine) they might have seemed.

PRESENT: REFLECTIONS

As ancestors [the old ghosts] live forth in the present generation, while as ghosts they are compelled to haunt the present generation with their shadow life. Transference is pathological insofar as the unconscious is a crowd of ghosts, and this is the beginning of the transference neurosis in analysis. . . . In the daylight of analysis the ghosts of the unconscious are laid and led to rest as ancestors whose power is taken over and transformed into the newer intensity of present life, of the secondary process and contemporary objects.

— Hans Loewald, "On the Therapeutic Action of Psychoanalysis" (1960)

The potential downsides to working in the context of a medical illness are legion and obvious. But the supervision challenged me with the question: can one, *when* can one or *how* can one, understand the effect of illness (and I'm speaking here of chronic or recurrent illness that doesn't preclude clinical work but has the potential to affect it) in the way one might understand that of any other aspect of the therapist's life and person—the fact of being male or female, old or young, married or single, pregnant or bereaved, in the midst of a divorce or about to get married, inexperienced or aging, in turmoil or at peace—of which the patient might have occasion to be or become aware? Or, as a life stressor like many others—having recently been mugged, having a sick child, being under extreme financial stress, or having received a time-consuming grant—that can affect our level of availability and receptivity to patients at any given time? Can one understand it as affecting the treatment, sometimes enlivening, deepening, or moving it forward, sometimes getting in the way, making it more difficult or even impossible; opening up some aspects of the patient's psychic life, calling to mind some aspects of his/her history while obscuring others?

I was reminded of the patient/analyst of Dr. A who said that, for him, for all that was *wrong* with how Dr. A's treatment of him progressed, there was a positive aspect to the role reversal that occurred with Dr. A: it made the patient/analyst feel valuable and like a doctor again and reduced *his* sense of helplessness.

It has been said before that illness tends to induce regression—to earlier modes of functioning and to the use of more primitive defenses, such as splitting, idealization, and omnipotent control. While at moments I was dumbstruck by the similarities between my supervisee's experience and mine, there were other moments when the differences were equally striking and caught me off guard. That both were true relates to the operation of such defenses and to how the world appears more polarized when one's safety is—or has recently been—at stake.

The neuroscientist Joseph LeDoux (1996) describes the fear system in a way that sheds light on the workings of primitive defenses such as splitting, idealization, and devaluation. In situations where we are threatened, we do not stop to make fine distinctions or perceive nuances that under other circumstances would be apparent to us. We are hardwired to react instantaneously rather than reflect and take our time. To a person running in fear from poisonous snakes, any squiggly stick in his path is a snake until proven otherwise; to a person alone at night in an unfamiliar, creaky old house, any sudden noise could be an interloper or a ghost. We see things in black and white: dangerous or safe, good or bad. We scan the world for sources of protection versus sources of danger, and we polarize what we see. Those in a position to help us may be apprehended as larger than life.

The tendency to idealize those whom we perceive as being in a position to "save our lives" was brought home to me recently as I was reading a paper on "Life-Threatening Illness in the Analyst." In it, Barbara Fajardo (2001) speaks of the necessary conditions for continuing analytic work during illness, which includes ensuring the meeting of selfobject needs outside of one's work: family support, a trusted medical team, a network of friends and colleagues with whom one may consult, and, often, personal therapy or analysis. I was struck by the inclusion of a trusted medical team in her list, given that doctors are not infallible and, sometimes, as was the case for me, the illness is undiagnosed and there is, as yet, no medical team in place. Nonetheless, those who play a significant part in our healing or consolation during illness more easily become selfobjects to us, and it is tempting to idealize them.

Crisis also breeds intensity of attachment: those who are nearby and empathic at a time of tragedy in one's life become especially important to us. I recall my fellow resident, the one who had died of AIDS the year before I got ill, bursting into tears when I brought him a gift, bought with money collected from the residency group, of a tape player, headphones, and books on tape, so he could "read" to himself in the hospital, having gone blind from an AIDS-related CMV infection. He said: "I didn't know you guys cared so much about me." And I felt a pang of guilt, because this seemed the least we could do, knowing that he was dying, yet to him it held the significance, or so it seemed, of a deep connection between us. I felt I didn't care *enough* to warrant such gratitude.

Like any other trauma, the processing of a severe illness experience is ongoing, shaded differently at different times in one's later life, as new life experience accrues atop it . . . And for all the anguish it may involve for us, it does confer a window, I think, into some deeper levels of the psyche, and it resonates with other developmental watersheds—infancy, adolescence, old age—in which one's body undergoes similarly profound and rapid changes.

Sharing an unusual illness or trauma such as what I shared with the resident is like sharing a secret, very private part of oneself; like finding someone in a foreign country who speaks one's own language. I felt I could understand my supervisee at this time in a way that no one else could.

I felt intensely protective, almost maternal toward her, a feeling that I see now was intensified by "ghosts" from my own past. My supervisee was not the only person with whom I'd shared my birthday; I had also shared a birthday with my mother. Shortly before the supervision began, my mother had died, following a protracted illness. Perhaps the wish to witness and even facilitate the healing of my new birthday-sake propelled me more than I recognized. Certainly it added to the weightiness of the supervision in my own life story.

What good came of the fact of our shared illness? My supervisee gave to me the satisfaction of putting my own hard, sad experience to generative use; I gave her the gift of feeling recognized and valued and of access to medical care she might not otherwise have found, which restored her functioning, enabled her to complete her training, and perhaps saved her life. She could confide in me, safely, things she could confide in few others, things that helped me do my job better and enabled me to supervise her in a more deeply informed way. This confidence in the supervisory relationship contributed, I imagine, to her poignant awareness—as reflected in her clinical work—of the potential power of the therapeutic relationship.

In what ways did I, perhaps, fail her? I did not do a good job modeling for her the professional boundaries she needed to learn. Perhaps she did not feel the same acuity of need for her own therapist that she might have felt without me. Perhaps some deep anxieties, operative in her and in me, could not be clearly articulated but instead remained enfolded in—and eclipsed by—our shared illness.

I did not then yet know that, even when one suffers from a "real" (medical/physical) illness and not a psychosomatic (or psychiatric) one, one's experience is formed equally by the physical reality *and* the web of meaning associated with it. I did not recognize that the physical changes carry with them a complex intertwinement of feelings, memories, and body memories that inform one's experience. I did not know as well as I thought I did what my supervisee's illness meant to *her* or indeed the myriad individual pressures in her own life that shaped the experience for her: specters from the past and pulls toward the future.

And I am still learning—and shaping—what my illness means to me. I do not have power over the facts of my illness or over the "ghosts" of my past, but I can alter my perspectives on these things, and I have the power to claim them as my own, to carry these memories into the future in a way that transforms them, bears the stamp of my individuality, and, perhaps, touches the life of someone else in a meaningful way.

NOTE

1. A note on confidentiality: Identifying particulars regarding both the resident and her patient have been changed. The supervisee has read and approved this chapter, and I am grateful to her for her memories and feedback at various points in the writing process. The patient whom she treated, were he to happen upon it, might perhaps recognize and remember the charged interchange highlighted in the chapter (details of which have been changed), although it took place many years in the past. I trust it would be recognizable to no one else.

REFERENCES

Abend, S. M. 1982. "Serious Illness in the Analyst: Countertransference Considerations." *Journal of American Psychoanalytic Association* 30:365–375.

Arlow, J. A. 1990. "The Analytic Attitude in the Service of Denial." In *Illness in the Analyst: Implications for the Treatment Relationship*, ed. H. J. Schwartz and A. L. Silver. Madison, Conn.: International Universities Press.

Baranger, M., and W. Baranger. 2008. "The Analytic Situation as a Dynamic Field." *International Journal of Psychoanalysis* 89: 795–826.

Bleger, J. 1967. "Psychoanalysis of the Psycho-analytic Frame." *International Journal of Psychoanalysis* 48: 511–519.

Carroll, L. 1865. *Through the Looking Glass*. London: MacMillan & Co.

Dewald, P. A. 1990. "Serious Illness in the Analyst: Transference, Countertransference, and Reality Responses—and Further Reflections." In *Illness in the Analyst: Implications for the Treatment Relationship*, ed. H. J. Schwartz and A. L. Silver. Madison, Conn.: International Universities Press.

Fajardo, B. 2001. "Life-Threatening Illness in the Analyst." *Journal of the American Psychoanalytic Association* 49: 569–586.

Freedman, A. 1990. "Death as a Form of Termination of Psychoanalysis." In *Illness in the Analyst: Implications for the Treatment Relationship*, ed. H. J. Schwartz and A. L. Silver. Madison, Conn.: International Universities Press.

Lasky, R. 1990. "Catastrophic Illness in the Analyst and the Analyst's Emotional Reactions to It." *International Journal of Psychoanalysis* 71: 455–473.

LeDoux, J. 1996. *The Emotional Brain: The Mysterious Underpinnings of Emotional Life.* New York: Simon & Schuster.

Loewald, H. W. 1960. "On the Therapeutic Action of Psychoanalysis." *International Journal of Psychoanalysis* 41: 16–33.

Schwartz, H. J. 1987. "Illness in the Doctor: Implications for the Psychoanalytic Process." *Journal of the American Psychoanalytic Association* 35: 657–692.

Silver, A. L. 1982. "Resuming the Work with a Life-Threatening Illness." *Contemporary Psychoanalysis* 18: 314–326.

CHAPTER 9

THE LOSS OF AN INSTITUTION

Mourning Chestnut Lodge

RICHARD M. WAUGAMAN

OCTOBER 9, 2009—LETTER from RMW to Harold F. Searles: *I got asked last week to contribute a chapter to a book on* The Therapist in Mourning. *Since then, I've told myself I'm probably still grieving leaving the fallopian tube for the uterus and much since then, so I'll have to condense. The editors loved my idea of writing about leaving the Lodge. I'm hoping that writing about it will help resolve some of the grief.*

Okay, I was exaggerating ever so slightly about mourning the lost fallopian tube I left as an embryo. But I doubt I am alone in my attraction to the long-term work for which Chestnut Lodge was famous, partly because I am constitutionally unsuited to coping with separations. A colleague at the Lodge once gave an aptly titled paper on "Chronic Patients and Chronic Therapists." Perhaps Joanne Greenberg's memoir *I Never Promised You a Rose Garden* was so powerful in its emotional impact on millions of readers because she projectively identified into us her mourning about leaving the Lodge, along with her intense longing to return. Her unique experiences had a universal appeal because each reader resonated with her story, unconsciously linking our own lost people and places with her loss of her famous analyst (Frieda Fromm-Reichmann) and of her famous hospital.

It is easy to underestimate the emotional importance our institutions have for us. Losing them confronts us, in fact, with just how much they mean to us. I left the Lodge in 1999, after spending thirteen years on its staff. The hospital closed two years later. Within a few days of the editors' invitation to contribute to this book, I wrote an initial draft of this chapter. In a volume that addresses such tragically devastating losses as the death of a patient, a therapist, a family member, and soldiers at war, this chapter on the loss of an institution may seem trivial. However, the editors' invitation tapped into my deep need to rework my feelings about losing the Lodge. In allowing us to re-create our lost objects, writing can be therapeutic, and I am grateful for this opportunity to share some reflections on my grief. I hope my comments will be helpful to others.

After trying to convey some of the reasons that working at the Lodge had such a powerful emotional meaning for me, I will then explore my mourning process after I left the Lodge in 1999 and after it closed in 2001. I will draw extensively on my personal correspondence with Harold Searles, my well-known predecessor at the Lodge, to illustrate my process of grieving and working through.

STEPPING INTO A NOVEL WORLD

As I later had a chance to tell Joanne Greenberg at a Lodge event in 1999, I read her powerful *Rose Garden* when I was sixteen, thinking it was a highly imaginative novel. It was a few years later that I learned it was not in fact a novel but a memoir. Her book thus shaped my institutional transference to Chestnut Lodge, so that the Lodge came to represent for me a partly real, partly imaginary place. When I joined its staff in 1986, I realized there was some truth to this perception of the hospital as not fully part of the conventional "real world." Patients and staff would speak of "going into Rockville" when they planned to go to its nearby commercial district. Literally speaking, the Lodge was squarely in the middle of Rockville already. Alluding to the word "wavelength," one patient observed that the Lodge seemed to be on a different "timelength" from the rest of the world.

Rusty Bullard (Dexter M. Bullard Jr.) was the Lodge's medical director and owner. He once quipped, "The Lodge, like the unconscious, is timeless."[1] Gail Hornstein captured the Lodge perfectly in her biography of Fromm-Reichmann[2] when she called it a "kind of analytic think tank." Rusty Bullard grew up on the grounds of the Lodge. His father, its previous medical director, grew up on the grounds of other psychiatric hospitals that Rusty's grandfather had directed. This intimate contact with psychiatric inpatients from their earliest years no doubt did much to shape the unique humanity and respect with which the Lodge's patients were treated.

A teacher in my psychiatric residency who had worked at the Lodge during its "golden years" of the 1940s and 50s warned me that it had lost ground since his time there. So I began working at the Lodge in 1986 with a complex brew of feelings about it—it was a half real, half imaginary place that was already mourning its lost youth. Yet it was still magical. I had never been part of an institution that showed such deep respect for the most severely ill, treatment-refractory patients. The work was intensely demanding, but the mutual collegial support helped make those demands bearable. As the years went by, the Lodge evolved to adapt to the diminishing external resources for long-term psychiatric inpatient treatment. I left the Lodge not long after the Bullard family sold it, three generations after they had created it. I had hoped to remain there for the rest of my career. Two years after I left, it closed for good. "Bereft" ultimately comes from a word that means "rob," and we certainly felt robbed of our beloved hospital. My chapter will elaborate on this nearly unbearable professional loss.

The loss of an institution leaves each person with a unique experience of bereavement. This personal grief is shaped not only by subjective elements but also by the nature of the lost institution. Here again, the Lodge was unique. One goal of analysis is to help the patient find and become her true self. The ego's mechanisms of defense are directed not only toward inner dangers but serve to protect the person from interpersonal experiences of shame, criticism, and rejection. Soon after I arrived at the Lodge, I sensed that I could be myself there in a way that felt new and liberating. For the first time, I realized that I had always felt subtly stifled by the pressures of conventionality in my past educational and work environments.

I felt drawn to work at the Lodge for fifteen years before I finally did so. As a medical student, I contacted the Lodge about a residency position but learned they did not offer a full psychiatric residency. As I was finishing my residency at Sheppard-Pratt Hospital, I applied for a staff position at the Lodge. But I turned down their offer, since the low salary would have made it extremely difficult to finish the analytic training I had recently begun. When I explained this, John Fort, the Lodge's clinical director, suggested I give him a call when I finished my analytic training. I did, ten years later.

It was a dream that finally prompted me to reapply for a job at the Lodge. My private practice was at that time equally divided between doing analysis and doing mostly once-weekly psychotherapy. I found the latter increasingly frustrating, as my analytic training and practice had convinced me of the greater therapeutic power of more intensive treatment. In that context,

I dreamed that I yelled at an especially recalcitrant patient, "You don't want to know the truth about yourself!" Pondering this dream made me realize that the truth about me was that I wanted to spend more of my professional time treating patients intensively. Part of my idealized image of the Lodge was that it was the place where all patients could be seen four times per week by their therapists.

By the time I was assigned my Lodge patients, this had changed. An elderly patient had refused to meet with her therapist for the past few years. Robert A. Cohen, the director of psychotherapy, asked me to become her therapist but to see her only twice per week. This was a significant departure from the Lodge's tradition of more intensive therapy for each and every inpatient. I mention this anecdote to highlight the fact that the Lodge as a real place was in constant flux, however much we viewed it as an idealized institutional transference object eternally immune to the vagaries of time. The elderly patient agreed to come to my office, and we met twice weekly for many years. (At that time, we were all on salary, so I met with two other Lodge patients five times per week. Two years later, when Rusty Bullard suggested we question whether all our patients needed therapy four times per week, I began seeing one patient six times per week.)

After an unusually contentious team meeting, where bitter disagreements about clinical issues were aired, I confided to Rusty Bullard, "This place really is like a family!" It was. Not only in terms of rivalries and conflicts but also like a family in providing a sense of common identity and purpose, with the emotional intensity and intimacy that grew out of our collective professional commitment to our deeply ill patients. Transference reactions were intense, multiple, and convoluted, contributing to the unique intensity of the place. Each patient had a range of transference feelings to his or her therapist as well as to the other members of the treatment team.

During my first years at the Lodge, all therapists were required to have a personal analysis, and most were either in analytic training or were graduate analysts. So it was natural for some of our transferences toward our own analysts (and toward our fellow analysands) to become displaced onto one or more colleagues at the Lodge. In addition, there was the complex totality of patient and staff institutional transferences toward the Lodge. I became a training analyst during my third year at the Lodge. Soon after, I shared with Rusty Bullard my impression that my new role was making me a target of colleagues' displaced transferences toward their analysts and the analytic institute. Rusty, as a senior training analyst, our boss, and the hospital's owner, looked at me as though I had just stated the obvious—and as though he had had considerable experience of being such a displaced transference target. Our familial transferences toward the Lodge would later complicate and intensify our experiences of its loss.

LIFE AT THE LODGE

I often heard one patient telling another patient at the Lodge, "Have a good hour!" That is, all the patients there recognized the importance of one another's individual psychotherapy. This is a stark contrast to our private practices, where even when we have a shared waiting room, most patients politely avert their gaze from one another and certainly do not wish one another a good hour.

Among other distinctive characteristics of the Lodge were its somewhat idiosyncratic therapeutic boundaries. Many of us, when we were new, felt put off when we first saw therapists ambling around the grounds with their patients rather than staying put in their offices, where we firmly believed they belonged, so that true psychodynamic psychotherapy could take place. Each of us eventually yielded to the Lodge tradition of peripatetic sessions. Among other things, we learned that our patients' comfort took precedence over our own. Since the days of Fromm-Reichmann, it was also common for therapists to take their patients on brief car trips. There was usually not sufficient nursing staff for them to take individual patients off the grounds, much as these chronically hospitalized patients benefitted from a change of scene.

Going off-grounds put the therapist in the role of a mediator between the psychotic patient and the surrounding community. Once, a schizophrenic woman was reacting delusionally to her husband's plan to divorce her. As we were sitting in an upscale coffee shop near the hospital, she told me the news that her husband was seeing another woman. She then added, loudly, "I told him, 'Don't do that, John—your sperm is precious to me!' " That moment tested my comfort with unconventionality.

Another chronically psychotic patient had been a champion swimmer in his youth. He was hospitalized because he had become violent, and he was restricted to the unit much of his first year at the Lodge. During his second year, his violence had lessened enough that I felt comfortable taking him off-grounds. So we walked together to the community swimming pool, half a mile away. We paused on a bench near the pool before he took a swim. This usually mute, often incoherent patient then made one of his most lucid and eloquent comments: "It's good to get away from the doldrums of the mental hospital."

Therapists who needed to maintain a more classically analytic distance from their patients faced many challenges at the Lodge. Our patients were highly perceptive and were usually not inhibited about candidly confronting staff with their impressions of us. The six or so inpatients who were in four-times-per-week psychotherapy with a given therapist had many opportunities to compare notes, act out rivalries, or conspire together. This led to enactments that are unusual in a typical private practice. However, they had some features in common with more subtle enactments among psychoanalytic candidates who share the same teachers, supervisors, and training analysts. (Soon after I left the Lodge, I published some reflections on these enactments in an article titled "The Analyst's Caseload as a Family: Transferences to Fellow Patients.")[3]

Early in my indoctrination as a new Lodge therapist, a colleague's patient noticed I always locked my office door, even if I was away for only a few minutes. Once, when I was unlocking my door upon my return, he commented, "Suspicious, aren't you?" Our medical director, by contrast, had an open-door policy. That is, he always left his office door wide open—when he was not there. Even our cars, parked in their assigned spaces, were the targets of our patients' curiosity. I formed the habit of putting any mail or papers in my car face down, after learning that patients might otherwise read whatever was visible. In other ways, though, I learned to accommodate myself to the relative lack of privacy at the Lodge. I noticed instances where patients seemed to benefit from their opportunities to see me as a real person. For example, one patient in the day treatment program told me, "I notice I'm not having as many fender-benders in my car, since I saw that you always put your emergency brake on, even when you park where it's level." That is, she was identifying with me as a cautious driver, and she had fewer accidents as a result.

What I treasured most at the Lodge were the people, and the fact that the Lodge's milieu allowed more of their "true selves" to emerge, with less pressure to present their false selves. I gradually concluded that the magical atmosphere that made the Lodge unique had a lot to do with a lesser-known adage carved over the Temple at Delphi: "Be Yourself." As I have said, nowhere else have I found it so easy to be oneself, shielded from the usually intense societal and collegial pressure to put one's "best" but false self forward. A schizophrenic patient, in an ostensible compliment, said of a new staff member she had just met, "She has a *perfect* façade!" This patient was an articulate if idiosyncratic social commentator. Another time, she deadpanned, "The way to get along in high society is to have an expensive timepiece and look at it frequently." The head nurse of her unit was something of a Nurse Ratched. My patient told me one morning, of this nurse, "I think she made a kill last night," eloquently reducing this nurse to being less than human— instead, a predatory animal. The father of a fellow patient was visiting his daughter on my patient's unit. When my patient could no longer stand the way he was loudly arguing with his schizophrenic daughter about her delusional thinking, my patient calmly advised him, "If you want to bring her back to reality, you have to enter her world first."[4]

My thirteen years at the Lodge included a series of ongoing losses of colleagues there, many of whom died prematurely in their sixties—John Fort, Erich Heydt, Rusty Bullard, and David Feinsilver. So, once again, it would be misleading to imply that my sense of loss began only when I left the Lodge. As the Lodge evolved to adapt to changing times, our work as psychiatrists also changed, which meant the loss of some of the Lodge's valued traditions. Like mental health professionals everywhere, we were expected to do more with less. Lengths of stay in the hospital dropped precipitously. The intensity of psychotherapy diminished. Various aspects of ancillary support for the patients (and staff) were withdrawn. Finally, the beginning of the end was the terminal illness of Rusty Bullard. The moment he told us he had lung cancer is seared in my memory. I had an instantaneous premonition that this spelled the end of the Lodge. A couple of years earlier, he had mentioned to me, seemingly out of the blue, that there was no one among the next generation of Bullards who was interested in succeeding him in running the Lodge. Rusty Bullard's death led his family to sell the hospital to a nonprofit outpatient clinic that had no experience running a hospital. The hospital (as well as the clinic that now owned it) closed in bankruptcy a few years later.

In writing this account of leaving the Lodge, I have to resist a strong pull to spend all my time reminiscing, trying to recreate this lost world, and trying to recapture the deep satisfaction of working at the Lodge by telling (selected) stories about my time there. Shifting to the actual topic of my chapter— my grief over losing the Lodge—is more painful. Yet maladaptive efforts to evade grief simply prolong our mourning, while facing grief creates more mental space for our memories of the person or place we have lost.

Temperamentally, I try to use humor when I'm confronted with a problem. So I spoke of feeling "dis-Lodged." I thought of the transition back to conventional logic, after I had spent thirteen years adapting to "Chestnut Lodg-ic." Considering how much the Lodge changed during my time there, I maintained that *it* left *me* before I left *it*.

Being at the Lodge meant being part of an intense milieu of patients and staff. Leaving it felt like far more than just ending a job. It was more like leaving one's family to attend college, or, later, like graduating from college. I tried to expand my world beyond my new office in Chevy Chase. I eventually became intensely involved in literary research. Nature often gives solace to those in grief. I set up a birdfeeder on my balcony and learned to identify a dozen or so species of birds I saw. Instead of just trying to rescue chronically psychotic patients from their illnesses, I tried to protect the birds' food from the marauding squirrels. (More on that later.)

MY CORRESPONDENCE WITH HAROLD SEARLES

Sigmund Freud conducted some aspects of his self-analysis through his correspondence with Wilhelm Fliess. Although I am no Sigmund Freud, I have been fortunate to be a friend of Harold Searles. He had worked at the Lodge some sixteen years (that was well before my time there). He retired and left the Washington, D.C., area in 1993.

During my second year of psychiatric residency, I read several pages of Searles's book, *Collected Papers on Schizophrenia and Related Subjects*, each morning before driving to Sheppard-Pratt Hospital to begin my workday. Searles is a gifted writer whose unique insights into the unconscious made him world famous in our field.

I sought supervision with Searles as a psychoanalytic candidate. Although that was not possible, he was assigned as my advisor a couple of years later. After I graduated, I again asked him for supervision, and this time he was able to see me. He supervised me weekly on my work with a patient I later concluded had dissociative identity disorder (formerly known as multiple personality). Because of scheduling problems, I ended this supervision when I began working at the Lodge two years later. But before long I returned to him for weekly supervision on one of my schizophrenic patients at the Lodge. We coauthored an article about that work.[5] Apart from one chapter in *Countertransference and Related Subjects*, this is the only time he coauthored an article, so I felt deeply honored.

Since I first began reading his work, Searles has been one of the analysts whose writings have most influenced me. I once took an excellent course on psychoanalytic writing, taught by my former institute classmate Judith Viorst. She asked each of us to choose a writer we admired and to imitate their style in our writing assignment. After she read my paper, she told me I needed to take more risks in my writing if I wanted to emulate Searles. Just as my former training analyst never told me when to stop saying whatever came to mind, Viorst never told us when to stop emulating, so I find I have been following her advice during the ensuing thirty years.

When I began submitting articles to psychoanalytic journals, I often sought Searles's comments on my drafts. He was consistently generous with his time and encouragement. After his retirement, I exchanged frequent letters with him. When I left the Lodge, I drew on our respective feelings about the hospital to keep re-creating it and letting go of it in my mind. Some of my most painful feelings about losing the Lodge got displaced onto other topics. Preparing this chapter led me to review my correspondence with Searles, since it served as something of a diary, recording a range of feelings about my loss over several years.

In many ways, Searles was the ideal interlocutor. His renown did much to enhance the Lodge's reputation. I suspect my feelings toward him included some of my institutional transference toward the Lodge itself, so he served as a surrogate for what I had lost. As you read selections from my letters to Searles, keep in mind Judith Viorst's advice about emulating Searles. As Viorst once observed, Searles made her feel he expects people to be slightly more self-disclosing than they are comfortable being. Since Searles developed a reputation for self-disclosure before it was in vogue in analytic circles, my disclosures to him were naturally influenced by competitive feelings that sometimes resulted in hyperbole.

June 10, 1999, HFS [in response to reading my discussion of a case presentation by a social worker who was still working at the Lodge]: *The Lodge can't have plummeted out of sight, or material like this wouldn't be getting heard there. Reading all this stuff is, for me, like water to a man who is parched with thirst. . . . Frequently I dream about the Lodge. Some day, if we ever get together again, I'll tell you what it was like for me, when I left there in early '64.*

January 21, 2000, RMW: *I'm still getting a wide variety of songbirds at the birdfeeder* [outside my office's sliding glass door]. *I've had a running battle with the squirrels who do not realize that my birdfeeder is squirrel-proof. I've tried everything—greasing the pole from which the feeder hangs; futilely shooting rubber bands at them; spraying them with wasp spray, which doesn't seem particularly toxic to them, but the spray travels some 20 feet, unless there's a northern wind that blows it back in my face. . . . Now, knowing you, you're probably formulating all sorts of notions about displaced countertransference, which I honestly do not believe I had had a single thought about until writing this to you and imagining your reaction. So, perhaps there's a paper in this, though I suspect all extant analytic journals take themselves a bit too seriously to publish a paper on "Squirrels as a Target of Displaced Countertransference." Speaking of underlying sources of my anger, I did go ahead and cut the cord to the ECEC* [the steering committee of training analysts in my institute]. *I had just completed 10 years on it, and I decided it was time for a break. The many contentious administrative issues were getting to me, and I decided I was losing too much sleep over them. I've felt much more relaxed since resigning. . . . That paper on displacement of countertransference from one patient to another is due out shortly.*[6]

This letter illustrates the benefit of conversations, whether in person or through letters, in helping us deepen our self-understanding as we're coping with loss. As you can see, when I imagined Searles reading my letter, it brought to mind a fresh perspective on my thoughts.

March 29, 2000, HFS: *I was unable to subject to my usual flawlessly objective scrutiny the data you sent me last time about the songbirds, the birdfeeder, and the squirrels, for the reason that my medical school roommate regularly addressed me by the name "Squirrels." I'm sure this did not allude to any tendency on my part to dart about incessantly in a seemingly patternless way, but was based solely on the similarity to my actual last name. . . . Your having left the ECEC reminds me of my own having avoided taking on any administrative post at CLS[7] after the requisite two years of being administrator of one or another ward. I also held aloof from getting involved in various movements at the Lodge, sure that I would never do the writing that I was determined to do if I got involved in them. I'm still sure that this was wise of me. It is clear from your most recent letter how much you love to write. . . . I greatly miss my long-time profession, and dream more often than not about it. . . . This leaves me . . . immersed in analyzing myself, and I'm fortunate in having bottomless riches of psychopathology. . . . I miss the long-gone CLS a lot, too. . . . I'm an expert in not realizing how much I miss various persons and places.*

Note that it is the "long-gone" Lodge that Searles misses. One way to attenuate acute feelings of loss is to convince ourselves that the Lodge's best years were already but a dim memory. Rereading Searles's letter, I suspect that he was one important influence on my subsequent decision to become less active in the institute during the ensuing years and instead to spend much more time writing. And my writing has been central to coping with the void that the Lodge left in my professional life.

January 9, 2001, RMW: *Well, I finally got rid of the squirrels who were vandalizing my birdfeeder. Now if I could only get some birds to visit it. . . . I've also made some progress with the Institute. By the time you receive this, I hope to have been promoted to Emeritus S&TA [Supervising and Training Analyst] status. My competitive nature being what it still is, I've now got my heart set on becoming the youngest Emeritus S&TA in the history of the Institute. Withdrawing from active status has brought enormous peace of mind. As I'm less burdened by the enormous time commitment and financial sacrifices that the Institute increasingly demanded, I've enjoyed devoting my energies to other interests. Maria, the patient you supervised years ago, had to stop seeing me in '97 for financial reasons. I have resumed treating her, at no fee, now that I'm not having to do so much low-fee work with candidates. . . . The Lodge keeps plugging away, and may survive its current bankruptcy.*

February 3, 2001, HFS: *I'm very glad to hear that you have found greater equanimity in the changes you've made in relation to the Institute. . . . I was interested to hear about Maria. She can only assume that you're hopelessly psychotic, treating her for nothing.*

May 4, 2001, RMW: *I'm feeling the need to ventilate some about the closing of the Lodge last week, which you may have heard about already. We had earlier exchanged some of our sentiments about what it was like to leave the Lodge. Having it leave us is another matter. If misery loves company, there is some perverse satisfaction in knowing that Menninger's is also closing during the next few weeks. . . . A couple of weeks ago, my son and I spent two hours in the medical library at the Lodge, helping pack four tons of books. . . . The books seem like a tangible representation of the old Lodge, which I hope will be carried like the embers of a fire to some new location. And I hope that new place will be more fire-resistant.*[8] *. . . Some good news professionally is that an article in the current JAPA, by a retired engineer, presents actuarial evidence that psychoanalysts have half the mortality of control groups.*

June 9, 2001, HFS: *For me, not only so many decades of time, but also thousands of miles of geography, lie between me and my separation from CLS, that it greatly mutes my present feelings.*

Even in going back to the term CLS, Searles was time-traveling to the era when he worked there (he left in 1964). His emotional connection with that earlier era "muted" his feelings of grief about its closing. Around the time I joined the staff, the Lodge started calling itself "Chestnut Lodge Hospital." As seemingly minor as this change was, it offended me—I thought it smacked of trying to sound more conventional and was thus contrary to an essential aspect of the Lodge's identity, so I never used that new designation. I treasure some old hospital letterhead I saved, which called it simply "Chestnut Lodge." That sounds much more welcoming to me. It reminds me of a patient who told me she had considered other hospitals before deciding to come to the Lodge. Their glossy brochures compared unfavorably, for her, to the simple photocopied sheets of information the Lodge sent her. She was uninterested in attractive façades.

December 9, 2001, RMW: *I'm about to leave for the analytic meetings in New York. I'll spend the first four days on the Certification Committee. I'm due to stay on that committee an additional three years, but I'm not sure I'll make it that long. It's beginning to feel all too much like serving as a training analyst locally—more or less like being a lightning rod, to attract and safely siphon off massive volts of widespread anger and frustration about analytic organizations, the paucity of analytic patients, the general state of the world, etc. The former Lodge medical staff continue to get together. I just got an announcement about the "Lodge Group Associates," eight former staff members who still operate the [former Lodge's] day treatment program for borderline patients in their private offices in Rockville. Seven of us have been meeting for lunch here in Chevy Chase every Monday.*

We know that contiguity of associations conveys underlying connections. So, rereading my words, I notice an unconscious implication that those of us meeting for lunch were trying in our own way to fill the void by creating something of a day treatment program for the Lodge's former staff members.

October 22, 2007, RMW: *I'm enclosing a reprint of my latest publication.[9] . . . As you will see, it was a welcome opportunity to ventilate. I have definitely arrived at the old codger stage, having been precocious since childhood. Colleagues my age agree that the younger generation not only has no respect (we didn't either at their age)—they have an astonishing level of entitlement. It's a blissfully conflict-free form of entitlement. Occasionally, they seem to manifest signs of acute dysphoria if they are temporarily disconnected from the nipple, or if the flow of milk does not start and stop on demand. . . . I already feel better having spoken more candidly to you. Naturally, there is another side to this, if we were to ask the nipple-suckers. They would probably critique the milk quality, quantity, and flow control. They would be nonplussed, however, at the very idea of the nipple talking back. They've learned to ignore such aberrations. . . . Part of the pleasure of writing this commentary* [the reprint I was sending Searles] *was collaborating with my co-author* [who was] *teaching and supervising psychotherapy, while simultaneously struggling with her first year of classes in the analytic institute. So she was candid in describing the various role conflicts she experienced—critiquing her teachers, while acknowledging the irony of being on the receiving end of what felt like unfair but similar critiques from her students. She helped me avoid ranting too one-sidedly in our commentary . . . I saw* [the ninety-seven-year-old] *Bob Cohen in August . . . he's clearly as sharp as ever, since he agreed with my articles attributing two anonymous 1585 poems to Edward de Vere, a.k.a. Shakespeare.[10]*

November 12, 2007, HFS: *I particularly enjoyed the reprint of your well-written article, and your having found occasion to refer to my writings in your article. . . . Sylvia* [his wife] *and I are each planning to stay around till* *about 110 years of age.*

My letter of October 22 stirs up more thoughts than any other. I am ambivalent about including it, given its intemperate diatribe. The reader must take it with a grain of salt. Ironically, my ill-fated first attempt at supervision with Searles ran aground on similar rocks. A master at reading the unconscious of the other person, Searles told me early in our first meeting that he thought I was really seeking supervision with him in the hope that he would refer me a control case. I had explained to him that a new institute policy required that candidates discuss potential cases with a supervisor before recommending analysis to the patient. (Previously, more experienced candidates were allowed to begin some analyses before seeking supervision.) Although I already had a patient suitable for analysis to present to Searles, I was naturally delighted when he began referring several analytic patients to me during the ensuing years.

My venting about the entitlement of the younger generation has echoes of Searles's initial perception of me as his would-be supervisee. At the time of my letter, I was more aware of feelings that contributed to my earlier decision to step down as an active member of our institute's education committee. Now, I wonder if I was also trying to project onto "the younger generation" my own feelings of longing for the "nipple" of the Lodge.

When I left the Lodge in 1999, I assumed that my work at the analytic institute would continue to consume much of my time and that it would serve as my surviving institutional home. This was not to be. In 2000, my colleagues on the education committee became acutely worried about the continuing drop in applications for analytic training. I tried to inject some of the Lodge's contrarian spirit and dark humor when possible. For example, I pointed out that if we had no candidates to teach on Saturday (when institute classes met), we could play more golf. However, the mood seemed too somber to be lifted by my feeble attempts at levity. Eventually, a radical overhaul of the role of training and supervising analysts was approved. I should mention that during my thirteen years at the Lodge, our salaries and fringe benefits were steadily eroded, then eliminated altogether. In my final years there, we were paid about sixty dollars per session (less than half of standard private-practice fees at that time) to conduct psychotherapy, with no additional benefits (in fact, we now had to pay rent for our Lodge offices). As a result, I had steadily decreased my work for the Lodge and increased the private practice we were always allowed to conduct in our Lodge offices.

So when I saw the details of the new requirements for training and supervising analysts, I had a painful feeling of déjà vu, and I felt unable to go along with these new policies. A sliding-fee schedule would be administered by the institute's executive secretary. I calculated that it would force me to grant a reduced fee to candidates whose family income was twice that of my own. One of my children was planning to go to graduate school, and I wanted to help her pay for it. I concluded that the institute's new policies were not for me. It felt too much like a repetition of the steady devaluation of therapists in the final years of the Lodge.

It seemed to me that my institute reacted in both adaptive and maladaptive ways to the decline in demand for analytic training—much as the Lodge itself reacted both adaptively and nonadaptively to the declining number of referrals of patients suitable for long-term hospitalization. It is to be expected that psychoanalytic candidates will have parental transferences toward their training analysts and other members of the institute. But I thought my colleagues were enacting unconscious group dynamics in assuming parental-like financial responsibility in subsidizing the educational costs of their trainees to an extent that seemed masochistic on the part of training analysts who did not have independent means.

Relinquishing my role as an active training and supervising analyst was acutely painful. During the two years afterward, when my feelings about it were still most intense, I reflected on many of the factors that influenced my decision. But it is only in writing about it now that I wonder about yet another factor. I suspect I was unconsciously coping with the loss of the Lodge by turning passive to active, in voluntarily giving up a prestigious position in the psychoanalytic institute.

March 26, 2008, RMW: *I happened to be near the Lodge yesterday, so I forced myself to go have a look. I usually rely on others to give me updates. It wasn't a pretty sight. Main Building, Little Lodge, and Upper Cottage have survived the ravages of time. . . . There is a weird website on closed psychiatric hospitals, that has many photos of the Lodge. . . . It seems to be sponsored by actively paranoid patients, some of whom suffer from psychotic transferences to the Lodge. It's a strange way for the Lodge to be a presence on the web. . . . Well, the feelings stirred by stopping by there yesterday moved me to get back in touch with you.*

October 9, 2009, RMW: *I visited Bob Cohen two days ago. He's now in a hospice. He hasn't always been alert when people visit him. When I greeted him, he opened his eyes and immediately began talking about the Lodge. He realized he'd been dreaming about the Lodge. He then said "But I know it's true that I'm about to turn 100."*

I quoted the first part of this letter at the beginning of my chapter. As it turned out, my visit with Bob Cohen was three days before he died (I had not yet heard the news when I wrote this letter to Searles). Robert A. Cohen, M.D., Ph.D., linked Searles and me to each other and to the Lodge.[11] Bob had first worked there in the 1940s, alongside his training analyst, Fromm-Reichmann. He supervised the psychotherapy of Searles's first Lodge patient. He was then invited to become the first clinical director of NIMH. He supervised me weekly for five years on my second analytic case while he worked there. Upon retirement from NIMH, he returned to the Lodge as director of psychotherapy, the same position he held during Searles's first years at the Lodge. Searles was ninety-one when I wrote him this letter. One of my goals was to make him feel younger, by giving him news about his near-centenarian colleague.

I was, in fact, profoundly moved to share with Bob Cohen that moment of his mourning for the Lodge, as he was anticipating his own impending death. Bob had the emotional resilience courageously to face painful feelings from which many of us retreat. The group process of mourning is naturally influenced by the cumulative impact of the various "vectors" of each individual's unique ways of handling loss in general and the specific loss in particular. Bob's dream about the Lodge so soon before his death also underscores the way that we cope with death partly by investing ourselves emotionally in people and institutions that will survive us.

Our hopes for the future naturally go beyond our hopes for individual people and institutions, no matter how much we might cherish them. Yet, however much the Lodge was "merely" a symbol of a certain approach to intensive psychotherapeutic work with difficult patients, real places serve a different purpose for us emotionally than does the more abstract, if still important hope that the future will continue to value the ideals embodied by the Lodge.

REPLACING THE LODGE

As I said earlier, what I valued most about the Lodge were the people. So coping with the loss of the Lodge meant doing my best to preserve and enrich my connections with people. The long work hours at the Lodge meant sacrificing time with our families. Leaving the Lodge gave me more time to spend with mine. During the first year after I left, my son met me for lunch every week at a restaurant near my office, and I deeply appreciated having that time with him. My wife and I had lunch once a week with her mother, who lived in a nearby retirement community. Two colleagues who had left the Lodge for private offices in Chevy Chase had been meeting for lunch weekly, and they invited me to join them. Eventually, other former colleagues from the Lodge joined us. As of this writing, these weekly lunches continue, as one example of the collegial connections we valued at the Lodge and that we have maintained. I also branched out, inviting many other non-Lodge colleagues to lunch. (Yes, there's a lot about food here— further evidence that I was indeed projecting onto the younger "entitled . . . nipple-suckers" in my letter of October 22, 2007.) As I became less active in our psychoanalytic institute, I found these lunches and other social contacts with colleagues offered a vital replacement for both the Lodge and for my former institute committee work.

I felt fortunate that I was continuing to treat some of my Lodge patients. One of them, who reacted poorly to change and found fault with many aspects of my new location, loved the beautiful view of the woods and creek outside my office's large sliding-glass door. She took one look outside and told me, "This view will add years to your life." I was struck by her generosity in stepping outside herself to put herself in my shoes.

Writing has been one of the most important ways I have coped with my grief. We are all sustained by being part of a fabric that will outlive us, helping us cope with our mortality. The Lodge encouraged us to publish, offering unlimited secretarial assistance and other support. We gave hour-long presentations to the entire professional staff about once a year on our Lodge patients. In addition, I gave five presentations at the fall symposia during my years on the staff. These annual meetings drew audiences of up to four hundred mental health professionals (along with international visitors throughout the year), which helped validate our sense that our hospital was widely respected. Before I joined the staff at the Lodge, I had only two publications.

I then averaged two publications per year during my thirteen years there. With the void left by leaving the Lodge, I had more time to write, and I felt more of a need to do so, to help cope with this loss. My publications increased to an average of five per year since 1999. Some of this writing has been directly about the Lodge.

So, writing and connections with colleagues have been two important ways I have dealt with my grief. Collaborative writing has been a natural melding of these ways of coping. The only co-authored publication I wrote at the Lodge was the one I mentioned earlier, written with Harold Searles. After I left the Lodge, writing and presenting at professional meetings with colleagues became a welcome way of re-creating the lost collegiality of the Lodge. An art therapist and I gave presentations at two national meetings on our collaboration in the treatment of a former Lodge patient who had dissociative identity disorder, as did a couples therapist and I at two local meetings, about our collaboration in working with that same patient.

A colleague who had left the Lodge ten years before I arrived there co-authored with me a commentary on borderline personality.[12] While my daughter was pursuing a master's degree in international relations, she and I reviewed a book on the psychological consequences of war.[13] The refugees described in the book make me think of those of us who are "refugees" from the Lodge. Another colleague who was at the Lodge two of the years I was there invited me to co-author a paper on the value of psychological testing.[14] I wrote two book reviews[15] with a younger colleague I had taught, after we discovered we had common interests. As I included Shakespeare research in my writing, I was delighted when one of the leading authorities on de Vere as Shakespeare agreed to coauthor a paper with me.[16] This collaborative writing, which includes one co-author who is thirty years my senior and two others who are more than twenty years my junior, enacts the intergenerational transmission of clinical experience that the Lodge once provided in abundance.

Our institutions elicit both forms of familial transferences, with the institution as both a surrogate parent and a surrogate child. The loss of an institution thus ruptures one thread that connects us with a future that will outlive us. I lost a unique and beloved institution, one with which I had fused a large portion of my professional identity. It has left a void. Although the world of a great novel is timeless, Chestnut Lodge was not. Yet every reminder of transience enriches all that remains in our lives. My relationships have been imbued with an extra measure of meaning since losing the Lodge.

The fragility of what we value in life can inspire us to make the most of the relationships, time, and opportunities that remain. Writing this chapter has, as I had hoped, helped me continue to mourn the loss of the Lodge. If aspects of the chapter strike the reader as unfinished, it may mean my grieving process is still incomplete.

NOTES

1. It was not, but approaching the work as if the Lodge was timeless is reminiscent of Fromm-Reichmann's advice to therapists that we approach our work with patients as though we will have all the time we need.

2. See my review of Hornstein's *To Redeem One Person Is to Redeem the World: The Life of Frieda Fromm-Reichman* (New York: The Free Press, 2000) in *The Psychoanalytic Quarterly* 71 (2002): 367–374.

3. R. M. Waugaman, "The Analyst's Caseload as a Family: Transferences to Fellow Patients," *Psychoanalytic Quarterly* 72 (2003): 575–614.

4. R. M. Waugaman, "If You Want to Bring Someone Back to Reality, You Have to Enter Their World First," *Psychiatry* 68 (2005): 236–242.

5. R. M. Waugaman and H. F. Searles, "Infinite Reflections: The Opening Phase of Intensive Psychotherapy with a Chronically Schizophrenic Patient," *Journal of the American Academy of Psychoanalysis* 18 (1990): 99–114. Also published in *Psychoanalysis and Severe Emotional Illness*, ed. A.-L. Silver and M. B. Cantor (New York: Guilford, 1990).

6. R. M. Waugaman, "Displacement of the Countertransference from One Patient to Another," *Journal of Clinical Psychoanalysis* 9 (2000): 113–120.

7. CLS stands for Chestnut Lodge Sanitarium, as it was called when Searles first worked there. I usually refer to it in this chapter as simply "the Lodge," as we called it among ourselves.

8. Little did I know at the time I wrote this that the Lodge's original building (the "Main Building") would in fact burn down in June 2009.

9. R. M. Waugaman and J. Lhulier, "'And Gladly Wolde He Lerne and Gladly Teche,'" *Psychiatry* 70 (2007): 221–228.

10. R. M. Waugaman, "A Wanderlust Poem, Newly Attributed to Edward de Vere," *Shakespeare Matters* 7, no. 1 (2007): 21–23; R. M. Waugaman, "A Snail Poem, Newly Attributed to Edward de Vere," *Shakespeare Matters* 7, no. 2 (2008): 6–11.

11. R. M. Waugaman, "Robert A. Cohen: A Remembrance," *Psychiatry* (in press).

12. R. M. Waugaman and W. N. Goldstein, "The Pivotal Role of Interpersonal Relationships in the Outcome of Borderline Patients," *Psychiatry* 66 (2003): 129–132.

13. R. M. Waugaman and A. Waugaman, "Broken Spirits: The Treatment of Traumatized Asylum Seekers, Refugees, War, and Torture Victims," *American Journal of Psychiatry* 162 (2005): 1768–1769.

14. M. J. Peebles-Kleiger, L. Horwitz, J. H. Kleiger, and R. M. Waugaman, "Psychological Testing and Analyzability: Breathing New Life Into an Old Issue," *Psychoanalytic Psychology* 23 (2006): 504–526.

15. R. M. Waugaman and J. Lhulier, "*Putnam's Camp: Sigmund Freud, James Jackson Putnam, and the Purpose of American Psychology*, by George Prochnik," *Psychiatry* 70 (2007): 374–381; R. M. Waugaman and J. Lhulier, "*The Psychiatric Interview in Clinical Practice*, second edition, by Roger A. MacKinnon, Robert Michels, and Peter J. Buckley," *American Journal of Psychiatry* 165 (2008): 271–272.

16. R. M. Waugaman and R. A. Stritmatter, "Who Was 'William Shakespeare'? We Propose It Was Edward de Vere," *Scandinavian Psychoanalytic Review* 32 (2009): 132–142.

CHAPTER 10

THE DEATH OF THE ANALYST, THE DEATH OF THE ANALYTIC COMMUNITY, AND BAD CONDUCT

ROBERT M. GALATZER-LEVY

WHEN DR. P died suddenly, he disappeared. There was a memorial service, and those patients who could be identified were offered help by other analysts. But after that, not a word. Though Dr. P had been a central figure in his society and institute, his name never came up again, even in relation to projects he had initiated. Study groups to which he belonged became inactive and dissolved for no apparent reason. He disappeared from institutional awareness as if he had never existed.

Dr. P died from a brain aneurysm that had been diagnosed several years before and for which surgery was being contemplated. He told neither his colleagues nor his patients about it, though in other respects, he was the soul of care in his treatment of patients. His own life experience was marked by the death of his training analyst. His own analyst had died suddenly from a complication of a medical condition that he, too, had kept as quiet as he could.[1]

In this chapter, I address the issue of our communal response to the problem of the medically ill analyst in light of the psychoanalytic community's resistance to mourning and denial of grief. Physically ill analysts are often significantly impaired in their analytic function, and not uncommonly ethical lapses emerge in the context of the analyst's illness. The link between failed mourning and troubling analytic behavior is strong. Clinical experience clarifies it. Several facts became obvious a few years ago, when I described a series of cases involving the death of the analyst during the course of treatment (Galatzer-Levy 2004). First, my ability to collect so many cases as part of a general psychoanalytic practice suggests that similar clinical experiences are far more common than our literature suggests. Second, the frequency with which the death of the analyst is preceded by extended periods of professional dysfunction is reflected neither in psychoanalytic publications nor community discussions. Third, this problem goes unaddressed in psychoanalytic education, both during training and throughout continuing education. Finally, psychoanalytic institutions rarely deal with these problems effectively. They are ignored and effective action is seldom taken.

My widened experience of consultation and treatment in this area, which resulted from the publication of my article on the death of the analyst, supports these impressions. At professional meetings, when I spoke about the challenges posed for analysts, analysands, and the analytic community by an analyst's illness or death, colleagues came up to me or contacted me later confirming these impressions from their own experience. I heard many supporting stories during consultations. Discussion at national and international meetings further confirmed that psychoanalytic institutions shy away from these problems even when failure to address them has led to shocking experiences in those institutions.

The death of a working analyst is a common occurrence. My earlier report (Galatzer-Levy 2004) indicated that the cases fell into roughly three categories. Analysands whose analyst died unexpectedly in the midst of a good analysis seemed to do best. Another group involved pathological analytic stalemates, often including slavelike transferences that only came to light by virtue of the analyst's death. These cases overlapped with the most malignant ones, in which gravely ill and impaired analysts continued to practice. These analysts involved patients in complex situations transparently intended to soothe the analyst. Patients became slaves whose life function was to care for the analyst. Not surprisingly, some patients' lives collapsed under these arrangements.

These experiences led me to doubt whether any analyst, no matter how disciplined, could maintain an analytic attitude when gravely ill and to be skeptical of the ideas put forward by authors like Barbara Fajardo (2001), who, working in the shadow of her own advanced ovarian cancer, suggested that analysis with a dying analyst provided analytic opportunities that were unique, especially if one thought of analysis from a relational point of view. While her theoretical exposition was attractive, it did not jibe with my clinical experience.

As I study the cases I reported and learn more information about the dying analyst, I am less certain whether good work can be done by dying analysts. As I have gotten to know more about some of the cases I reported and the analysts involved, it has become apparent that some of their practices were extremely problematic long before they became physically ill. For example, one of the analysts in the series, who from the patient's report and by reputation had been an outstanding practitioner until becoming ill, turned out to have had multiple sexual relations with patients decades before his illness. This suggests that at least some of the cases I described could be better understood in terms of the analyst's characterological deficits than in terms of their illness. In addition, in none of the cases I reported did the analyst adequately use the assistance that might have been available within the analytic community. A few sought consultation. Some others sought personal therapy. However, these efforts were focused on the analysts' personal distress (the consultations focusing on medicolegal issues) rather than the needs of the patients. I think it is an open question whether even an analyst with truly adequate assistance from the analytic community can serve analysands well during a terminal illness.

THE ANALYTIC COMMUNITY'S FAILURE TO ADDRESS THE PROBLEM

Why, despite the obvious harm to patients and the profession, do analytic communities remain ineffective in addressing the problems that arise when colleagues become too ill to practice safely? Superficial reasons are often given: the privacy of the psychoanalytic process precludes monitoring (unlike, for example, surgery), no one but analyst and analysand knows what happens behind closed psychoanalytic doors, anything that interferes with privacy is unethical and detrimental to analysis, and monitoring psychoanalysts' competence is far more difficult than monitoring other professionals' work. Yet there are ways that analysts could be better monitored, and our failure to use such methods suggests that the issues mentioned are not a sufficient explanation for the failure to safeguard patients. Readily available, if problematic, means to assess broadly analysts' competency include formal complaints to ethics or "analysts' assistance committees" (a telling euphemism for committees on impaired analysts); recertification; participation in continuing education, including presentation of clinical work to colleagues who are expected to address evidences

of significant impairment; evaluation of all analysts in small self-monitor-
ing groups; and requirements of regular physical examinations. Committed analytic communities can monitor members for significant impairment and intervene when necessary. My experience, confirmed in conversations with analysts from around the country, is that the problem lies
not in the difficulty of detecting analysts' impairment but in a profound
reluctance to do so.

Reluctance to address one's own death is easy to understand. Denial and/or disavowal are commonly used and often adaptive (Bonanno
2009). It has even been suggested that the analyst's impending death can
stimulate psychoanalytic work and provides one of the few opportunities
to address these defenses effectively and urgently (Fajardo 2001). Often,
problems associated with excessive use of denial-disavowal are partially
neutralized by the social surround. Institutions commonly respond in
ways that elicit resistance but nonetheless often provide help, comfort,
and solace, thus allowing the person to avoid some of the consequences
of undue denial and disavowal. Sometimes, the social surround supports
denial and disavowal in ways that make these defenses more adaptive.
The most obvious social supports can be seen in traditional religious beliefs and rituals that institutionalize the denial of death through concepts
like the immortality of the soul. This can allow dying individuals and
those close to them the opportunity to avoid a confrontation with the finitude of personal being while facilitating adaptive responses to physical
death. At the same time, mourning rituals such as funerals, wakes, and
memorial services provide community emotional support that makes the
loss less terrifying.

Social configurations such as "life" insurance, hospice care, and the medical rituals surrounding death in the United States similarly support terminally ill individuals and those close to them, by limiting the material and
psychological damage of death and providing clear pathways through its
predictable emotional and material trials. Much of contemporary medicine
can be regarded as simultaneously confronting the material problems of serious illness through effective treatment and palliation and denying other
problems—the unlikelihood of recovery and the inevitability of death. Hospitals provide a separate place, where death can occur apart from the world
of the living. Alternatively to denial, death may initiate pervasive depression, which, by denying all hope, spares the pain and frustration that comes
with the realization of the limitations of realistic hope.

Analysts tend to think about loss, grief, and mourning in terms of the individual's experiences. Commonly, psychoanalytic formulations about loss are based on Freud's (1917) intrapsychic model. Most of us have experienced individual loss and are aware of its profound effect. Some of us have experienced the loss of entire communities when wars, genocide, or natural disasters destroy them. But there is another sort of loss that, despite its gradualness and lack of clarity, is no less profound. This is the loss of communities, in particular the psychoanalytic community, as members of a particular cohort gradually die, retire, or leave the field. This loss of community is often experienced as a series of individual losses, which obscures its larger nature. In the absence of a psychoanalytic community, the larger context for the analyst's identity is lost. This loss is particularly well defended against both because of its gravity and because of the lack of institutional and social defenses that typically support bereft individuals. In other words, the death of individual analysts comes to represent, albeit out of awareness, the demise of psychoanalysis itself. In the absence of adequate adaptive defenses, primitive and maladaptive denial and disavowal take their place. I believe that the tragic inattention to the problem of the severely ill and dying psychoanalyst arises in large measure from this denial.[2]

Communities can adapt creatively to devastating loss by using higher-order defenses, as Myerhoff (1978) and Lear (2006) have shown. Myerhoff describes how very elderly, impoverished Jews living in a culturally alien environment and isolated from normal social supports reestablished a sense of community through shared stories that helped them comprehend their current reality. Although psychoanalysts share a fondness for nostalgia and commonly recount tales of colorful characters encountered in bygone psychoanalytic days, the sort of rich and meaningful narratives that sometimes appear in communities facing destruction are not evident in these stories. Nostalgia—sentimentally holding on to trivial elements of the past—is a different process from a narrative reworking of history that includes an appreciation of tragedy, irony, and humor. This latter type of creative reworking can occur in response to the recognition of the past's inevitable loss. Cornel West (2004) describes this essential capacity to engage realistically and effectively the painful reality of mourning as a "blues sensibility."

ANALYSTS' RESPONSES TO THE LOSS
OF COMMUNITY

Since the 1970s, most American psychoanalytic institutes, including the Chicago Psychoanalytic Institute, from which I graduated and of which I am a faculty member, experienced a gradual decline in both the number of candidates we train and the esteem in which we are held within the larger community. This decline was and is, of course, the subject of numerous formal and informal discussions within my institute. One day in the late 1990s, during a faculty meeting devoted to the topic, a widely respected but characterologically gloomy colleague, then in his late sixties, rose to address the faculty. He said that all our plans and talk were pointless. We were avoiding the main problem, one about which we could do nothing—psychoanalysis is dying. Our collective task was to mourn the loss, not to attempt frantically to resuscitate our moribund field.

I was angry with my colleague. He had enjoyed a good life in psychoanalysis and was now willing to let the field die. He had gotten what he wanted from it. The death notice seemed premature and harmful. Though this colleague's attitude was extreme, at least in his willingness to express it publicly, I have repeatedly heard subtler variations on the theme. The idea that the game is over and therefore that there is no reason to continue to struggle seems to arise often in two situations. The first occurs in discussions of reform of psychoanalytic institutions, when it is put forward as a reason for avoiding the stress associated with attempting reform. The second is when dealing with the problem of an impaired colleague. The appeal of not addressing the problem of the dying colleague or the dying institution is the same. Neither will survive long enough to do much harm, and attending to the situation will, at best, exacerbate its inherent distress. As a colleague said to me during a committee discussion about a severely impaired analyst who had caused enormous harm to a patient, "Let it go. He's retiring soon anyway. He's basically a good guy. All we can do is make him even more miserable than he is already."

My own response to preparing the current chapter informs my thinking about its topic. My paper on the effect of the analyst's death during analysis was not only well received, but numerous analysts and analytic patients sought my advice and consultation as a result of it. The paper was clearly useful and pertinent to many analysts. Its topic is hardly upbeat, but then again, some of the things I study in the area of psychiatry and the law are far more objectively unpleasant. Yet anticipating talking about such topics does not necessarily produce the burdened feeling I experienced anticipating writing about the dead and dying analyst. I resisted writing on the subject. Neither my conscience nor my reason diminished that feeling. It now strikes me that my response reflects the central problem, the wish to deny the very existence of the problem about which I am writing, the increasingly conscious wish that ignoring it will make it go away.

INSTITUTIONAL AND COMMUNITY RESPONSES

I repeatedly found that even when there were institutional mechanisms to review these matters, they were seldom used, except in extreme cases, and even then they often functioned poorly because those involved often became confused and uncertain about their roles. In my earlier paper, I made several recommendations to analysts and analytic communities about the management of these situations. I pointed to the idea that several of the difficulties that arise in this situation can be anticipated, that the individual analyst should be aware of these difficulties, and that within the analytic community, norms need to be developed to handle them. As with many earlier, similar suggestions, I have seen little evidence that ideas designed to help analysands and analysts through these situations are effectively implemented.

In fact, community and institutional responses have frequently harmed patients. Often these patients, many of whom were themselves mental health professionals, became pariahs within the analytic community. Of course, the burden of having been gravely exploited in the service of the analyst's needs interferes with patients' capacity to use subsequent treatment. But the community's response often increases this difficulty. Patients often correctly anticipate that consultants, committee members, and potential new therapists would rather not hear their painful stories, especially when the analyst was held in high regard or enjoyed the friendship of colleagues. There is a grave risk that the consultant or new therapist may be torn between his alliance to the patient, on the one hand, and his allegiance to his troubled colleague, on the other.

The pressure put on the consultant to respond in a way that supposedly protects the analyst is both internal and external. Few of us hearing stories of misconduct fail to imagine how painful it must be to be in the offending analyst's shoes, and few of us have the hubris to feel confident that we may not someday actually be there. Indeed, effective superego function, by including the ability to appreciate one's potential for ethical lapses, thereby better protects us than the certainty, even if valid, that one would never behave unethically. As we are wont to say, "Pride goes before the fall" (Proverbs 12:18). Externally, even the possession of knowledge that another analyst has behaved badly can create conflict.

Often, consultants and committee members who address the problem of impaired analysts are explicitly told that taking any action that might harm a fellow analyst will have negative consequences for them, either personally or professionally. In one city, three analysts were part of a study group that they each valued highly. One of them was a leader in the analytic community; the other two were up and coming. One of the junior analysts consulted with a patient about her ongoing treatment with the other junior analyst from their study group. The patient said she was being bizarrely abused by her analyst and wanted help figuring out what to do. To complicate matters, the consulting analyst and the senior analyst both served on a committee that was to make an important decision about the purportedly offending analyst's career. Anxious about the outcome, the accused analyst sought out the senior member of the trio and said how much he feared that the consulting analyst would "tell on" him. The senior analyst approached the consulting analyst, who had kept the patient's communication in confidence, warning him that any leakage of the information he had could "do your career no good." The consulting analyst provided reassurance of confidentiality and, in fact, did not bring any of his patient's material to the committee, yet the senior analyst remained suspicious of him. Shortly afterward, the study group broke up for reasons that were never made explicit. After the breakup, the three were never at ease with one another again.

Sometimes, the consultants and members of committees addressing the problems of analysts are explicitly told that doing anything that might in some sense harm a fellow analyst is an indication of personal pathology.

Finally, there is a group of analysts who respond to the internal and external pressure to avoid harming another analyst with reaction formation. They seem to believe that any attempt to minimize the harm or pain that come to misbehaving analysts is a sign of corruption. For them, it is important to make sure that the offending analyst is effectively expelled from the analytic community, as if his continued presence in it contaminated the entire group. The rationalization that such expulsion is in the service of the protection of patients is transparently untenable since such expulsions rarely affect the analyst's ability to practice. But, much like sweeping the matter under the rug, this rigorous approach of expulsion has as its primary effect removing the offense and the offender from the community's ongoing awareness.

THE POSSIBILITY OF EFFECTIVE INTERVENTION

The following vignette brings us closer to the psychological problems faced by the analytic community when a colleague becomes impaired or is dying. At the same time, it provides an example of how working through the resistance to intervention can be helpful.

I had known Dr. T for many years as a friendly but dull individual, the sort of man one greets with genuine affection in the hallway but prays not to be seated next to at dinner. In seminars and his few publications, Dr. T gave the impression of not being terribly bright. He often adopted others' opinions, presenting them in a simplified and pedantic fashion. The high point of Dr. T's life appeared to have been his acceptance at a very elite college, where he did well enough to get into medical school and to follow an undistinguished path through residency and analytic training, eventually becoming a training analyst. Everyone described him as a "nice" man, and most of us attributed his mediocrity to neurotic inhibition for no particularly good reason. My relationship to Dr. T was complicated because for a time we were in analysis with the same analyst. Dr. T developed a manifestly warm fraternal transference to me, which I did not particularly enjoy.

Sometime in his late fifties, Dr. T developed a complex heart condition that seemed to slow him down. A few years later he developed Parkinson's disease, whose medical management was complicated by his cardiac condition. As might be expected, there was a certain amount of gossip about Dr. T's medical problems. These conversations always ended with the conclusion that beneath his mask-like face, Dr. T remained as vigorous as ever and that in his practice he was doing "just fine," though there seemed to be no evidence to support either of these ideas. In fact, as I learned later, his practice had dwindled during this time.

Among Dr. T.'s patients was a middle-aged mental health professional who had long been involved with the institute. A bright if somewhat idiosyncratic thinker, her reputation around the institute had suffered because she had publicly expressed increasingly unusual ideas. In addition, people noticed her increasingly odd appearance. When she applied to a training program, all three of her interviewers, including myself, thought that she seemed to be suffering from a pathology that was likely to interfere with her training, although her history suggested that she had at one time functioned at a much higher level. We turned down her application but, as is the custom at our institute, offered her the opportunity to meet with the chair of the admissions committee, who at this point happened to be me.

Ms. A was distraught by the committee's decision, not so much for herself, though she very much wanted the training, but for her analyst, who had wondered whether the committee had thought that he was conducting her analysis improperly. Indeed, he had explicitly told her that her entering training would be the crowning achievement of his career. In fact, the committee had not formed a negative opinion of the analysis per se, since we try to avoid intruding into applicant's personal analyses. However, all of the interviewers had commented on Ms. A's singular lack of insight and incapacity, despite a dozen years of analysis, to describe herself or her psychodynamics in any meaningful way.

I told Ms. A that while the committee had not, in fact, formed an opinion about the analysis itself, we did feel that she had not learned some of the things that one hopes to learn in an analysis. She said she wanted to tell me about the analysis. Much of her adolescence was devoted to caring for her invalid father, who was slowly dying of a chronic illness. She deeply resented this role and acted cruelly toward her father in a multitude of ways. When her analyst became ill, the two of them decided that his illness constituted an opportunity to relive the experience of the father's illness and this time "to do it right." The transference was not to be interpreted nor worked through; it was taken as an opportunity to reenact the patient's adolescence. Part of this reenactment included staying with the analyst until he died, avoiding being "mean" to him (i.e., avoiding saying anything negative about the situation), and keeping the analyst's spirits up. The therapeutic intent was to play out this drama. The patient felt that it had, in fact, been highly therapeutic, although she was able to recognize that her life had fallen apart during this treatment.

Ms. A asked me what she could do to get into the program, and I said that I didn't know if there was anything she could do, but possibly she should consider a consultation regarding her analysis, since, from what she told me, it appeared to be both unconventional and unproductive. Ms. A left the session in tears.

A few days later, I got a call from her analyst, who said that he knew it was against institute policy for analysts to intervene in administrative situations involving their patients but that he wanted to talk to me about what I had said to Ms. A. He had her permission. Would that be all right? He told me that the last thing he wanted to do was to hurt his patient, and I explained that I knew full well that an analysand might describe an analysis quite differently from the way it would be seen by the analyst. If they both wished, I would speak with him, but that if I did so, I would have to recuse myself from any administrative decisions about Ms. A. He said sadly that Ms. A had completely given up on training, so no administrative issues regarding her would come up. Ms. A told me the same thing when I talked to her on the phone.

My meeting with Dr. T was one of the most painful professional experiences of my life. Dr. T said that he knew that he was functioning poorly as an analyst and believed that behind the encouraging words of his colleagues lay an unspoken conviction that he was not fit to practice. He had not received a new referral in six years. In fact, on many days Ms. A was his only patient. He would have ended his practice but for her, yet he often fell asleep during her sessions and did not recall what she had said between sessions. Ms. A had a longstanding and extremely intense paternal transference to him. When in the past he had attempted to interpret her deep attachment to him as transference, she had always agreed, but the interpretations seemed to have no other effect. He had given up on making interpretations years ago, thinking that they were "premature." He spontaneously confirmed Ms. A's idea that she was very special to him and that her becoming a candidate would be proof that he had made a contribution to psychoanalysis. He had analyzed another candidate, but that person had told him at the end of the analysis that the analysis had been useless, that he had only tolerated it to fulfill the institute's requirements, and that he had then gone on to adopt a theoretical position antithetical to that of Dr. T.

Dr. T then looked at me with tears in his eyes and asked, "Do you think I'm hurting her?" I said, as gently as I could, "Well it doesn't sound like things are going well." Now Dr. T was crying, "You know I've been very sick." "I know." "It's not fair," he said. I said, "No, it isn't fair." He shook my hand and left. Two weeks later, he sent me a note saying that he was retiring from practice and thanking me for the interview. He died eighteen months later.

I was distressed but not surprised when several colleagues became angry at me about my handling of the situation of Ms. A and Dr. T. Some of them explained their displeasure, saying that it was important to keep institute and analytic functions separate, but I found their statements less than credible since these same analysts commonly talked about candidates' personal analyses in other administrative contexts. Others were more direct—how would I feel if I were in Dr. T's shoes? "We are all vulnerable to having our careers ruined by a misstep." "Ms. A was borderline. We all get into trouble with borderlines."

Although I simply did not agree with most of these criticisms, they worried me. I felt sorry and guilty toward Dr. T, even though he expressed his seemingly appropriate gratitude for being spared doing further harm, not to mention risking a malpractice suit.

In other words, I and others responded to my actions as though they reflected hostile aggression rather than an effort to help both analyst and patient in a difficult situation. As I had occasion to observe and participate in the dynamics of similar situations involving ethics committees and analyst assistance committees, I became aware of how profoundly analysts are influenced by concerns about hostility in these situations. A small number of colleagues use their administrative power simply to enact hostile fantasies, attacking the impaired analyst with moral indignation and medical authority. One analyst even referred to himself as the "prosecuting psychiatrist" during a hearing in which he was supposed to play the role of neutral evaluator. Various forms of reaction formation and disguised hostility are much more common, in which committee members and colleagues consciously attempt to be kind while acting in a way that leaves the problematic analyst in worse shape than he was before their kindness.

For example, an analyst who years previously had been involved in a serious boundary violation responded to a life-threatening illness by repeating this boundary violation with another patient. Interviews with the analyst suggested that there had been other boundary violations, that he had little insight, and that he was at profound risk of reoffending. Despite the seriousness of the situation, several members of the Impaired Analyst Committee who reviewed the case advocated kindness—or at least what they saw as kindness—out of pity for the analyst. They recommended that he only have minimal additional supervision, in no way restrict his practice, and enter into a nonintensive therapy. Strikingly, these half-measures closely resembled those imposed earlier, which left the analyst vulnerable to committing another serious boundary violation. This would almost certainly bring his career to an end and carried a high risk of a malpractice suit that could wipe out his savings, since after his first violation he was no longer able to get adequate malpractice insurance. The committee left him with essentially no tools to prevent catastrophe.

It strikes me how frequently administrative attempts at supposed kindness in fact leave analysts more vulnerable and contribute to more severe problems down the road. During the 1990s, a distinguished analyst took it upon himself to try to help colleagues who had behaved unethically and their patients come to mutually satisfactory agreements to avoid the pain and danger of legal or ethics committees' processes. In several instances, although patients willingly entered into these negotiations, the process backfired badly because the patients came to believe the mediator was using his position to protect the analyst. Now the analysts were attacked with even greater vigor.

The supposed kindness often punishes the analyst's remaining patients. One patient complained that Dr. W, a respected member of an analytic community, had sexually molested her. With the patient's permission, the matter was referred to the Analyst Assistance Committee instead of the Ethics Committee because Dr. W was known to be recovering from major cardiac surgery and had been observed by several of his colleagues to be "out of it." They "kindly" did not call that situation to the attention of the Analyst Assistance Committee, even though their society's bylaws required them to do so. Dr. W readily admitted his conduct and attributed it to "pump head," a form of dementia observed after an individual has been on a cardiopulmonary bypass. He said he was getting better and indeed appeared to be. The committee accepted a note from his cardiac surgeon saying that the analyst's brain function was fully recovered, even though the surgeon was not nearly as qualified as the committee members to assess the state of the analyst's dementia and even though the medical literature is gloomy about the prognosis of pump-head syndrome (Alston 2005).

About six months later a second patient came forward to describe her awful experiences with this analyst, who would fall asleep during sessions and fly into rages when confronted about his behavior. In these rages, he would yell at the patient that she was "just like the other cunt" who ruined his life. The patient felt at a complete loss about what to do because her previous work with Dr. W had led to an enormous transformation for the better in her life. The ongoing sessions were tormenting her, and her extra-analytic life became ever more constricted, as she did not want the world to know about what was going on with her beloved analyst.

I have increasingly come to think of "kindness" in the context of these problems as a symptomatic act in which the "kind" analyst, while convincing himself that he is sparing the impaired colleague and his patients pain, in fact intensifies that pain. I believe these situations are much more common and harmful than we realize or want to admit. Obviously, ideas about the dynamics of those involved must be largely speculative. But I suggest that we consider the possibility that these behaviors reflect unconscious rage at both the analyst and the patients who force their problems into our awareness, thereby interfering with our denial of the effect of the analyst's impairment and death on the patient. I think these responses are of a piece with the angry responses toward analysts who do not cooperate in denying the severity of the problems posed by the severely ill, impaired, or dying colleague. These analysts have brought the bad news into awareness.

Even discussing a colleague's serious illness or impending death, much less taking action, is often experienced as a hostile act. Retrospective discussions of the consequences of a colleague's death are seen as defamations. Talk about these matters is often unwelcome and experienced as hostile because it punctures a common defense. The fantasy that "we could all be in his shoes" hides the reality that we all are already in his shoes. We are all going to die, and many of us will become too ill to practice before we are ready to give up our beloved work. Every confrontation with a colleague's death is a confrontation with our own mortality and thus is experienced as a hostile attack.

It is in the nature of denial that speaking about the denied situation is equated with causing that situation. The emotional response to the death of a colleague and, hence, the recognition of one's own inevitable death is displaced onto the individual who speaks about death and forces awareness of it. What is merely painful and unpleasant for the analyst who feels himself forced to confront these matters with colleagues becomes truly horrific for the former patient who must speak of these matters with subsequent analysts. My findings are that many of these patients are treated harshly when they seek consultation or attempt to resume analysis. Some of these patients' chronic vigilance for evidence of their new analysts' physical deterioration can be exhausting to analysts who are already aware of their vulnerability.

But for both patient and new analyst, when a patient has been severely injured by the treatment he received prior to his first analyst's death, the work is particularly delicate. The analyst is susceptible to making the patient feel unwelcome, as he is a harbinger of the nightmare of how an analyst may be remembered. The situation is complicated because such patients often have significant masochistic trends in their personalities, which lead to their continuing analysis with an impaired analyst. Yet analysts are accustomed to dealing with difficult and confronting personalities, so the characteristics of these survivors of the death of an analyst does not sufficiently explain the widespread negative reactions they receive. This leads me to wonder whether the deaths of individual analysts meant more than the loss of the individual.

THE EXPERIENCE OF THE DEATH OF A COLLEAGUE: MOURNING A PERSON, MOURNING A COMMUNITY

One morning I learned that William Meissner, M.D., S.J., had died. Bill was an extraordinary man who went to medical school and became a psychiatrist and a psychoanalyst as a Jesuit. He was both intellectually and clinically productive, writing twenty-nine books and more than 250 papers. He taught at Harvard and at Boston College, where he was the first professor of psychoanalysis in the United States, with the exception of Franz Alexander's brief tenure at the University of Chicago in the 1930s. His encyclopedic knowledge of psychoanalysis made his writings both synthetic and absolutely reliable but also, to the distaste of some, rather Jesuitical. He was simultaneously a committed Jesuit, a committed psychoanalyst, and a caring physician. It was my good fortune to get to know Bill through the Center for Advanced Psychoanalytic Studies (CAPS) program, an organization in which small groups of analysts meet together twice yearly for decades. When I joined my CAPS group, I was not only its youngest member but also a "young Turk" fascinated by then-deviant ideas of self psychology and the possibilities of applying the new mathematics of chaos theory to psychoanalysis. The welcome I received was mostly warm and collegial, but at the same time it became fairly clear that I should correct my odd and mistaken ideas. Bill, too, was clear in his disagreement with some of my thinking, but his attitude was unique in the degree to which he at the same time took me

seriously and felt no need to educate me to "proper" psychoanalytic thinking. Respect and curiosity about ideas that differed from his own seemed to
come naturally to him.

Despite his enormous sophistication about psychoanalysis, philosophy,
and religion, he was in some ways remarkably unworldly. When, after one of
our meetings, the CAPS group retired to a second-rate Chinese restaurant, I
was amazed to discover that this was the first time in his seventy-three years
that Bill had eaten Chinese restaurant food.

Bill was not above bending rules for a higher good. After Massachusetts
passed laws that effectively made it impossible for individuals who engaged
in illegal sexual acts to seek treatment without fear that the therapist would
become an agent of the police, Bill continued to see such patients but re-
defined his role as that of a priest and thus not required to report to the
authorities.

I got to know Bill better after a series of painful and appalling events.
Bill had written a well-regarded text on psychoanalysis and ethics, which
covered ground similar to that of another author. Both had written scholarly
works that included extensive paraphrases of Freud. The other analyst al-
leged to the Boston Psychoanalytic Society and Institute Ethics Committee
that Bill had plagiarized his work. Bill denied the allegations but failed to
provide the strong evidence he possessed that clearly would have exoner-
ated him because, being old and ill, Bill did not choose to spend his time defending the accusation. The Boston Society retained the services of an editor
of psychoanalytic books who had no particular expertise in plagiarism. He
located several similar passages in the books. Disregarding the possibilities
that the similarity of the passages might have arisen as a result of both analysts paraphrasing very similar material in primary sources and ignoring the
possibility that the other analyst might have worked from materials that Bill
had previously published, the editor concluded that Bill had too extensively
paraphrased the other analyst's work. The committee issued a reprimand,
even though there is no reference to plagiarism or similar issues in the ethical principles of the American Psychoanalytic Association. The committee
did, however, decide to hold the opinion in confidence, and Bill, having
better things to do and already ill from the cancer that would ultimately kill
him, decided against appealing a decision whose only effect was to lie in a
file cabinet somewhere. However, someone telephoned a reporter from the
Boston Globe, who contacted the Boston Society and Institute, asking for
confirmation of the report of the finding, which he was given. Now Bill's

supposed misconduct appeared as a leading article in the second section of the paper, much to Bill's embarrassment and distress. Many colleagues, including myself, were infuriated about what had happened, but Bill's attitude was that despite his distress, he did not want to spend the limited time he had on earth battling this foolishness.

I learned of Bill's death by e-mail and felt the particular pain that comes when such news arrives in this inherently dissociated fashion. That night I had a dream. *I was packing for a trip, but somehow was already on the train on which I was to take the trip. I was discussing with my wife whether or not I needed to take a suit with me, and there were images of her folding the suit so it would fit in a suitcase. There was some indistinct conversation about whether the suit would really be necessary, and in some vague way the train started on its journey.*

Besides Bill's death, day residues for the dream included that I was to speak the next day at a conference where I anticipated that conventional dress for presenters would include a suit and tie. Since I find these uncomfortable, I debated whether I could "get away with" my usual outfit: wash pants, dress shirt, perhaps a blazer.

Representing death as a train journey has idiosyncratic meanings for me. As an adolescent, I was deeply impressed by this idea as it was portrayed in John Huston's 1962 film *Freud*. The source for the vivid imagery in the film was Freud's *The Interpretation of Dreams*, which I read somewhat later. It struck me as implausible that train trips could universally be interpreted as representing death or dying, because to my youthful mind death was associated with an abrupt, violent disruption of ongoing life. Trains also evoked the memory of being four years old and sharing a train berth with my mother, which was "Freudian" not only in the sense of referring to a classically oedipal situation but also in that it allied me with Freud, who describes a somewhat similar experience. My choice of a train to represent death and dying in my dream refers to Freud and the world of classical psychoanalysis, a world in which Bill was, to my mind, not only more firmly attached than myself but also which he epitomized. I also associated trains to my teacher Heinz Kohut. Kohut had gone to the Vienna train station when Freud was fleeing the city and saw Freud through a train window. He thought Freud looked at him and he thus felt connected to Freud and the Freudian tradition, an idea that paralleled my sense of connection to the classical tradition by way of Bill.

The image of the suit and the question of whether to wear it refer to a symptom, which I carry with me to this day: an aversion to wearing wool, which I find unpleasantly itchy. This symptom is also associated with oedipal-period experiences of sexual frustration. While I have found a "work-around" for this symptom (cotton or fine wool clothing), it remains with me, as does a fantasy of how awful it would have been for me to live in times when people had to wear coarse wool garments. A particular version of this fantasy concerns the dreadfulness of being a monk forced to wear itchy clothing, i.e., to be in a state of perpetual sexual tension. In other words, the dream spoke to a conflict about identifying with Bill the Jesuit. At the same time, it referred to the issue of being part of a community, be it a conventional religious order or the psychoanalytic community.

In sum, at this level of analysis, Bill's death stimulated not only grief about the loss of a friend and anxieties about my own finitude but also a whole series of ambivalent attitudes about membership in the psychoanalytic community. I had a sense that the entire community was dying.

The widespread concern among psychoanalysts that the entire field is dying reflects not only the reality that, at least among some groups of analysts,[3] fewer people are seeking analysis or analytic training but also a feeling, particularly common among senior analysts, that the analytic world they knew is disappearing and that with each individual death that world is being diminished and brought closer to an end.

In disciplines like psychoanalysis that engage their practitioners in depth, practice and membership in the community commonly become central to practitioner's identities (Aegele 1961; Erikson 1963, 1968, 1978) and, in conjunction with relationships to mentors, colleagues, and students within the profession, constitute central supports of the self through adulthood (Galatzer-Levy and Cohler 1993). Thus the death of the psychoanalytic community as it resonates with the deaths of its individual members is a source of intense anxiety.

It is this anxiety, I believe, that drives us to primitive defensive operations of denial and projection in dealing with dying colleagues and the people who have been injured by them. As a community, we either turn away from the problem as rapidly as possible or approach either the dying analyst or his analysands with rage. Denial and projection are commonly combined in actions that expel the offending presence from the community, at the same time symbolically destroying them and making them invisible. Insofar as these defenses operate, both mourning and thoughtful efforts at reparation become impossible.

The work of mourning is thus a necessary prerequisite for working with the problem of the dying analyst, and the recognition of what is mourned, which I believe includes the community of analysts, is essential if our reactions are not to be dominated by primitive defensive operations.

NOTES

1. The cases described in this chapter are disguised or are composites of actual cases. As with my earlier publication, I urge readers not to attempt to identify the subjects or to assume that similarities to identifiable subjects provide adequate clues to who they are. I have found that guesses about these matters are almost always wrong.
2. This is not to say that other maladaptive defenses are not at work. Those analysts who maintain their medical identity often continue the common medical defense that death is something that occurs to patients, a group that is quite distinct and different from us. Like other physicians, we feel ashamed and diminished by illness, which moves us from the group of elite, illness-free doctors to the mass of suffering sick humanity.
3. Whether it is actually the case that there are fewer analysands and trainees is unclear. The sense of the decline of psychoanalysis is strongest among the conservative, still medical-dominated institutes and societies associated with the American Psychoanalytic Association. To what extent there is a decline even in psychoanalysis as a treatment is very much contingent on how rigidly one defines psychoanalysis and what sort of training is regarded as essential for psychoanalysts.

REFERENCES

Aegele, K. 1961. "Youth and Society: Some Observations." In Youth: Change and Challenge, ed. E. Erikson, 43–63. New York: Basic Books.
Alston, T. M. 2005. "Pumphead—or Not! Does Avoiding Cardiopulmonary Bypass for Coronary Artery Bypass Surgery Result in Less Brain Damage?" British Journal of Anaesthiology 6: 699–701.
Bonanno, G. 2009. The Other Side of Sadness. New York: Basic Books.
Erikson, E. 1963. Childhood and Society. 2nd ed. New York: Norton.
——. 1968. Identity: Youth and Crisis. New York: Norton.
——. 1978. Adulthood. New York: Norton.
Fajardo, B. 2001. "Life-Threatening Illness in the Analyst." Journal of the American Psychoanalytic Association 49: 569–586.
Freud, S. 1917. "Mourning and Melancholia." In The Standard Edition of the Complete Psychological Works of Sigmund Freud, ed. J. Strachey, 14:237–258. London: Hogarth.
Galatzer-Levy, R. 2004. "The Death of the Analyst: Clinical Experiences with Patients Whose Analysts Died During Their Treatment." Journal of the American Psychoanalytic Association 52: 999–1024.

Galatzer-Levy, R., and B. Cohler. 1993. *The Essential Other: A Developmental Psychology of the Self.* New York: Basic Books.

Lear, J. 2006. *Radical Hope: Ethics in the Face of Cultural Devastation.* Cambridge, Mass.: Harvard University Press.

Myerhoff, B. 1978. *Number Our Days.* New York: Simon & Schuster.

West, C. 2004. *Democracy Matters: Winning the Fight Against Imperialism.* New York: Penguin.

CHAPTER 11

THE ANALYST'S DEATH—
APPREHENSION YET NOT COMPREHENSION

BARBARA STIMMEL

To anyone who has listened to us we were of course prepared to maintain that death was the necessary outcome of life, that everyone owes nature a death and must expect to pay the debt—in short, that death was natural, undeniable and unavoidable. In reality, however, we were accustomed to behave as if it were otherwise. We showed an unmistakable tendency to put death to one side, to eliminate it from life.

—Sigmund Freud (1915)

It might be thought the height of poor taste to ascribe good fortune to a healthy man with a young family struck down at the age of sixty by an incurable degenerative disorder from which he must shortly die. But there is more than one sort of luck. To fall prey to a motor neuron disease is surely to have offended the Gods at some point, and there is nothing more to be said. But if you must suffer thus, better to have a well-stocked head.

—Tony Judt (2010)

FREUD WAS first operated on for jaw cancer in 1923. In 1939, thirty-three operations and sixteen years later, he died. Within the breadth and depth of his powerful theoretical and clinical output during that decade and a half, Freud never makes reference to his illness, his disfigurement, his pain, or his looming death. The political historian Tony Judt transformed some part of his own death into a compelling memoir, one that extols the wonder of looking at the streams of consciousness wandering through his reservoir of memories. Both psychoanalyst and historian kept working while dying. This chapter considers how the analyst, when attempting to integrate the misfortune of dying with the good fortune of engaging in significant work, offers her patients, and herself, the opportunity for growth and heart-lifting farewell.

Taboos disappear as zeitgeists transform. Parsing death was done in private in Freud's time; now, during that of Judt, it is often a public event. And the consulting rooms of therapists who are dying themselves may be seen as public places, even if only two are in attendance. There has been an explosion of intense discussion as to the role of the therapist's "reality" in the life of the patient. Death, the ultimate reality about which the least is known, presents the greatest challenge to the therapist regarding the judicious use of herself in the therapy of another.

Although in the end we all die alone, most have others in their lives as this final separation occurs. The hope is that the dying therapist will meet her patients with a minimum of denial, hypomanic displacement, or embellished clichés. How the patient is helped at this moment of disruption and loss remains the central question in a query that reaches for answers not easily found, at least not specifically. The aim, hopefully, is to enable the patient to move on with an incorporated imago of the helpful, loving therapist as one aspect of her continuing self.

When best applied, psychoanalysis describes rather than prescribes; its explanations, which occur in the form of interpretations, are endlessly unique to each therapeutic dyad. In paying attention to details large and small, the individual couple interprets what is at hand, not what is in the text. This close process, which attempts the understanding of psychic reality, is perhaps most fully comprehended when facing the inexorability of death. This is the template of what follows—description, not prescription; interpretation, not regulation. To try to do more would be to reject the basic tenet of psychoanalytic therapy, which is that each analytic dyad encounters a brave new world, one to be discovered together.

There are several aspects to contemplating the significance of the loss that death brings to a therapeutic relationship. Death may send one into therapy, past deaths resurface regularly and meaningfully throughout treatment, loved ones die and patients may face death themselves while in therapy, and so, of course, may the therapist. As this book demonstrates, therapists grieve just as do their patients, for all the same reasons, and their grief has a profound influence on their work. Therapy, like life, has no guarantees regardless of the arduous efforts of both players to create a stronghold of respect, shared aims, and attachment. And, although it offers one of life's most profound relationships, therapy must end, with death being one way for that to happen. So that even before the inevitable conclusion of the work and the relationship, illness and death may rear their fearsome heads. Of course, the most powerful interaction between patient and therapist occurs when one or the other of them is dying, and dies.

The patient, an analyst himself, was worried. His analyst had missed sessions often and erratically that spring. Then, just as summer arrived, cancellations occurred on a regular, weekly basis without much information to allay expected and predictable fantasies. In the fall, the analyst called to say that he would be away longer than his planned summer break, returning mid-autumn. In October, the call included the information that the analyst had cancer but with an optimistic prognosis by his physicians. Did the patient want a referral so that he could resume therapeutic work without further interruption? "*No*," was the patient's emphatic response, "I'll wait for you." Without dragging the reader through more months of waiting, wondering, hoping, we jump forward to February, when the analyst called once more, for the last time. "I want to say good-bye and to tell you how special it was to know you." And then, three months later, he died.

It must be true that if the analyst chooses the best course of handling his or her life-threatening illness, the analysand may be spared, if only a little, some of the inevitable pain and anguish associated with the loss of such a pivotal figure. But, as in all of life's major moments, there is not one way or, especially, one right way to make these choices. Psychoanalysis is not a monolithic profession with one clinical theory that serves as an adhesive among competing models of the mind. Rather, it stands for a shared commitment to helping others know themselves, amend their characters, enhance their pleasure, and become (more) mature members of their families and communities. Or, as Freud said many years ago, the aim of psychoanalysis is to help with work and love.

At the center of work and love are attachment and loss. Relationships require enough attachment to keep things going and enough love to keep things strong; psychotherapy is no different. The most powerful inhibitor of the deepening of attachment and love between people is the fear of loss. There is no relationship that does not end—the passage of time sees to that.

Whether through geography, development, or death, people separate from one another throughout life. This most painful of experiences hovers such that the essential aim of therapy, the strengthening of our patients' capacity for work and love, is confounded by the state of its essential need, deep attachment, existing under the shadow of impending loss. In other words, a successful therapy endeavor depends upon a relationship determined and destined to end.

It is argued that psychoanalysis has undergone a sea change with regard to the locus of its interest: that a migration has occurred from a one-person psychology, with the patient at the heart of the matter, to that of a two-person psychology, in which patient and therapist share the co-created center. Others rely on the basic tenets of psychoanalytic clinical theory: transference and countertransference, action and reaction, repetition and enactment. In this reading, the therapist, whose inner life exerts a major influence on the therapeutic endeavor, is obviously a key player, but the focus of inquiry remains the inner life of the patient.

One significant difference between these two scantily contrasted clinical perspectives is manifest in the therapist's attitude toward her personal disclosure of facts, states, and emotions. Obviously, where one places herself on the continuum of therapist disclosure in the face of illness and death is most keenly meaningful. What the therapist tells, how she tells, and to whom she tells comprise the hallmarks of the drama in which patients and therapists find themselves when the therapist's death is near.

In the context of therapist disclosure, we find almost all that is written about this uniquely demanding subject is organized around what is revealed to the patient versus what is kept secret from him. The element of secrecy is crucial to thinking through one's attitude toward revealing personal information to the patient. An analyst broke his leg skiing, had surgery, and expected to return to his practice within a day of his hospital discharge. His patients, thoroughly informed of the accident, were given this timetable, and all—analyst and patients—expected soon to return to work. However, to his astonishing dismay, the analyst found that when Monday rolled around, he could not imagine moving from home. His pain and discomfort were too great. He chose to tell his patients that he had erred and that he could not easily move about, leading him to fear that this inability would distract him and interfere with his listening to them; he returned to work the following week.

His patients' reactions varied regarding their ability or willingness to balance their needs against his at this time of the analyst's personal travail.

One patient, though, hit the nail on which hung the analyst's true needs directly on the head. "I know that you stayed home an extra week because you were in pain, so why did you say you were concerned about me; why didn't you tell me the truth?" The analyst was stunned into silence and contrition. In an attempt to preserve some secrecy regarding his personal experience, both for himself and because he assumed it would interfere with his patients' inner lives, the therapist confused at least one patient. He had been open and forthcoming, just not quite enough. This patient spoke up. Others either chose not to or did not have access to what they possibly had discerned. In any case, the therapist had drawn a line: to some, crossing it would have been a boundary mistake; to others, it was an error of deception.

Analyst vulnerability is the fulcrum of this and other more disabling conditions, certainly including impending death. All manner of narcissistic shocks assault the therapist's—and patient's—system. Unsurprisingly, induced passivity, incapacity, diminished control, financial loss, neglect of the care of others, and separation from loved ones and life too often lead to disavowal, denial, and reaction formation, among a myriad of responses. Even though it is obvious that the manner in which the therapist handles his disability will have a significant effect upon the patient's response not only to this drama but also to future therapeutic possibilities, it is almost impossible to prescribe one particular course of action.

Although the admonishment "first, do no harm" goes without saying, how can we be sure which of the therapist's actions aid in carrying out that dictum and which may be determinative of the patient's next steps? Perhaps more significant still, would we all agree on what those next steps should be? And finally, death can occur without warning, without preparation, without the possibility of farewell. The two perspectives brought to bear on the issues of the therapist's death, the therapist's technical choices when aware of what looms ahead and the patient's responses, are those that are the most idiosyncratic and least generalizable beyond the superficial.

Though the complexities of such disruption and loss are universal and therefore "ordinary," each event is "extraordinary" in its form. By this I refer to the particular interaction between the two individuals who comprise the remarkable (in its singular nature) relationship confronting this challenge. Each will have his or her unique intersections between reality and fantasy, past and present, acceptance and denial. Therefore, when speaking of illness and death, we are really talking about these "facts" in the face of the psychic reality, the inner construction each player brings to bear on a shared yet separately experienced set of events. What we do know is how little we can predict or prescribe regarding each therapy couple's encounter with death. We are left with overall generalities, superficial similarities, but that is always the way in analytic discourse about the human condition.

Although late in coming, there is a growing body of literature dealing with the analyst's illness and its effect on both patient and therapist.[1] Illness, an anlage of death in a given instance, also serves as a template of the challenge to the afflicted therapist's existential balance. We need and rely on the reports of colleagues to invite inquiry into a clinical conundrum by stimulating thought and discussion. Impending death noticeably is a very special topic because of its essential confrontation to the therapist's neutrality and judgment. Looming death disarms the therapist in the very moment of threatening the dissolution of his professional identity. In what follows, I will discuss in depth several papers: two serious and thoroughgoing reports of serious illness in the analyst, two papers presenting an overview of the analyst's death, and four compellingly courageous reports by seriously ill analysts.

Abend (1982) and Dewald (1982) opened the discussion of the therapist's illness in provocative and productive ways. Their titles are almost identical—Dewald's "Serious Illness in the Analyst: Transference, Countertransference, and Reality Responses" and Abend's "Serious Illness in the Analyst: Countertransference Considerations"—and they reveal the importance of illness's effect on both members of the couple.

Dewald, and undoubtedly many others, consider that the real assault that illness wreaks upon the analytic pair deserves its own set of considerations. This view holds that there is a general or universal set of variables in confronting illness and death, and these variables require recognition and respect in their own right. In other words, first we ought to acknowledge these challenges and then investigate the particular meaning they hold for the individuals involved. Abend, on the other hand, asks us to consider that reality, no matter how profound (or even insignificant), can never be understood as a thing apart from the inner life of both participants. In this context, nothing, not even death, has its own meaning but always must be understood, at least in the consulting room, as refracted through the personal psychic prism of each partner.

Here, Dewald (1982, 349–350) gives a straightforward depiction of the therapist's dilemma inherent in this clinical conundrum.

One important issue is the question of how much factual information to provide for the patients while the illness is acute. In terms of the future of the therapy, the more extensive the reality information the patient is given, the less free and uncontaminated are the transference distortions likely to be. Detailed reality information may interfere with the subsequent evolution, analysis, and working through of the patient's unconscious fantasies and affect reactions to the illness. On the other hand, to leave the patient without factual information when there are no analytic sessions in which the transference implications can be brought to conscious awareness and ultimately analyzed, may overburden the patient's adaptive capacity. To give extensive factual information may unnecessarily allay anxiety and the occurrence of transference fantasies if the illness turns out to be relatively benign. But to provide detailed factual information may further activate and intensify frightening fantasies if . . . the illness becomes increasingly life-threatening.

Abend (1982, 369), through a slightly different lens, further explicates the conundrum.

The crux of the matter rests in how much factual information should be provided. It is my contention that the chief significance of the powerful countertransference elements mobilized by the analyst's experience of serious illness is their tendency to influence analytic technique. This means, among other things, that the very clinical judgment relied upon to assess the specific needs of patients . . . is exactly what is under pressure from the countertransference; at no other time is the analyst's judgment about this technical problem less likely to be objective and reliable. Countertransference reactions are liable to affect the analyst's perception, understanding, capacity for instinctual control, and judgment in subtle, or sometimes not so subtle ways, and therefore may well color his opinion of his patient's need and capabilities.

The essence of the problem lies in what occurs outside the therapist's conscious awareness. What becomes abundantly clear when considering giving information about her illness is that the therapist can never be sure of why and what to disclose. Since every conscious decision to describe an aspect of her experience is freighted with unconscious aims, she can only hope that all her disclosures (not to mention interpretations, clarifications, questions, and suggestions) are primarily in the best interests of the patient.

Again, since no analyst can do better than that, times of great, even unbearable, stress further jeopardize the likelihood that the patient's needs will be sufficiently safeguarded. How much of what the therapist discloses is to enlist the succor and sympathy of her patient, how much is to repel the patient's needs in favor of her own, how much is to dilute her attunement to the patient in the service of lessening his attachment toward her and, conversely, what she feels toward him? In other words, how much is the analyst protecting herself as she narrows her interventions in the service of warding off the heartrending pain (hers and her patient's) that follow upon separation and loss?

And of course, not all paths traveled at such times by therapist and patient is lovingly paved. We cannot ignore in such a discussion the often less available feelings of envy and rage in the therapist toward the patients who will survive her, toward the therapists to whom her patients may turn in the future. Conversely, what of the sense of good fortune, even superiority, in the patients who know it is not they who are dying but the therapist? Giddy acting out will often accompany this good fortune in the patient, while bizarre options may accentuate the bad fortune of the therapist. Both will be prone to suffer from destructive guilt, which in turn leads to further acting out. And what may occur will do so in the already brewing stew of the transference/countertransference matrix of love, aggression, altruism, and guilt that comprises all analytic relationships.

In writing of self-disclosure in these circumstances, some attempt to categorize and then prioritize such decisions as, for example, inescapable, inadvertent, or deliberate (Aron 1992, Pizer 1997). However, we are forced to acknowledge that attempts at harnessing subjective insights and narcissistic needs in the service of the therapy are imperfect at best and destructively self-serving at worst. Are we then doomed always to mistake our own needs for those of the patient? It seems that the best, and possibly truest, answer is yes and no. To the extent that the therapeutic relationship relies on the personal analysis and education of the therapist being as thorough as possible, there is a chance that most often things will be tilted in the service of the patient's favor, and to the extent that it does not, no set of circumstances will be free of the top-heavy needs of the therapist. We are required to be vigilant regardless of life's dictates and no more especially so than when we are ill or, especially, dying.

These, then, are the primary concerns of the "heroic" analysts, as Galatzer-Levy (2004, 999) aptly describes those who have written movingly and honestly of illness while contending with the possibility of their deaths. These authors moved from the inner safety of their consulting rooms to the larger community in our literature. This chapter focuses on four such papers (Clark 1995, Fajardo 2001, Feinsilver 1998, Morrison 1997), in part because of the searching questions they raise. What each of us stands to gain in reading these reports from the front lines are questions to ask ourselves when, and if, we find ourselves in similar situations some day. They can provide a spur to the unfolding of the intellectual and emotional strategies with which we can, if need be, help ourselves and our patients face the unbearable. And we can hopefully empathize a bit more supply with the dying therapist when we meet their bereft, angry, and mournful patients in our own consulting rooms.

All four therapists shared much data from sessions with patients, including those who knew and those who did not know, presumably, that they were seriously ill. Some patients spoke freely of their fantasies and feelings, while some sailed along as though their therapist's illness was of little or no concern. The therapists' attempts both to generalize and to particularize their own fears and solutions in the face of life-threatening illness are as informative as they are uplifting. These papers are characterized by the humility and uncertainty of their authors, each of whom is aware that what he or she has to impart is useful but limited, universal but specific, professional but personal.

In writing of the Pope's need for a confessor of his own, Clark (1995) wonders what the analyst should do to preserve her stability and therapeutic identity when serious illness strikes. "What happens when the analyst's part of this instrument is out of order, broken, or just not functioning well"? "Do not analysts sometimes need repair work?" (138). "Why do we not do the same [ensure our physical health] for mental well-being for the protection and preservation of our analyzing capacity?" "Is this seen as a further narcissistic blow on top of the physical illness"? And finally, "Who might volunteer for such a difficult duty, and how would it be organized, and what about confidentiality?" (148). Clark's questions refer to therapists living with a potentially fatal disease, who might have a profound need for assistance from perhaps hesitant colleagues, while at the same time clearly conjuring the difficulty for the therapist at such moments.

Fajardo, Feinsilver, and Morrison did not survive their illnesses. It is an extraordinary privilege to observe the determination with which they, our colleagues, contended with the concluding moments of their lives.

Fajardo's (2001) forthright description of her treatment for cancer reflected her thinking and behavior in the consulting room, as she remained actively engaged in treating her patients, during this ordeal. She formulated two essential questions, which helped guide her actions: "Would I survive my illness and be there for him?" (579) and "Whom [do I] tell what?" (582). In confronting head-on these pressing issues of her death and its disclosure, Fajardo convincingly and movingly alerts us to an easily overlooked but central concern: the multilayered nature of the doctor/patient relationship fluctuates wildly when the "doctor" is ill. As the opportunities become rampant for confusion (even fusion) of roles, one finds that caretaking activities are shared while therapist/patient identities merge.

Morrison (1997) modestly described her thinking and her work ethos during the period in which she battled cancer: It "has been to be sensitive to and value my patients' needs with respect to my disclosures. I have not done this perfectly but here have chosen not to overly elaborate my mistakes. I do not set myself forth as a model, nor do I advocate that other therapists follow my example, because I think reactions to such events as life-threatening illness are individual and idiosyncratic" (240). She admits, "It may not be humanly possible to handle a frightening event or illness in a way that is ideal for each of our patients" (239). In the same vein, she asks the important question as to whether it is moral to take on new patients when struggling with serious illness and death. The ramifications of this concern extend beyond its context to include the larger issue of when to stop working altogether.

In his evocatively titled paper, "The Therapist as a Person Facing Death," Feinsilver (1998, 1133) posed several trenchant questions about the therapeutic process as he approached the end of his life.

> Am I witnessing a valid enhancement of therapeutic processes? Are they truly psychoanalytic processes? (2) If valid, why so? What are the primary significant factors responsible? (3) Are there other important factors? (4) Can anything like this powerful mobilization of analytic process occur under ordinary circumstances? Are my observations capable of validation by others?

Although he concludes his paper with an attempt at answering these questions, his answers of course reflect his own particular approach to work and technical choices.

One of the most important lessons to learn from these, and all the papers in this body of literature, is that there are no clinical dicta that could possibly hold true across the board. Thus, while the "answers" in these papers are limited to these particular authors' experience, there is much to ponder in the questions asked by our colleagues in the middle of the maelstrom. The imperative to the rest of us is to reflect upon the inescapable effect upon the patient of the therapist's life, and no time more so than when it is threatened.

Two important papers (Lord, Ritvo, and Solnit 1978; Galatzer-Levy 2004) are compendia of reports about sick and dying analysts and the patients they left behind. They present helpful clinical data sets with which to consider the range of reactions analysts bring to the confrontation with their own deaths and those of their patients in the wake of such significant loss.

Lord, Ritvo, and Solnit (1978) studied a group of twenty-seven patients whose analysts died during the course of their analyses. Some of the information was gained directly from the patients, some from their subsequent therapists. Not much is known about the analysts' behavior during the period leading to their deaths, although most patients chose to wait for and with their therapists during the course of their illnesses. The reactions to the deaths of their analysts by the twenty-seven patients studied varied widely depending on history, age, marital status, length of treatment, level of psychological health, and so on. The intensity of the patients' mourning reactions, veering from none at all to years of deep anguish, were diverse in their content and disparate in their effect on functioning. Nonetheless, all but one of those studied sought further treatment; that stands for something.

Twenty-six years later and in the wake of much analytic debate about the peeling away of the analysts' anonymity, Galatzer-Levy (2004) described his contact with patients whose former analysts had died. He attempts to offer a systematic glance into the actions of these analysts and the effect they had on their patients. Since this study occurred in the context of the patients' reports, here too it is impossible to know the state of mind of the analysts, beyond inference and assumption. Additionally, Galatzer-Levy makes the speculative point that his data are skewed in that they were gathered from those who "had problems serious enough to merit further analysis" (1007). Should we not assume that some patients who had undergone such trauma might decide to find help elsewhere, independent of diagnostic labeling?

Also in this construct, Galatzer-Levy goes on to diagnose the difference between those who can and those who cannot develop new therapeutic relationships as reflective of the intensity of their selfobject transferences.

Regardless of whether one would agree to the use of this schema to characterize the ease with which patients could continue in new therapeutic relationships, one should be wary of collapsing the limitless array of patient choices regarding follow-up treatment. Whether their problems are "serious enough," their reality testing clear enough, their egos strong enough, or their treatments complete enough can only be answered on a case-by-case basis.

Given the possibly limitless range of degrees of incapacity and resolution that patients evince in the face of the death of their therapists, of course it is impossible to predict or prescribe the patient's next therapeutic choices, if any. Galatzer-Levy addresses this in a footnote when pointing out simply that "[other] patients dropped out of treatment when their analyst died" (1007). While we have no way of knowing what happened next for these particular patients, I would suggest that this is not the most interesting point of inquiry. What matters more is that the patient and analyst have the best chance possible to look reality square in the face together as they attempt to cope with the overwhelming loss facing them. Beyond that, as with any other death, life offers many ensuing possibilities. There really is no equation as to which behaviors of the analyst are more likely to ensure ongoing analysis with a different analyst and if that is indeed the best course anyway.

But what does emerge unfailingly in the Galatzer-Levy data, some of the Lord et al. cases, and the myriad tales we, therapists and patients alike, have been told is a disturbing picture of analysts frequently acting poorly, angrily, and in denial. The papers describe therapists who repeatedly break the therapeutic trust, leaving little room for working through, even preliminarily, of the transference configurations of their patients as they live through their therapists' deaths. Dying therapists commit boundary violations of all sorts and magnitudes: they see patients in their homes, give them unwanted and overloaded autobiographical data, speak out of turn about other patients, and, sadly and unsurprisingly, often enter into sexual encounters with their patients. Also described are the strange and disturbing behaviors of the analysts' families and their colleagues: gossip, broken confidentiality, material transactions, unseemly familiarity, and inappropriate referrals, all amid other bizarre doings that characterize many experiences to which the patients were exposed. All in all, the reports present a portrait of chaotic acting out among all levels of participants, with the centrally disheartening image of analysts and patients colluding in myriad ways to ward off the doom hanging overhead.

Here, then, is the overarching problem. The ability to make deep, rather than simply broad, statements about the interrelationship between the analysts' technical choices and the patients' responses is limited by the report, the reporter, the observer, and even the reader. If we cull from papers that purport to reflect generalized behaviors and those that relate individual accounts of patients' managing, working, and reflecting, we still find ourselves without anything more than guidelines. And is this different than when observing, writing, and reading about any aspect of the therapeutic endeavor?

It is clear that those who have written of their own challenging encounters with illness and death have a special body of knowledge to impart. We must not assume, though, that these authors have perhaps worked things through with more surety than their counterparts from whom we have not heard. For we also know that there are a vast number of therapists who become sick acutely, have chronic illnesses, are aging, and perhaps dying but who are hanging on, against overwhelming odds, to their professional identities, with their challenges and gratifications intact. The number of those who do not share publicly these experiences is greater than those who do.

The gripping point is that, while under the relentless stress of illness and death, our unsung fellow professionals grindingly, haltingly, sometimes soaringly, work away at integrating the needs of their patients with their own. They fail or succeed to the extent that they are able to maintain a careful process of close listening, free association, dream analysis, and reconstruction. These tried, true, and reliable mechanisms are the surest tools we have through which to monitor and work through impending loss and all its attendant affect. The nuanced use of these tools, colored by self-disclosure, gives patients the best chance of finding their footing in the face of such powerful loss.

The rules we seek, the answers for which we strive, the authority in the written word all reduce to two observations that capture the entire therapeutic dilemma at such a dire and dramatic point in the treatment relationship. The first is that the death of the analyst stimulates in the patient the expected and unavoidable responses of astonishment, anger, ambivalence, faith, guilt, hatred, humiliation, heartbreak, longing, and love. Wait, there are still other reactions, you say. And so there are, and if one can think them, then they are inescapably part of the human condition. The profound yet perilously ignored fact is that the analyst is susceptible to the exact same responses—those named and those still to be identified.

This conjures up the second observation, which is that two people are caught in the same moment of a story, one over which they have no control.

In other words, they are in life together when death comes calling. In the face of that, which is unlike anything else they will have to fear, fight, or forgive, they have only, but powerfully, their resolve to keep searching within to find parts of their pasts, their personal myths, and their plans for perseverance. The hope is that each of the two can play his or her part, helping the other with dignity, respect, and intelligence, until the time to stop is clear. And then mourning can fully begin.

Our task as therapists is to tolerate life's storms when they appear. We try our hardest to stay steady for our patients, whether we are the ones sick and dying or the ones who continue the work with patients caught in such a tempest with their former therapists. Paradoxically, in this way the greatest test is also the most ordinary. And that fact lends strength to the determination to stay with the work, actually to choose life in the face of death. The analyst's perseverance in work in the face of life's storms is captured dramatically by Melville's (1851) description of the fight against that which looms large:

> "Hear him, hear him now," cried Peleg, marching across the cabin, and thrusting his hands far down into his pockets, ". . . hear him, all of ye. Think of that! When every moment we thought the ship would sink! Death and the Judgment then? What? With all three masts making such an everlasting thundering against the side; and every sea breaking over us, fore and aft. Think of Death and the Judgment then? No! No time to think about death then. Life was what Captain Ahab and I was thinking of; and how to save all hands—how to rig jury-masts—how to get into the nearest port; that was what I was thinking of."

The analyst I described earlier who died in May after that long summer and fall when his faithful patient/analyst awaited his return was a wonderful man and a gifted therapist. But he made some "mistakes." First of all, might he have brought on his own death through his possibly unanalyzed habit of smoking? Then, he succumbed to the waves of denial that kept his own and his patient's hopes afloat. Then, he promised to return. Then, he said goodbye in an altered state of consciousness. And finally, he abandoned his patient without a last chance for the patient to look upon him, his office, or his smile again. The patient did not go to the funeral or the memorial service and did not speak of his analyst or his loss for many years. As a matter of fact, in spite of feeling helped by his analysis, the patient assumed he knew what he felt, what he needed, and what had been accomplished. The patient's ego strength, his own gift for the work he did in his office, and his full and rich life had allowed him, temporarily, to fill the hole in his heart.

Then, some years later, the ground started to shift, and his steady gait became wobbly. Something was amiss, and he realized that there was un-finished work to be done about his loss and all else that it had stirred up. Throughout his ensuing therapy, both his choice of a new therapist and his continuing reasons for attendance remained an enigma to the patient. All the while, though, he made headway in several directions, worked through with more conviction some unresolved issues from childhood, reorganized key relationships, uncovered recalcitrant memories, and even found new successes at his advanced age. It was not until his mother died and his wife became ill that he finally came to understand the role of his "new" thera-pist, the man whose meaningfulness and helpfulness he continued to doubt. And, as is often the case, this discovery came to him in his own office, with a patient of his own.

She, also a therapist, had been in therapy some years before when her therapist retired, delivering a deathblow to the treatment. After a year and a half in her new and stormy treatment, she began dreaming about her former therapist. Dredging up feelings of anger and guilt, her associations unleashed a train of images that brought the therapist to an interpretative brink. He said to her, "We have understood that you could not bring yourself easily to replace Dr. J with me because of the guilt you felt at betraying her. But also, now we can see that if you allow me to become important, perhaps more important than Dr. J, the guilt you will be colliding with has another level of meaning. As you become attached to me, you find yourself that much closer to the rage and sadness you harbor toward Dr. J for having abandoned and rejected you. The oppressive guilt you are desperately trying to avoid is re-taliation for your frightening, aggressive fantasies, all of which helps account for the six years you waited before entering therapy again. This was your penance as well as the cauldron within which your fury at Dr. J could brew."

The patient's tearful response paved the way for her to add several hours to her therapy schedule, allowing her to come in every day. Thus she found herself more committed to one treatment as she enlarged the potential for working through the loss of another. Her melancholia would give way to mourning and the liberation it brings in its wake.

And our therapist realized in a flash that this interpretation was aimed also at himself, another therapist/patient. In his own session of the day before, his therapist had pointed out to him that he had not used the word "love" when speaking of his wife, but only "attachment." Something was unleashed, and in the recursive state of treating–being-treated–treating, he found an important link between his understanding of his patient's warded-off anger and mourning and his own. This work was no different, really, than that of the work he might have done with Dr. S in the first place, had they but room enough and time. They would have found their way through the anger and the rejection, the loss and the heartbreak they were each experiencing in their own way and for his own historical and psychological reasons. In other words, another day(s) in the office. Just one with greater finality.

NOTES

The title of this chapter follows Kant's definition of that which is sublime in *Critique of Judgment*.

1. This chapter focuses on several papers in this expanding bibliography. Other key papers include those of Craige (2002), Dattner (1989), Gervais (1994), Hoffman (2001), Morrison (1990), Schwaber (1998), Schwartz (1987), and Van Dam (1987), as well as an important compendium by Schwartz and Silver (1990).

REFERENCES

Abend, S. M. 1982. "Serious Illness in the Analyst: Countertransference Considerations." *Journal of the American Psychoanalytic Association* 30: 365–379.

Aron, L. 1992. "Interpretation as Expression of the Analyst's Subjectivity." *Psychoanalytic Dialogues* 2:475–507.

Burton, A. 1962. "Death as a Countertransference." *Psychoanalytic Review* 49: 3–20.

Clark, R. 1995. "The Pope's Confessor: A Metaphor Relating to Illness in the Analyst." *Journal of the American Psychoanalytic Association* 43: 137–149.

Craige, H. 2002. "Mourning Analysis: The Post-Termination Phase." *Journal of the American Psychoanalytic Association* 50: 507–550.

Dattner, R. 1989. "On the Death of the Analyst: A Review." *Contemporary Psychoanalysis* 25: 419–426.

Dewald, P. A. 1982. "Serious Illness in the Analyst: Transference, Countertransference, and Reality Responses." *Journal of the American Psychoanalytic Association* 30: 347–363.

Fajardo, B. 2001. "Life-Threatening Illness in the Analyst." *Journal of the American Psychoanalytic Association* 49: 569–586.

Feinsilver, D. 1998. "The Therapist as a Person Facing Death: The Hardest of External Realities and Therapeutic Action." *International Journal of Psychoanalysis* 79: 1131–1150.

Freud, S. 1915. "Thoughts for the Times on War and Death." In *The Standard Edition of the Complete Psychological Works of Sigmund Freud*, ed. J. Strachey, 14:275–300. London: Hogarth.

Galatzer-Levy, R. 2004. "The Death of the Analyst." *Journal of the American Psychoanalytic Association* 52: 999–1024.

Gervais, L. 1994. "Serious Illness in the Analyst." *Canadian Journal of Psychoanalysis* 2: 191–202.

Halpert, E. 1982. "When the Analyst Is Chronically Ill or Dying." *Psychoanalytic Quarterly* 51: 372–389.

Judt, T. 2010. *The Memory Chalet*. New York: Penguin.

Lord, R., S. Ritvo, and A. Solnit. 1978. "Patients' Reactions to the Death of the Psychoanalyst." *International Journal of Psychoanalysis* 59: 189–197.

Melville, H. 1851. *Moby-Dick; or, The Whale*. London: Penguin, 2010.

Morrison, A. 1997. "Ten Years of Doing Psychotherapy While Living with a Life-Threatening Illness: Self-Disclosure and Other Ramifications." *Psychoanalytic Dialogues* 7: 225–241.

Pizer, B. 1997. "When the Analyst Is Ill: A Dimension of Self-Disclosure." *Psychoanalytic Quarterly* 66: 450–469.

Schwaber, E. A. 1998. "Traveling Affectively Alone: A Personal Derailment in Analytic Listening." *Journal of the American Psychoanalytic Association* 46: 1004–1065.

Schwartz, H. J. 1987. "Illness in the Analyst: Implications for the Psychoanalytic Process." *Journal of the American Psychoanalytic Association* 35: 657–692.

Schwartz, H. J., and A. L. Silver, eds. 1990. *Illness in the Analyst: Implications for the Treatment Relationship*. Madison, Conn.: International Universities Press.

Van Dam, H. 1987. "Countertransference During an Analyst's Brief Illness." *Journal of the American Psychoanalytic Association* 35: 647–656.

PART IV

WHEN DISASTER STRIKES A COMMUNITY

It may happen on a day
Of ordinary weather—
The usual assembled flowers, or fallen leaves
Disheveling the grass.
You may be feeding the dog,
Or sipping a cup of tea

—Linda Pastan, in *Traveling Light*

THE FIRST three authors in this section bring us into their experience of working in the midst of tragic events. They each describe their efforts to maintain a therapeutic framework in the face of a global devastation that affects clinician and patient alike. Such large-scale catastrophes underscore the reality that we are limited in our ability truly to provide the protection and stability that we strive for in our ordinary clinical practice. No one is immune to unexpected tragedy—neither patient nor therapist.

In her chapter on the effects of Hurricane Katrina, Sylvia Schneller invites the reader into the post-Katrina world of New Orleans, challenging us to imagine the experience of being completely cut off from one's home, family, and community. She relates her personal journey through the destruction and gradual rebuilding of her home and her clinical practice. With aching clarity, she describes losing contact with each and every one of her patients. While some patients eventually return, the fate of many others remains unknown.

Schneller examines the spectrum of depression and anxiety one experiences in the face of a catastrophe. In its direct aftermath, it is impossible to distinguish between an expectable and universal response to trauma on the one hand, and on the other, the response of an individual suffering from post-traumatic-stress disorder. In the end it is clear that everyone, in one form or another, suffers the effects of overwhelming trauma. Schneller's reflections reveal that, even as the process of rebuilding unfurls, the fragments of ruin remain.

Billie Pivnick relates her experiences as a therapist in New York City on 9/11 and her subsequent involvement in the development of the memorial at the site of the Twin Towers. She describes her disorientation and dislocation on that day and her efforts to be present for her patients while simultaneously being bombarded by her own fears. Pivnick tells us about her work with a mother and her child who saw the planes hit the towers and witnessed their collapse. She contrasts this treatment with that of an American man of Muslim faith who had lived and married in an Arab country. Following 9/11, he returned to the United States, fearing for his life had he remained in the Arab village where he was living. He sought treatment around his conflicts as a Muslim American. Pivnick demonstrates how the events of 9/11 and her work with these patients reawakened traumatic childhood memories of her own.

Pivnick brings the reader in as a witness to these moments, pointing out that bearing witness to traumatic events is an essential part of the process of mourning and recovery. Traumatized mourners often experience guilty self-recrimination, which gives rise to a tension in their inner world between a never-ending search for answers and a nonverbal, largely somatic experience of intolerable pain and grief. She views the therapeutic relationship as a means of opening up what she refers to as "memorial space," creating a "metaphoric container—a safe space in which faint and dissociated memory traces can be etched more deeply; connected to other memories, feelings, and sensations; and then linked to symbolic meanings in imagistic or narrative form." This idea of a memorial space parallels what we have called the middle-distance, a space that allows for integration and narrativization.

Russell Carr relates his experience as a military psychiatrist during the wars in Iraq and Afghanistan. He writes about feeling isolated and set apart from his civilian counterparts. He experiences the war through the eyes of his wounded patients, feeling a complex blend of emotions, including rage and shame. As a result, he finds himself reluctant to connect with old friends, neither trusting that they would understand what he had been through nor be able to bear the recounting of his wartime experiences.

Carr poignantly remembers the pain of seeing young men with limbs torn off, traumatic brain injuries, and PTSD. In the face of such horrors, he is acutely aware of his own helplessness and vulnerability. He points out the necessity of finding what he calls a "relational home," where traumatic experiences can be processed and borne. Carr writes, "I mourn the loss of a fully integrated sense of time, where part of me is not trapped with a traumatic past." In this way he captures how trauma ruptures the continuity of time—what came before and what comes after the trauma is permanently altered by events that shatter one's sense of self in time and in space.

In this section's final chapter, Robert Winer brings us full circle to the essence of our psychoanalytic work—that is, mourning what was and coming to terms with what will be. Whether patient or therapist, we are all caught in the inexorable progression of time and our growing recognition of its finite nature. In fact, all of life is organized around our struggle to reconcile ourselves with this awareness. Without such an awareness, we are unable to mourn, and our grief may become depression, rooted in a denial of loss that keeps us paralyzed.

Psychoanalysis, for Winer, is about mourning and the recognition that our time is limited. Within this frame, he suggests that we try to do the best we can—to take hold of every moment and experience life to its fullest. He writes, "Analysis manifests itself as the cure for great expectations. . . . Some things happen for no good reason, and others for deep and complicated reasons, and getting our minds around that isn't exactly pleasant or satisfying, but becoming reconciled to the truth, as best we can understand it, is what's possible."

As analysts, it is incumbent upon us to enter into the world of our patients, to bear witness to their trauma and loss, and to help them make the world whole again. Yet, as we have seen in these chapters, there are times when we too have been swept up by the same disastrous forces as our patients. Then we must attend to our own grief while simultaneously providing a space to connect with our patients—one where they can begin to heal their wounds. It is in the context of this unfolding connection with another who listens and tries to understand that transformation can begin.

CHAPTER 12

BROKEN PROMISES, SHATTERED DREAMS, WORDLESS ENDINGS

SYLVIA J. SCHNELLER

THERAPISTS INVOLVED in a long-term dynamic treatment process commit to their patients, either verbally or nonverbally, that the work will continue until completion of the therapy. When something unexpected occurs, such as illness or trauma in either the therapist or the patient's life, the disruption of that process is frequently experienced as a broken promise. Often, dreams of a fantasized good outcome are shattered. This chapter deals with one such life situation: Hurricane Katrina and the levee rupture that inundated the city of New Orleans in late August 2005. All members of the community, patient and therapist alike, experienced a shared trauma, a trauma some researchers describe as apocalyptic.

THE SITUATION

On August 29, 2005, Hurricane Katrina and the subsequent levee failures interrupted my thirty-five-year analytic practice. All the citizens of New Orleans, my patients and myself included, lived through the sudden and complete disruption of citywide and governmental services, those considered usual and essential to the conduct of daily life. We either experienced at first hand or through television and media coverage the same chaos as did the rest of the country. However, the immediacy of the despair, lawlessness, and anarchy happening to our homes, to our city, and to our neighbors left us marked in a profound way.

In some form or another, my patients and I shared the trauma of massively flooded neighborhoods and homes. In one instant, we lost our city, our sense of home, and that feeling of rootedness so essential to the conduct of a successful treatment process. More importantly, we lost the illusion that life was somehow within our control. Although this belief is naught but a fantasy, the maintenance of the illusion of control over our environment is necessary to feel internally safe. Without it, my patients and I experienced a sense of chronic and unremitting vulnerability, which laid the groundwork for subsequent feelings of hopelessness and despair—what we clinicians call post-traumatic-stress disorder.

I invite you to share with me the few weeks following Hurricane Katrina.

Imagine the abrupt rupture of all means of communication: telephone lines down, cell phone towers underwater, families separated, neighborhood alliances split, and the town under martial law.

Imagine water covering most of the homes in your city, up to the second story or even the roof.

Imagine that water staying in place for two to three weeks while experts devise methods to repair the two-block-long levee breach and then pump a lake's worth of water back over that levee.

Imagine sitting, sleeping, and eating in a relative's home or disaster shelter, desperately watching television, searching websites for satellite images of your neighborhood. Are the news helicopters flying over your street in their endless search for tragedy? Is that your home, safe at the edge of the blackened pool of water, or is it that one, devastated in the midst of the flood?

Three weeks after the storm, when the National Guard opens the unflooded portion of the city to business owners, realize that you have left your medical license identification card in your other purse the morning you evacuated. Wonder if you will be able to convince the police officer guarding entry into your city that you are a physician wanting to retrieve your patients' records.

Imagine spending part of that morning getting those records but also sneaking around police roadblocks to reach your neighborhood, which had flooded and was recently drained, because for three weeks you have lived in fear that your house was indeed under water.

Imagine you cannot reach your house because your street is impassable, crowded with a tangle of fallen trees. Search for another route. Find your house standing intact at the edge of the floodwaters, one blessed foot above the flood zone.

Imagine driving back to your son's home in Houston, patient records sitting untouched in the backseat. Find those records still there the next morning on your way back from a Houston Starbucks. Gratefully recall how the baristas there kindly comped your coffee and muffin every morning of your six-week-long evacuation.

Imagine reaching for those patients' records, wondering again what happened to them when your relationship was unexpectedly ruptured. Look through the charts, trying to match addresses with your knowledge of the extent of the waters.

Imagine knowing the futility of calling landline numbers, because you continually call your own home number praying for the restoration of electricity and phone service. But you call a few anyway. Feel the frustration when your response is an incessant bleep or that robotic voice spouting, "This number is no longer in service."

Realize you are using a cell phone to call them and that, like you, perhaps one of them is fortunate enough to have a workable cell phone number. Search their files to see if any of them has left a cell as well as a home phone number.

Realize your old charting system does not have a space for patients to leave both their cell phone and their landline numbers, so you have very few cell phone numbers. Think of how many times you saw a patient turn off their cell phone before or during a session. Wish you had asked more often for that number.

Feel that sense of loss when you recognize you have no realistic or simple way to contact most of your patients. Search your memory for the personal details of their lives and imagine where those patients might be.

⸭ ⸭ ⸭ ⸭ ⸭

I did find some of my patients. One I reached after several days of fruitless calls that occurred while the cell phone towers were still underwater. This patient had evacuated to Maine. Though still there, she planned to return in another two or three weeks. We spoke as if we were long-lost relatives. I shared my evacuation situation with her, and she shared hers with me. There was no room for treatment-room formality. We decided to meet when I reopened my office, likely in another month or so. Four weeks after the hurricane, I still did not know when I would be able to return home.

I also reached another patient, a medical student, via cell phone. Tulane Medical School, the school she attended, was flooded and not expected to reopen until the following September. All their students transferred to the Baylor School of Medicine in Houston for the remainder of the school year. My patient was involved in moving her world and her senior-year education to a new city and hospital. We spoke twice on the phone, but I was in such a state of flux, I did not have anything stable to offer her other than phone sessions.

My neighborhood, within a mile of the largest levee break, had flooded even though my home did not. The city was uncertain when electrical service would return to that area, as the entire electrical grid supplying that portion of the city had been underwater for three weeks. I was still living in Houston, so I offered to arrange to see her at least as long as I was there. However, since I planned to return home as soon as Entergy repaired the major electrical grid (estimated to take from one to four months), I could not guarantee anything, even the length of time I would be in Houston. We decided to suspend treatment. What a strange and abrupt way to say goodbye to someone I had known intimately in analysis for three years.

I discovered another patient, a lady whom I had treated and worried about for years, at her married daughter's home in Destin, Florida. She was a very dependent individual who, throughout treatment, took few independent steps without first consulting me. She often visited her daughter, and I was certain that she would have evacuated to there. Needless to say, I did not have her cell phone number, she did not have mine, and I did not have her daughter's number. From time to time during the sessions, she had used her daughter's last name, but I could not recall it. For several days, I tried desperately to remember. Finally, I suspended attention, thinking that if I did not try so hard, the name would come to me. Indeed it did. I searched the Destin phone book, obtained her daughter's number, and called. Recognizing that the boundary issues with this patient were different from the ones with the earlier patient, I was careful to share only basic information about my safety with her. I listened, helped her contain her anxiety, and validated her experience, particularly her fears that she had lost me. I told her I expected to resume practice on November 1, two months after the storm, and we arranged for periodic telephone sessions until then.

One long-term analytic patient elected not to return. She wrote a short note telling me she had lost her house but was safe. She left the letter in my waiting room a few weeks after I resumed practice. As she and I had worked together for a number of years, the brevity of her note and the fact she did not come in to see me was surprising. I knew the flood was massively traumatic for her. Part of the work of analysis was to help her disengage from a dysfunctional family situation in which she was belittled and verbally abused. In addition, her elderly parents controlled her separateness by threatening to disinherit her from their significant fortune if she did not do what they demanded. Buying her own home, renovating it, and decorating it with her own earned income were significant to the development of her independent self. This home, in the flooded area, was submerged under eight feet of water for three weeks. To add to her trauma, the family's business ventures were in the most severely flooded area of New Orleans and would require significant time to repair. Four years later, I accidentally met this patient at the symphony. We spotted each other at the same time. We shared the usual "haven't-seen-you-in-a-long-time" greetings, and she spontaneously volunteered that she did not return to treatment because she did not "want to bother me." Startled, I accepted that reason without comment and went on to talk about the music we had just heard. It was a comfortable conversation. She ended the encounter telling me, with an embarrassed look, that some months after the flood, she sought help from one of New Orleans's better-known psychopharmacologists and was doing well on antidepressant medication alone. Indeed, she looked quite well and was spontaneous and cheerful.

Remembering her treatment, I recalled that she knew I lived in the same area of town as did she, and she probably assumed my home was also flooded. With the hostile dependency and separation issues she and I worked on throughout her analysis, I postulated she had overidentified with the possibility that she and I were in the same boat (so to speak). Made anxious by that idea, she rationalized it by not wanting to "bother me." However, more importantly, a few months earlier she had tentatively brought up the possibility of terminating the analysis, and we had agreed to think further about that. The ruptured levees provided her an opportunity to do what she had never been able to do with her parents: extricate herself from a dependent relationship. Indeed, she did it on her own, without my permission. For her, this was an important step. In not following accepted "psychoanalytic rules," she found a way to separate from me on her own terms.

When mail service resumed, I received a letter from the parents of a mid-adolescent girl I had treated analytically for three years. In order to remove her from the trauma of living in New Orleans, they decided to send her to boarding school on the East Coast to complete her education. I never saw or heard from her again—a wordless ending beyond both of our control.

Several other patients whom I could not contact by phone disappeared into the morass of evacuation and lost homes. As landline phone service was not to be restored to the flooded areas of the city for three to six months, I resorted to rather primitive, old-fashioned means of communication. Six weeks after the levee failures, I left a note on the door of my office informing patients I would resume practice on November 1 and would see them at their regular appointment time. As the AT&T cell phone towers still did not function, I obtained a Houston-exchange cell phone number and left that on my note. A few patients called to confirm their appointment; others simply showed up. Almost half my practice disappeared.

THE TRAUMA

Many New Orleanians, myself included, still experience the flood's consequences on a daily basis. We overreact to large, as well as small, situations. When the BP oil spill occurred, we dreaded and fantasized the worst. Prominent in our thinking was a total lack of trust in the possibility of an effective government response. For many, the spill recalled post-Katrina events. The same feeling permeated the area on the fifth anniversary of the levee ruptures, when every newspaper and every television anchorperson descended on our city to report on our recovery. The tone of coverage was positive and focused on our resiliency. Yet people I knew and spoke with wanted to hear and see none of it. We turned off the news programs and stopped reading the newspaper. I heard many say, "I hate all this coverage. I don't want to be reminded of what happened."

It is difficult for me to describe my mental state during this five-year period. A recent experience at a concert captures the essence of my sometimes fragile emotional state. During a symphony performance of Shostakovich's First Symphony and Tchaikovsky's First Piano Concerto, I overreacted to an incidence during the performance when my pleasure in the music was shattered. It was like the moment when the storm and the flood splintered my world.

As I sat in an acoustically sound theater for the performing arts, eighth row, left of center, I became riveted by the right hand of the pianist, Yefin

Bronfman. His five fingers seemed aglow in the spotlight. Struck, paralyzed, I stared. The five fingers dangling from that hand awaited the moment when they could fall unimpeded onto the keyboard and release a cascade of sound.

How can I depict this moment? At first, the fingers resembled a white daisy, heavy with droplets from a stormy rainfall, the petals bent forward and downward. Then, abruptly, the image shifted to one of a floating jelly-fish, a man-of-war, whose tentacles dangle limply in a blue-green sea. These creatures seem harmless, even poetic, as they glow, glide, and drift unfettered in the ocean waters. However, entangle them around an unsuspecting, vulnerable man, and their poison leaves welts in the aged and tears and fear in the young.

I was momentarily aghast. How did Bronfman's poised, creative fingers lead to this seemingly unrelated image of a poisonous, white, gelatinous, umbrella-like sea creature? Drooping flower petals are innocuous, but stinging tentacles not so. My still overwhelmed mind could not protect itself from the intrusion of frightening or dangerous images.

I sat in that theater, expectant, waiting. This evening, I was confident that the artist's hands floating above the keyboard would strike a resonant chord. After all, Bronfman is a much-acclaimed pianist. I expected and hoped the music would sweep me away.

I glanced at the couple in front of me. I had already been distracted by the woman's restlessness. She chatted with her spouse, she thumbed through the pages of the program, she shifted about in her chair rearranging her dress, and she fluffed her hair. She seemed to have little interest in the music. Earlier I had politely asked her to be quiet, and her response had reassured me.

Now, caught up in my reverie I watched Bronfman's fingers. The opening strains of the music swelled from keyboard to audience. For the first time that evening, the woman in front of me seemed to have recognized a piece of symphonic music. She jumped halfway up from her chair, waved her arms wildly, and embraced her husband. Shattered, my moment was lost.

I became angry, murderously so. In that moment, I discovered a metaphor for my post-levee-rupture life. I never knew when feelings and images of disaster would swamp me, forcing me again to claw my way to the surface.

I describe this to demonstrate how the hurricane and flood affected and continue to affect even the most simple and pleasant of life experiences. Shattered moments, shattered lives and murderous rage were displaced from the government, the Army Corps of Engineers, FEMA, and God onto this woman sitting in front of me at the symphony. I had to swallow the urge to strike her head, pull her hair, and scream obscenities at her. For what? She only expressed in her own way the same enjoyment I hoped to experience. She had no inkling of the effect she had on me—how could she have? Indeed, this event was not related in any way to the levee failures. How then can I compare it to such?

It makes no sense in the normal everyday world, where what you see is what you get. It makes no sense in a world where the government functions, where lights come on when you flick a switch, where dialing a telephone results in a voice on the other end, where mail appears at approximately the same time every day, where the grass on the median is cut, where broken and downed trees are removed. However, in a world where refrigerators filled with rotting food line the sidewalks, where sheetrock and carpet are piled high along the curbside, where children's soggy dolls, broken tricycles, waterlogged games fill your view as you drive daily to work, perhaps it is conceivable. This symphony patron for a moment stood in for all those elements of nature and man who at an earlier time had torn my pleasant life out from under me.

Interested in other therapists' response to the trauma, I recently attended a conference sponsored by the FAR Fund Foundation and the New Orleans/Birmingham Center for Psychoanalysis entitled Stretched Thin. It explored the therapeutic consequences of shared trauma following the levee ruptures. Ghislaine Boulanger, author of *Wounded by Reality: Understanding and Treating Adult Onset Trauma*, was the main speaker. The panel included four therapists from New Orleans. The conference addressed the ongoing process of healing and presented the results of a three-year study grant based on interviews with treating therapists. The study focused on the way Hurricane Katrina and the failed levee system affected the treatment of patients with whom the therapists had shared trauma. The fact that all the patients and all the therapists had similar stories to tell is the remarkable part of the study. Some therapists reported anger and jealousy that their patients had fared better than they did. Some wanted to say, "You think that's bad. Listen to what happened to me." Others envied their patients' ability to get a better response from their insurance agent or FEMA and wanted to ask, "How did you manage that?" All suspended the usual boundaries of the treatment situation (some with more guilt over relaxing the rules than others) and shared their own experience of the storm. Apparently, experienced therapists felt more comfortable with this kind of shared response and often saw it as enhancing the therapeutic alliance.

As I listened to one of the panelists at the FAR Fund Conference describe the post-Katrina treatment of one of her patients, I recognized myself in the data. This patient, after several phone sessions, finally shared her
evacuation experience. Hers was not unusual: worse than some, better than
others, but uniquely tragic for her. When she waded out of her home, her
beloved dog held securely in her arms, she saw a couple of her neighbor's
dogs tied to long tethers. They were floating dead in the water. Should we
blame the owners for cruelty, or should we recognize they chose the better
of two equally bad alternatives? Either they could take their pets with them
into a two-state long traffic jam to search for a motel that allowed animals,
or they could leave them in the yard with enough food for a few days. After
all, according to the Army Corps of Engineers, the levees were safe, and no
one expected them to fail. The owners probably planned to return the next
day after the hurricane blew itself out to untie and feed their pets and clean
fallen debris from the yard. We who live in hurricane-prone areas expect to
do the same.

Certainly, everyone can identify with this patient's pain as she swam to
safety with her pet. As she clutched her dog, she wondered if they would
both drown. The image of the dead dogs was seared in her mind and underscored her helplessness, wounding her to the core. When the patient
finished telling her story, she wailed, a loud piercing scream her therapist
thought would never end. As the therapist recounted, it was the most horrific sound she had ever heard. Finally, the patient stopped screaming and
said, "That was how it was."

As I listened to the speakers, two salient features became apparent. First,
shortly after the hurricane, each of the panel members found a support system that provided him or her with a sense of belonging to a larger group.
The psychoanalyst on the panel began to work more closely with her office
staff and the New Orleans Center for Psychoanalysis. The school counselor
found support from the teachers and other counseling staff at her school.
Even though students did not return until January 2006, the school personnel involved themselves in plans to reopen the school. Another psychologist on the panel maintained stability by contacting and reinstituting her
five-year-old study group and meeting weekly with them. The fourth panel
member sought out, applied for, and organized the FAR Fund Grant project
between the New York grantors and the Psychoanalytic Center.

The other important point, summarized by Boulanger, was that all the
therapists were aware that they were emotionally fragile. They reported that

listening to their patients tell stories so similar to their own experiences threatened to overwhelm them. Boulanger noted the high number of psychiatrists, psychologists, social workers, and mental health professionals that either retired or permanently left New Orleans. She remarked on the courage of those who stayed to deal with the illness created by what she termed an "apocalyptic trauma."

I can identify feelings in myself much like the ones noted in the conference. Some two to three months after the levee failures, the executive director of the Jefferson Parish Medical Society invited me to speak to the Ladies Auxiliary about how to cope with the stress following the break. As a psychiatrist and past president of the society, I was a logical choice. The director had noted how many of the physicians and their families were affected by the hurricane and sought a way to address some of their needs.

I remember quite plainly that moment sitting at my computer, composing my talk, when I realized the meagerness of what I had to offer. I could barely tell myself the basics: put one foot in front of the other, live in the moment, develop a support system, express your feelings to someone else, and, if you find yourself with symptoms of severe depression and anxiety, seek help. Everyone I knew had symptoms of anxiety and depression. It was impossible to say how much of that was normal under the severely traumatic circumstances and how much was symptomatic of illness. I called the director and told her I was unable to speak to the group. I remember my words, "I'm having trouble coping myself. How can I tell someone else what to do?" Yet I had begun to treat those patients who had returned. As I look back on that time, I wonder how well I did and what I accomplished. From time to time, I want to call one of them and ask, "How was I in those days?"

Although I needed the FAR Fund Project to put it into words, I too developed a support system, a "home, a community." My post-Katrina practice situation was complicated by the fact that a year and a half prior to the flood I had made the decision to retire in May 2006, which turned out to be nine months after the levee ruptures. The week prior to the hurricane, I had initiated postretirement plans by enrolling in the MFA creative writing program at the University of New Orleans. I had always wanted to write a novel about the French-Creole history of the city and believed I needed to develop crafting skills with which to accomplish this. Besides, I had read that one should not suddenly retire without interests to substitute for the work. Thus, in the year and a half after making the decision to retire, I limited my acceptance of new patients to those needing short-term work. When one of my analytic patients finished treatment, I did not accept another long-term patient to fill that time slot. I had planned to advise my remaining patients of my upcoming retirement sometime that fall. Thus, when Hurricane Katrina arrived and the levees broke, I already had one foot out the door of my practice. Fall classes had begun at the university a week prior to the flood, and by now I had started one of the reading assignments. In preparing to ease my patients—and myself—into my retirement, I carefully thought out everything except the fact that the world that my patients and I knew was soon to end.

When my world exploded, I lost my retirement home on the Mississippi Gulf Coast, my close proximity to my younger son and most recent grandchild, my neighborhood, my routine living situation, and almost half my practice. I felt as though I was lost. I recall telling a colleague that I imagined myself floating inches above the ground. She identified with the image. Although I tried desperately to picture my feet touching solid ground, I could not. My family and I, uprooted, became part of the diaspora. For several weeks, unable to return to our flooded neighborhood because of the lack of essential services, we wandered from my older son's home to motels and ultimately to what turned out to be a crack house, the only place we could find to rent near New Orleans.

The New Orleans Center for Psychoanalysis experienced its own disruption. Almost half of the training analysts moved to Birmingham. New Orleans had sponsored the Birmingham Center and all of us had taught or supervised those analysts living there. Thus it was logical for those members of the center who lost their homes and their practices to seek help from colleagues in Birmingham. In fact, some moved there and never returned. Some months later, with half its colleagues practicing in Birmingham, the New Orleans Center formally became the New Orleans/Birmingham Center for Psychoanalysis. This added to my sense of confusion and loss.

As per Boulanger's study, I did find a place to set down my emotional self. The University of New Orleans, like all the universities in the city, had closed its doors. Uncertain when they could or would reopen, the University of New Orleans offered online courses. The English, creative writing, and sociology departments combined to offer a course in which students interviewed ten survivors and wrote up their narratives. In addition, the students wrote their own story of the flood. These accounts were to be submitted in January for credit. The professors planned to publish some of the narratives as a book and collect the others for the university's archives. I sat down in front of my computer and began to write my story.

Tears in my eyes, I remembered the moment it began. Like the earlier patient, with her dog, I too screamed when I woke Monday morning, August 29, 2005. I turned on the television in my son's Houston guest room and discovered that the eye of Hurricane Katrina had passed directly over my retirement home on the Mississippi Gulf Coast. My husband and I had planned to retire there, and in anticipation of that, he and I had renovated and decorated the home with dedicated plans, thoughts, and care. Alone in my son's guest room, watching images of piled debris and reports of deaths, I remember punching the air, screaming, and running downstairs where the rest of the family gathered around the television set. A thirty-foot-high tidal surge had destroyed my home and everything in its path. The entire Mississippi Coast was wiped out, and with it a haven I had enjoyed for twenty-five years.

Difficult as that was, that day my family and I comforted ourselves with the fact that the hurricane had not hit New Orleans directly. We spoke to a couple that had not evacuated, and they reported the winds had not been too bad, the damage not severe, and that my daughter's home, and mine as well, were probably intact. My husband and I, my daughter and her family all planned to leave Houston the next day and return home.

The next morning, Tuesday, I awoke, turned on the television set, and saw a reporter standing ankle deep in water on Bourbon Street. He seemed confused and wondered, along with me, where this water was coming from. He told of vague reports of levee failures. Confused, uncertain, helpless to obtain reliable information, my nightmare began. I started again to scream, but this time silently. There was too much to cope with to break down openly.

The landscape of New Orleans resembles a bowl, the center section of which is below sea level. For many generations, levees as high as twenty-six feet have surrounded the entire city. Three major drainage canals pump rainwater out of the city into Lake Pontchartrain, a large lake on the city's northern boundary. Twenty years before the hurricane, the Army Corps of Engineers "strengthened" these canal levee walls and informed the citizenry that these levees now provided surer protection from future hurricanes. An investigation into the cause of the levee failures after the storm showed that the engineering studies used to design the walls were flawed. It was two of these three redesigned canal levee systems that failed.

If I again use the simile of a bowl, my home is on the northern rim of that bowl, along Lake Pontchartrain. The portion of the city most visitors are familiar with, the French Quarter, the Garden District, and the University Section is on the southern rim of the bowl, along the Mississippi River. My office is in that University Section, on the opposite side of the city from my home. The entire city, beginning four houses down from my house to within eight blocks of that southern ridge, was under water. The three-mile-long section along the lakefront where my home stood became an island initially reachable only by boat across the twenty-five-mile-wide lake. It took three weeks to pump the water out of the city and eight weeks to restore electricity to the one-square-mile area where my home stands. For several weeks, the surrounding area remained without power. We traveled through pitch-black darkness to return home six weeks after the storm.

We were the first of our neighbors to return, and we lived an isolated existence for the first two weeks before four other families came back. The rest of the homes on our street were flooded, and those neighbors returned sporadically over the next two or three years. Some gutted and repaired their houses. Others tore them down and built new homes or sold the lots. One-fourth of them never returned.

I returned with much optimism, determined to make the best of it. However, with growing dismay, I watched my daughter and younger son deal with the disruptions to their own lives. Each of them was faced with multiple disruptions: loss of employment, relocation, substantial loss of income, loss of schools for their children—indeed, loss of everything they previously knew. Like most New Orleanians, they had to rebuild from the ground up.

Watching this tragedy unfold was devastating. Yet I reopened my office not knowing how many patients would or could return. After a couple of weeks, I realized only half were going to make it. I already had an abbreviated practice in anticipation of retirement. Thus I now had many open hours. I considered my options. Knowing the mental distress that most citizens of New Orleans were experiencing, I rethought my approaching retirement. In looking back, I now realize I was too depressed to contemplate undoing the steps I had already taken. I was unable to imagine starting again with new patients. In addition, the nine miles I had to drive daily across the flooded remnants of the city to reach my office on the opposite side was itself emotionally draining, and after attempting for three months to deal with the daily sights, I found it impossible to continue without respite.

I could choose one of three routes to reach my office. There was the route through Lakeview, the site of the largest levee breach. Driving through it, I smelled the pungent odor of moldy houses whose owners had not yet returned to remove the sodden sheetrock that covered the walls of their homes. These houses, with what one reporter euphemistically called "a brown bathtub ring" circling their outer walls and black mold growing within, all displayed that familiar X mark with its coded information on the number of bodies, animal or human, discovered within. I recall one sad sight, that of a child's limp, soggy doll sitting astride a broken tricycle. I wondered what had happened to the little girl and what her parents told her became of her doll.

There was the Katrina landfill route. This one took me along a two-block-wide, seven-block-long, four-stories-tall mass of soggy sheetrock, piles of clothing, collapsed furniture, children's toys, and other discarded, decaying possessions of a bereft population. Refrigerators with rotting food, some artistically displaying their prior owner's thoughts on the disaster, lined the streets leading to the landfill. Deemed too toxic for exhibition, these often humorous comments on the horror were sorted out and eventually carted to another landfill outside the city limits. As I drove past this once green, tree-lined park, now a humanity-filled landfill, I became more and more saddened over the loss of my city, my neighborhood, my home, my younger son and his family, and my practice.

I continued to work but selected a third route to my office. Although longer, this alternative route through City Park was initially less painful than the other two. In fact, those others were so raw that I built in my imagination a twelve-foot high, three-foot thick, concrete-block wall around that area. One day, my husband inadvertently started to drive across the bridge leading into that section. I imagined the wall splintering, screamed at the thought of riding through there, and he immediately turned around. From then on, we took the much longer route to the grocery store and gas station. Even today, although much of that area has been rebuilt with large new homes, many citizens from the nonflooded "sliver by the river" avoid driving that way.

The hurricane winds felled many of the park's hundred-year-old oak trees, but that was usual following such a natural disaster. What were unusual were the consequences of the manmade levee failures. The grass died, and the remaining trees drooped from oxygen deprivation. All had suffered eight to ten feet of standing water for three weeks. The golf courses, the meadows, and the wooded trails were covered in a brown, powdery carpet of dead grass that gave off a macabre aura of dust and decay. The leaves on the oak and cypress trees hung limply, and I wondered if and when these trees would die. Muddy tire tracks from trucks used to clear debris scarred the soccer and baseball fields. In an attempt to stretch their maintenance funds to clean up the mess, park administrators started to rent space to the government and FEMA. These entities, without regard for the park's future, filled some of the meadows with tent cities for their workers, huge trucks, and debris-clearing machinery. Soon, these once lovely green spaces turned into a quagmire of mud, tire tracks, and litter. As FEMA doled out the money in dribbles, the park administration was forced to lay off its few remaining staff.

In desperation, the park sought what it believed to be a more reliable source of income. The city had lost an estimated eighty to ninety thousand homes, and citizens who wanted to return had no place to live. FEMA negotiated with City Park to build a trailer park on its main golf course to house some of these people. They wanted to excavate the eighteen-hole course, lay sewer and water lines, bring in trailers, and cover the remaining area with concrete and gravel. The trailer park was to cover several acres and would be directly across the street from the area of the lakefront where we lived. FEMA promised to restore the course at some undetermined time in the future.

Now, four months after the flood, my neighbors and I were weary of FEMA's promises and ineptitude. We did not trust them to reverse their planned destruction of the area. Therefore, our neighborhood association vigorously opposed the plan. My husband and I joined the "Save City Park Committee" and worked to squelch demolition of the course. After a number of weeks of futile effort, City Park personnel planned to begin excavation anyway. My husband, an expert in environmental law, along with an attorney on the committee composed a letter requesting that FEMA develop an environmental impact statement on building government housing on land that had been submerged under eight feet of contaminated water for three weeks. This effectively killed the proposed trailer park.

I, however, lost hope. The ongoing day-by-day, month-by-month struggle for normalcy surrounded by decay and ineptitude added to the sadness of my younger son's dire financial situation and the loss of my country home. My resiliency suffered; my emotional state deteriorated. I experienced anxiety, depression, and sleepless nights. During these few months, we had periodically visited my older son in Houston. The cut medians, the planted gardens, the intact houses, and the functioning government and police force comforted and delighted me. I discovered that my respite time there had made it possible for me to cope with the untenable situation in New Orleans.

In January, we rented an apartment in Houston, both as a place to relax and as a substitute for my lost home in Mississippi, a house we had decided not to rebuild. I began a weekly commute between Houston and New Orleans, a six-hour drive. In Houston, I started a new life freed from the constant everyday blight and decay of my neighborhood and city. I joined a writer's group in Houston associated with the University of Houston's MFA program. In New Orleans, I maintained my old life, treated my patients, maintained my practice and affiliation with the Psychoanalytic Center, and attended a three-hour writing class at the University of New Orleans. The insanity of living with one foot in Houston and one foot in New Orleans gives testimony to the fragility of my mental state.

The next several months are a blur. I was in a survival mode. Of the five intensive or analytic patients I treated before the storm, one analytic patient, whom I'll call Mary, and one intensive psychotherapy patient returned. The other three patients lost their homes and moved. A few of my short-term patients also had intact homes and returned. However, the decrease in my practice hours allowed me to split my days between Houston and New Orleans. I saw patients on Monday, Tuesday, and Wednesday and drove to and from Houston on Thursday and Sunday. Out of necessity, I had to decrease Mary's hours from four to three times per week. The intensive psychotherapy patient continued on three days a week, but I consolidated those days into Monday, Tuesday, and Wednesday.

Certainly, this decision to reduce Mary's treatment hours must have felt arbitrary to her. I cannot recall any discussion of it or understanding of what it meant to her. Knowing my commitment to analysis, I must have sought her associations to the disruption, but I am unable to comment on them at this late date. Indeed, it came at a time when her life was also in flux. Did she experience it as another loss of environmental and emotional stability?

I explained to Mary and my remaining patients my plans to retire in May. For the next few months, I helped them express and contain the anxiety and depression that the flood had caused in their lives. One patient, whose law firm relocated most of their associates to Dallas, feared she would also be forced to move. She worried over this possibility but decided to find a position with another firm and remain in New Orleans. None of my returning patients had lost their homes to the flood nor experienced the trauma of rescue from the roof of a flooded home. Perhaps one or two of those I never heard from again did experience that ordeal.

I regret that my years of analytic practice ended in such turmoil for my patients and me. I do believe I treated honestly those who returned until I retired. I respected their feelings about my retirement, helped them work with it, and transferred those who needed further treatment to colleagues who had returned to the city. The termination process was one I had worked with many times in my years of practice. Although different for each patient and associated with a sense of loss for me as each patient moved on in his or her life, the process was familiar. It provided a sense that the work was complete, like the ending of a good novel.

However, the levee rupture left me with a bad taste in my mouth. I did not know how to explain to Mary why I was cutting her hours back from four to three times per week. I did not say I had to do it for my own emotional survival. Yet I know that to be the truth. Such action was unlike me and must have confused her, but our work continued even as her fantasies about this remained unexamined. However, with the reprieve in Houston and the use of my writing classes to express my feelings and thoughts about the trauma, I gradually became more emotionally available to my patients.

I continue to have regrets about Mary. More importantly, I remain curious about her experience of the last several months of her analysis. I recall telling her about my plans to retire, with the hope of writing a novel, something I would not have shared under normal circumstances. She responded that while that was interesting, was not a life's work treating patients more important? Reflecting on that comment now, I wonder if she was relating a fantasy that she felt less important to me than she had hoped. In our many years of work together, she had expressed in word and life decisions her desires for closeness to me. Certainly, it was defensive of me to reveal my plans to her. I wonder if that interchange was reflective of my guilt that I was not living up to my own expectations of myself as an analyst, to complete every analysis and treatment situation as satisfactorily as one completes a novel, with all of the conflicts neatly tied up at the end.

Of course, this accomplishment is naught but a fantasy, unrealized and unrealizable in every analysis. However, with treatment situations that end in the usual manner, we analysts can comfort ourselves that all fantasies necessary for termination were expressed. When some trauma or unexamined life situation interferes with that process, then analyst and patient can be left with a sense of expectations unfulfilled. For me, I wonder what more could she and I have learned, if only I had asked about her feelings about the reduced sessions and further examined her response to my reason for retiring. What important fantasies went unexpressed, what conflicts unresolved? Actually, the patient was content with the analysis. We did examine whether she wanted me to transfer her to another analyst. She thought about it and decided she had achieved enough of her goals to stop.

Perhaps I am the only one in this analytic pair wondering about broken promises, shattered dreams, and wordless endings. Indeed, the levee breaches did shatter my dreams. The retirement house I loved disappeared, and my children scattered. I had no words, no power to affect that outcome. I did learn to write.

Even now, I remain curious about Mary's experience of our shared work during those several months after Katrina. Of all the analyses I conducted, this one feels most like an out-of-print novel that dropped into a lake just as I opened the page to the final chapter. I am left with a sense of unknowing. Indeed, I do not know what happened to many of my patients following Katrina, but that unknowing is the result of an uncontrollable environmental catastrophe. With Mary, my unknowing is the consequence of a shared apocalyptic trauma, too much of which feels unspoken. The abrupt disruption of our usual everyday lives left us both broken and speechless. The last chapter of the narrative of her life and of our work together shared the same fate as my long analytic career. Both were lost to the floodwaters of Lake Pontchartrain.

REFERENCES

Boulanger, G. 2007. *Wounded by Reality: Understanding and Tracing Adult Onset Trauma*. Hillsdale, N.J: Analytic Press.

Floyd, L., K. Nathan, D. Poitevant, and E. Pool. 2010. "Stretched Thin: Lessons Learned from Hurricane Katrina," The FAR Fund Project, New Orleans/Birmingham Center for Psychoanalysis, New Orleans, La.

CHAPTER 13

WHAT THE LIVING DID

September 11 and Its Aftermath

BILLIE A. PIVNICK

I am living, I remember you.

—Marie Howe, *What the Living Do* (1998)

TEN YEARS after the complex series of events we have collapsed into the phrase "9/11," many of my patients, especially parents with young children at the time, are still traumatized. Many were so distracted by the aftermath of the attacks that their lives became fragmented, more of a collage of snapshots—memories created as if by flashbulb—than a coherent narrative. With so many separate shards of experience to monitor, some could not recognize their grief. Others did not notice their sadness until many years later. When they did, they were startled to realize that they had somehow lost a decade of their life, along with their marriage, health, livelihood, or savings. Like mythic Orpheus heading underground to reclaim his Eurydice, hard luck awaited their efforts at reclamation. When they looked back, they found they had no one to bring back and often no memories to remind themselves of whom or what they had lost. And to make matters worse, they often felt it was their fault. Figuratively speaking, they had already lost their heads to the ravages of trauma when finally ready to grieve. The job of mourning for them was left to muses, museums, and musing therapists like me.

Traumatized mourners are often stuck in a divided inner experience of, on the one hand, an eternally looping search for answers and self-blaming explanations and, on the other hand, an active re-creation of subsymbolic sensations and somatic symptoms. These bodily experiences memorialize their intolerable pain and grief but do not give them the soothing that comes from making them meaningful (Bucci 1997, Shabad 2000). Psychotherapists hope that the transitional quality of the therapeutic relationship can open up "memorial space" and thereby bridge that gap (Bernstein 2000). In that manner, we wish to enhance the capacity for integrating seemingly incompatible opposites, characteristic of symbolic representation and healing.

In the therapeutic treatment of trauma and depression, the therapist creates a metaphoric container—a safe space in which faint and dissociated memory traces can be etched more deeply; connected to other memories, feelings, and sensations; and then linked to symbolic meanings in imagistic or narrative form. Aiming to disconnect fright from fact and to bring the past into contact with a more protected present and hoped-for future, the therapist and patient attend to the distortions produced by dread as well as the contortions that come from renewed renditions of painful experience. We accomplish this by using the therapeutic relationship as an emotional and conversational anchor during the inevitable reexperiencing of repetitive injury. We have discovered that bearing witness to patients' terror and grief renders traumatic loss less eternally damaging (Felman and Laub 1991, Gerson 2009) and that dialogue is essential to breaking up trancelike posttraumatic monologue (Boulanger 2007).

However, for the therapist, doing so in the face of one's own massive disruption is a challenge of another magnitude. For me, the aftermath of the terrorist attack on September 11 was such a test. The shock of this tragic event disoriented me, even as I tried to provide support and containment for my patients and their families. I write this paper to honor the rebuilding of familial and communal life that takes place after catastrophic events. We adults are also children at play; by continuing to play in the wake of destruction, we keep the social fabric from tearing. But our play is storied more by words than by toys. This chapter explores how I tried to keep my own sense of inner play at work during that difficult time, drawing on the dialogues I had with myself, as well as those with patients and colleagues, as my journey toward mourning unfolded.[1]

INTIMATE CONVERSATIONS

That bright and clear fall morning, I breathed in the crisp fresh air, glad to be alive. I had just dropped my kids off at their school in Brooklyn Heights and crossed the Brooklyn Bridge, admiring the glinting water and the view of the harbor to my left. The sky that morning was cerulean, a color I now call "9/11 blue." If you were in New York City on that day, you can probably picture that shiny, cloudless, cobalt expanse. Arriving at my office, I noticed my answering machine blinking. "*Beep. This is Ingrid; I won't be coming to my 9:00 session this morning because a plane flew into the World Trade Center and I'm going to go down there to see if I can help out.*" Oh, my. Why does she always need to be like a moth to a flame? I hope her impulsivity doesn't get her into trouble. Surely a small plane crash doesn't warrant civilian concern. There are firefighters and police officers for that job.

I called my husband: "Hi, honey. My first patient cancelled. Where are you? I thought you'd be on your way to Federal Court in Manhattan, but I can't remember whether you're going to the one in the World Trade Center? Someone told me a plane flew into it, so maybe you should avoid that area. I hope you get this message. Call me." While I didn't yet know it, I was beginning to search for my husband.

By 10:05, I began to realize that there was going to be more to this day than I had reckoned. My next patient told me anxiously that her partner, who worked in the Trade Center, was not answering her cell phone. She also informed me that a second plane had crashed into the buildings. Though restless, we sat together for fifty minutes. I listened to her worries about her partner, tried to be reassuring, didn't stop her from making occasional calls, and tried to help her anticipate what to do when she left. We talked about how she felt, but by now, I already knew. I was in the exact same boat. I had no idea where my husband was, he was not returning my calls, and he was likely in one of those buildings. My patient and I were both in a controlled state of panic. But I didn't share my own fears with her.

The end of the hour arrived in what seemed like glacial time. As soon as the door closed behind her, I tried to phone my husband again. No answer. I checked the Internet. I soon realized that no local calls or local Internet could get through. How was I to reach him? Other parts of the Internet were working, and, oddly, I received three e-mails from overseas. It seemed as if the whole world knew what had happened, while I, a mere twenty blocks away, had few clues. One was from the husband of a close friend who lived in London but was visiting New York that day. My friend was on the Upper East Side, but because of the shutdown of the city, she might as well have been across the sea. Still in London, her husband let me know that the two buildings had been struck and that the cell phones weren't working because the main antenna was on top of one of the towers. Improbably, I thought—maybe my husband is ok.

Finally, I managed to reach my housekeeper in Brooklyn on a landline. She told me that she had heard from my husband, who was on his way to pick up the kids from school. I wished I could have been the one who'd gotten to them first. Still, I thanked her profusely. She had told me everyone was fine, that my husband had gotten out of Manhattan just in time—running across the Brooklyn Bridge from the main Federal Court building just as the first tower fell. He was safe! They were safe! I was safe! But how I would get to them, I had no idea. I felt myself tearing up.

I was having trouble thinking about anything other than getting to my kids. I was grateful when my husband called, reassured by his familiar, sometimes annoying bossiness. He instructed me not to leave until the Brooklyn Bridge was less crowded, warning me that he had nearly been run over by panicked people trying to escape Manhattan. Still, in order to journey the four miles home to Brooklyn, I had to traverse the "frozen zone" of lower Manhattan, closed to all traffic, and then walk over the Manhattan Bridge. Perhaps this was the point at which I first realized how many must have died. In my mind I keep thinking "dead zone" rather than "frozen zone."

Traversing the bridge with a knot in my gut, I couldn't help but notice the smoldering ruins, nor could I escape the smoke blowing in my direction. When I was midway across, I turned to look back: a blackish-grey plume spread across the East River. A narrow column of smoke amassed near the rubble, broadening as it billowed over the water toward Brooklyn. A ghostly silvery-white disc of light shone bleakly through the black cloud. Beneath was a mirror image of the shape, in glinting grey-blue. The calm water reflected the sun and the part of the sky that was not concealed behind the cloud of smoke. The smooth surface of the water was marred only by a single black boat—an idling fireboat perhaps. The river thus made the yin to the sky's yang—the metaphoric shape of a mandala, joining opposite realities (Pivnick 2010a). There was something apocalyptic about it.

By then, I had begun to absorb that our country had been attacked, that our borders had been violated, that an unspeakable number of people had probably perished—that my husband had run across the Brooklyn Bridge with rubble chasing his heels to get to our kids. I was furious as well as sad and frightened. Although we still didn't know all the ways this event would transform the world, one thing was clear: we were inextricably linked to one another across vast distances. I thought that this day was the actual turn of the twenty-first century—a century in which we might be able to survive unspeakable disaster but would no longer be able to sustain our insularity. My personal world was also punctured by the terrorist attack. I was struggling to form some coherent way to comprehend this new experience. While I imagined that nothing would ever be the same for me or for most of the world, I pictured the image of the smoky mandala that I had glimpsed on the bridge, wondering if I could reassure myself that the world had not just shattered into pieces. But shock gave way to fear again. The smoke on the Brooklyn side was so thick I could barely see or breathe. Luckily, my husband was able to meet me at the foot of the bridge and drive me the rest of the way home. I was grateful for his embrace. Safe inside our car, I could finally let myself cry.

The next day, the bridges remained closed, preventing me from getting to my office. I spent the day fielding calls and speaking with patients from the landline telephone in my husband's office in downtown Brooklyn. All of my patients were alive and well, if shaken.

I started to get crisis calls, like this one: *"Dr. Pivnick, I am calling at the suggestion of Dr. R. My wife and two young daughters were at the WTC yesterday and saw the planes hit the towers. My wife hasn't been able to stop crying. I'm worried about her and our three-year-old. Can you help us?"* I agreed to consult with his wife, Natalie, the next day.[2]

Although it was three-year-old Callie who was referred, it seemed to me that the problem was in the relationship between mother and daughter, one that I came to understand as a "play disruption." With this in mind, I decided to work primarily with the mother, whom I call Natalie. Natalie had been taking Callie and her newborn sibling to daycare on that sunny 9/11 morning. Exiting the subway, they witnessed the plane hitting and being swallowed up by the World Trade Center. They saw the fireball explosion and were part of the horrifying mayhem that ensued. Certain that this was the start of a war, Natalie managed to have the presence of mind and good judgment to get them safely to their home in another borough, on the last subway train to depart from that station for many months. Once there, she was unable to contain her terror and grief. The children couldn't help witnessing that she cried inconsolably for two days. Although apparently coping well, Callie felt she had to take care of baby Hilary and of her mother. Her perception was exaggerated but true enough for at least the first hour, until a relative arrived to help. Her father, Steve, in a helping profession and isolated in Manhattan, did not make it back home until late at night. He was very involved in the family's subsequent recovery, so it would be years before Natalie could acknowledge her deep disappointment in his not putting her needs before those of his clients that first day. I felt it was important to repair the rift that was developing because of mutual recriminations.

At Natalie's request, I saw her and Steve together for a few sessions to help them find ways to manage their daughter's sudden fear of elevators. Later, after a year or more of exploring her own fears and childhood phobias, Natalie had learned to identify and separate her fears from her daughter's anxieties and had created a safe space, in a comfortable armchair, for the two of them to talk about the daughter's oft-recurring concerns. Now four, Callie felt secure enough to be able to enact her memories of the events of that day—actually a word-by-word and action-by-action account of who said and did what that entire day. This time, Natalie was able to help her daughter mentalize the feelings that accompanied the frightening events, providing comfort and reassurance without becoming retraumatized herself. The creation of such event representations by child and mother is a crucial step in normal language acquisition. A dialogue about their mutual memories enabled them both to gain the sort of perspective that would help conversation replace action as a form of communication.

Soon after, Natalie gave birth to a third child. Callie became extremely fearful and clingy. She was hypervigilant, shrieking if her mother left her side for even a few seconds in a store or at a birthday party. She was in a state that could easily be construed as PTSD. Natalie, who had worked so hard to soothe her daughter's fears, was again coming undone out of her fear, guilt, and frustration. So, although I believe in treading gently on the bond between parent and young child, I recommended that Natalie bring her daughter to a session. I wanted to assess Callie's apparent regression.

Callie, a spunky blonde whose smile was almost as wide as she was tall, walked into my office with her mother. She began by exploring the materials I'd left out for her to play with. Eventually, she chose paper and crayons and proceeded to draw sweet flowers and clouds. After a time, she created a picture of her and her mother, with the child's cartoon dialogue bubble saying "I hate you." "I understand you are angry at me, but I still love you," replied

Natalie, as a way of surviving her daughter's attack without falling apart or retaliating. Callie then crawled into her lap and snuggled up with her. They both wept. This was the one thing the little girl had needed after the scary events of that day and the one thing that was not available—a simple hug in her mother's lap.

While they were crying, so, quietly, was I. I felt deep respect for Natalie, who wanted desperately to "fix" the damage she felt she had caused by coming undone when her daughter had needed her and was now repeating with the addition of another baby. I, too, regretted not being able to be as available to my children as I had wanted to after the attack. But I also felt an uncanny sense of identification with Callie. Unbeknownst to them, I had "saved" my mother's life, when she suffered a grand mal seizure, when I, too, was not much older than four or five. Despite my desperate wish for comfort from my mother, my inability to make her stop shaking propelled me to leave her and my baby sister in order to run through the cold, dark Michigan winter to a neighbor's house for help. The neighbor, by chance a nurse's aide, identified my description of my mother's wild state as a seizure and came running. She stuck a hairbrush in my mother's mouth so she wouldn't swallow her tongue, as I comforted my little sister. All would have been well had my father not come home and blamed me for causing the seizure by being too "wild."

I had never experienced with my own parents such a forgiving scene as I now witnessed between Callie and her mother. Facilitating the mother-daughter rapprochement was a means of reparation for me. Rightly or wrongly, I felt as if I knew exactly what this little girl needed, *and* I felt gratified by the warmth of their embrace. This created for me a Proust-like sense of time, resulting in a resonance of emotions, both playful and mournful, within myself and among all three of us. Additionally, I realized how inflated was my own sense of importance to my mother, sister, and father; I began to find some humor where I had always felt terror and to let go of a bit of my own lifelong hypervigilance about others' emotional and physical states.

Callie came to the next session wanting to play "Mommy" and to discuss where babies come from. She also had a lot to say about her new baby sister. *"Everyone does whatever Mallory wants. All she has to do is cry and they run to her."* She had concluded baby Mallory was the real boss of the family, what with her noisy and tyrannical demands. After meeting with both mother and Callie separately and together, I came to believe we were witnessing a state of rage, toddler style—with the now older Callie utilizing all the behavior that had so successfully focused her parents' attention on her after 9/11. I now worked on helping Natalie reassert her proper authority by disillusioning somewhat the four-year-old girl's raging and competitive omnipotence. I felt satisfied that we had done enough conjointly for them to return to a more expectable, developmentally appropriate relationship.

I saw Callie and her mother together one more time, just before Callie started first grade. Natalie was very worried about how her daughter would manage the separation and the noisy lunchroom. She feared that she was too anxious to even read the teacher's advance letter properly and would therefore fail Callie as a mother. She wanted me again to assess the situation. This time Callie brought with her a *Finding Nemo* picture book. With her mother and sisters out of the room, she told me how frustrated Nemo was with his father, Marlin, because Marlin was too worried about Nemo starting school. She wanted me to know that Nemo would be okay at school and that his problem lay with Marlin. With that message received, Natalie and I could begin to explore her anxieties about Callie starting first grade. She felt helpless to protect her daughter at school. Natalie's painful memories of separating from home when she started first grade illustrated the sort of difficulties one finds in certain disorganized attachments. Understanding this allowed her to ease up on worrying aloud in her daughter's presence.[3] I hoped that this would help Callie and Natalie continue to create space for the dialogue that had been missing after the attack.

Over time, the need for this reparative dialogue emerged as a central theme in my post-9/11 practice. I noticed two types of reactions in my patients. Sitting with one sort of patient, I felt inundated with highly charged material that seemed difficult to organize. A second set of patients presented the opposite problem: although they spoke in a more organized and topical fashion, their constriction and withdrawal prevented me from identifying specific troubling symptoms other than a sense of great discomfort. This phenomenon reminded me of findings from my research on severely traumatized patients (Pivnick 1990, 2010b). I had found that, after a signal of threatened object loss—for example, the setting of a psychotherapy termination date—all patients in the study became more active in reaching out to their therapist, increasing the quantity of their talk, but that the quality of their conversation suffered, becoming either over- or undersymbolized. I understood this in light of the work of Freud (1920), Klein (1940), and Bion (1959). First, as these theorists suggested, symbolization and symptom formation varied inversely. Furthermore, though attempts at symbol formation increased, the linguistic links between patient's and therapist's statements were damaged, causing either a collapse at the representational level that led to increased symptomatology and concrete cognition or a defensive hyper-deployment of linking words that effectively kept the therapist "out," creating little room for dialogue. I had likened this dynamic to the protest of a child at the loss of a caregiver, rather than the actual mourning we expect during the termination phase of psychotherapy.

While Callie and Natalie had difficulty establishing space for dialogue, Brad, in contrast, showed affective flattening and cognitive collapse. Brad arrived in my office about a year after 9/11. A tall, slender young man, he stepped over my threshold as if wading warily into a scorpion-infested wadi. He seated himself on my couch so lightly that the cushions barely registered his presence. He was unmistakably stiff. He told me he was depressed but also that he felt uncomfortable in my neighborhood. Noting his handsome looks and conventional dress—a blue button-down shirt, khaki pants, and deck shoes—I was surprised. The only way he could disappear more successfully from view would be to turn sideways, like a shadow play puppet. Then again, this was Greenwich Village, so perhaps he could be forgiven for thinking he looked out of place.

A decade before, feeling welcomed into a Canadian mosque by some Muslim men, Brad had converted to Islam and moved to a predominantly Muslim country. He had an arranged marriage and learned the language and letter of the Koranic law. After some seven years, he'd been allowed to read some old English-language classics, which reawakened him to what he missed about life as an American. Although Brad had been a rebellious boy and was frequently humiliated by his father, his own biting sarcasm and pranks were not only tolerated but enjoyed by his mother and female teachers. But there was no room for humor in his new religion. Worse, he felt enslaved by the group; beheading was the punishment for renouncing his new faith—and daily beheadings in the local village confirmed that they enforced this law.

After 9/11, fearing for his life since his height and fair coloring stuck out in his town, he fled to America with his wife and children. But they were equally uncomfortable in post-9/11 America, where being openly Muslim could make one a victim of a hate crime. Ultimately, his wife and child returned to their former home—without him. He was deeply conflicted, feeling that the breakup of the family was his fault and that he deserved to be punished. He was particularly despondent over losing his young sons, who

were an ocean and a continent away and forbidden by his wife and her father to speak to him.

While Brad spoke, he placed his hands on his uncrossed legs—a posture somewhat reminiscent of psychotic patients who are concerned with
shielding themselves from intrusive thoughts (Freedman and Grand 1985).
He was also guarded in our conversations. He used few words and had to
be prompted to respond. But I noticed that whenever he expressed any humor, usually in the form of a criticism of his mother, he would relax, cross
one leg over his other knee as if to create a physical boundary, and begin to
gesture as if to reach out to me or to better demonstrate his point. I noticed
he repeated this sequence of posture and gesture over and over. At the same
time, he talked about how difficult it was to be living again with his mother,
whose emotional fragility made him fearful and submissive.

As Brad's posture, gesture, and narrative became more integrated, I
understood that his extreme self-consciousness related to his fear that
others would view him as "not belonging," which was in fact a repetitive
posttraumatic "perception." When I shared this interpretation with him, it
seemed to help him gather together many memories of how his appearance and sensibility, especially his sense of humor, didn't fit in and how that
endangered him, particularly at the end of his stay overseas. When I asked
some time later if he knew any other people who had gotten out or whether
there were self-help groups around so that he could begin to socialize, his
first really spontaneous gesture emerged. He laughed heartily and said, "I've
thought about contacting other people over the Internet, but first, I have
enough problems of my own, and second, when I think what it would be
like to get together, I realize that people would have to wear fake noses and
disguises so as not to be found out. Can you imagine what a room full of
people like that would look like?" As I shared in his hearty laughter, I felt
my first glimmer of hope for his sustained recovery—one that has, in fact,
continued.

After 9/11, I also worked with quite a number of adult patients who had
experienced childhood trauma. When describing their terror from that day,
rather then fearing their own deaths, patients related the fear of being separated from their loved ones, fear of punishment, or a memory of a childhood
death of a parent, who was imagined to be both alive and dead (e.g., "cold
and lonely"). This phenomenon is characteristic of a child's difficulty with
mourning, which often leads to rage and repetition rather than grieving
(Wolfenstein 1969). Attachment theorists might liken the resulting acting-out

behavior to a persistent period of protest, a term Bowlby (1973) used to refer to the child's initial response to separation from the caregiver. It can be diffi-cult to convert separation anxiety to grief and mourning without the feeling of security that comes from being in close proximity to a protective figure that can keep you in mind.

Nevertheless, on 9/11, many of these patients had risen to the occasion—just as I had. One man, who had grown up in Argentina during the disap-pearances, commented, "You know, it's odd, but I feel better since 9/11. I think everyone else is finally feeling the way I've felt my whole life." In the immediate aftermath of the attack, he was able to guide people to safety, help the injured walk, and monitor the doors of an evacuating building so that no one got trampled. I felt that I understood. I, too, had been strangely relocated. Perhaps my experience, like his, was of something found as much as it was of something lost. But a remnant of my frightened state appeared in a way that surprised me: On the first anniversary of the attack, I rounded the corner onto West Street from the Brooklyn-Battery Tunnel and saw thousands of lights, scores of fire trucks and ambulances, hurrying men in uniform—all on their way to the commemoration—and despite the absence of "the pile," I was certain I smelled that uniquely acrid chemical, electrical, and human burning that signaled a restimulation of the neural pattern acti-vated on the day of the actual attack.

TRAVELING TOWARD MOURNING

"This is not the first visit you'll make to this hangar," the conservator of JFK *Hangar 17 said—instead of "this is not the last . . ."* As a consulting psycholo-gist to Thinc Design, the lead exhibition designer partnered with the Na-tional September 11 Memorial Museum, I was touring the stored WTC artifacts—some six years after the attack. With that parapraxis, our host brought home to us the notion that we had already been there, we were part of a living past. Perhaps he showed me, in that moment, what it was a historian did. The hangar contained eighty thousand square feet of rusted steel beams that were salvaged from the towers. I remember the bike rack, as twisted as the bikes it somehow was still propping up—against all odds. The undulating waves of the rack and the circular wheels of the cycles created abstract shapes that distracted attention from the missing bike messengers.

I remember the autographed steel column full of messages from rescue workers to their dead brethren, embodying the hope that someone would read them. I remember the hangar door shaped like the fuselage of a plane—must we be reminded how easily we gave entry to rogue planes? I remember the photos of the burning potato-chip latticework and my wish to reassemble the buildings where they stood—to let the light stream through them as beautifully as I had seen it do one eerie Sunday morning. Oh, and I nearly forgot the meteorite-like molten residue of five floors sandwiched into a three-by-six-foot mound, garnished with still readable scraps of burnt ledger paper: "Expenses." Eighty thousand square feet of steel, and what I remember most is the lifelessness. A story without subjects and verbs is a list. In remembering, I am mourning again. My job would be helping the designers create a journey that would take visitors, like me, from a state of shock to a state in which they could reflect on their experience and honor the heroes while remembering the nearly three thousand people killed in the WTC bombings in 1993, on 9/11, as well as at the Pentagon and in Pennsylvania.

"Stay together," our guide instructed us, *"or you might get lost; stay with me, or you may never find your way back out."* Everything on this New York December morning in 2010 was cold and grey—the sky, the sidewalk, the concrete construction site, and the skin tone of the workers who'd spent so much time underground. Descending into the even darker underbelly of the site where the National September 11 Memorial Museum was being built for a guided tour of its still emergent structure was an eerie adventure. Like Orpheus mining the Underworld for a glimpse of his Eurydice, we proceeded glumly but expectantly through dust and debris. The guide hadn't said "don't look back," but I imagined that if I did, the confusion of "switchbacked" views would cause me to lose my place in the line and, in truth, become too disoriented to find my way to an exit. I stayed close enough to see her steamy breath.

The path we traversed was poorly lit, closed off in odd places, with steep cliff-like drop-offs overlooking vast indoor canyons four stories beneath us, with a bird's eye view of at least that many stories above us, as well. That the museum was going to be cathedral-like and awe-inspiring was clear. Its scale was breathtaking. I had been invited on this tour because the nearly four years of work with the exhibition design team was nearing its completion. It had been an unusual assignment for a psychoanalytically trained psychologist, but my background in dance and art therapy, as well as experience working with adults and children suffering from complex trauma and creative inhibitions, allowed me to envision the project not just as a psychic problem. It was also as a choreographic and narrative conundrum. As a storytelling museum, it must set up conditions for listening, for bearing witness. Because conversational discourse, like all narrative, is disconnected by trauma, "joint attention" is difficult to establish without a third (unifying, intersubjective) perspective. It was my goal to assist the team in imagining the museum as a "Third" that would help visitors "stand in the spaces" between trauma and dissociation (Bromberg 1998).

During my journey through this vast space, I was also reorienting myself in a world torn asunder. As I mournfully recalled the suffering of those who perished here, my joy at being alive ironically intensified. Trying to feel at home with my memories and beliefs about myself and my world, I also couldn't help letting my feelings of awe give me pause long enough to consider what was possibly new. The psychoanalyst Robert Langan (2000, 70) suggests that such a pause can help one cross over the concreteness of the known space to "someplace in mind—a new place to be a person." Marveling at the fact that someone as small as I could find a secure place in such a vast and often violent universe, I hoped a similar experience might help soothe the vigilant state many had carried with them since the day of the attack.

But transiting a place is not quite the same as transitioning in psychic space. Many parameters needed to be altered to create the conditions for communal mourning. Would architectural space—intersubjectively conceived—combine with emotional wisdom to create conditions for the emergence of what Avishai Margalit (2002) called "an ethical community of memory"? As our group moved together down this ramp, we also became a procession—not unlike one of the noninscribed rituals involved in enacting remembrance at funerals (Connerton 1989). Future tourists would traverse this same route. Perhaps for some visitors, this place would be a site for pilgrimage, an ancient practice of transformational travel in which the itinerant hopes to be changed by encounters with the unknown (Cousineau 1998). The ancient Greeks practiced *theorein*—a form of transit that involved leaving the *polis* to observe a religious ceremony. As the root of our word "theory," that custom reminds us that leaving home in some way is essential to finding the emotional and mental detachment necessary to the creation of new perspectives (Clifford 1989). Seeing our design coming to life was incredibly moving. We hoped the museum would recontextualize visitors' experience of 9/11 so as to help them move on.

Some scholars (see Tweed 2006) would consider these concerns to be less those of psychoanalysis than those of religion. I hoped there would be subjective room enough in this transitional space for the more religious visitor to attribute such a transcendent experience to the work of suprahuman forces and for the secular citizen merely to become someone other than he had thought himself to be. If, as Langan (2000, 77) posits, "where you choose to place your mind determines what place is," each visitor's unique intentions, beliefs, and lived experiences would shape their encounter (see Hennes 2009) with the tour guide's itinerary for our visit in idiosyncratic ways. I saw that even something as seemingly banal as tourism can be reimagined as a renewal of this wounded site. Scholars have said the relation between trauma and tourism was so close as to be like matter and antimatter (Nelson 2003). No wonder sites of cultural destruction and trauma so quickly become tourist destinations. Thinking we are merely crossing from one domain to another to find a place to dwell on the meanings of our lives and those of the people and places we had lost, we visitors are rather like blood cells rushing to repair a bruise.

The tour finally wended its way deep into the heart of this monument—the memorial exhibit designed to enhance the experience of the memorial aboveground. Mindful of research on mourning (cf., Silverman, Nickman, and Worden 1992), which found that bereaved children do not, as Freud thought, stop grieving but instead experience grief and remembrance as a lifelong developmental process in which internal representations change and evolve much as the living do, we conceived the memorial exhibit as a sanctum within a sanctum within a sanctum. On its periphery, additional information about the deceased would be accessible. At its core would be a room lined with benches for contemplation of the projected images and spoken stories of those who had perished in the attacks. The floor of this room consisted of the actual ground of Ground Zero. As I tried to make sense of this still raw, unfinished space, my heart missed a beat. The framed shape of the uneven terrain that would be seen by all who visited the memorial exhibit was unmistakable—a yin-yang mandala like the one I envisioned as I walked over the Manhattan Bridge on the afternoon of 9/11. Goosebumps formed on my skin. There was no explaining this coincidence in rational terms; Jung (1960), though, would consider it an example of the acausal connection he termed synchronicity. I then recalled a favorite verse from a Rilke poem about Orpheus, who lost his Eurydice a second time when he turned back to make sure she was present. Instead, he had to find her

image within—as memory—a task that preoccupied him until his life was
cut short by women alienated by his continued absorption with Eurydice.[4]

For to looking, see, there is a limit.
And the more looked-at world
Wishes to flourish in love.
Work of sight is done,
Do heart-work now
On the images in you, those
Captured ones, for you
Conquered them, but now you
    do not know them.

CONCLUSION

A great many of the patients in my practice—both old and new—are parents
of families torn asunder by the trauma of 9/11. Most are unaware until they
begin telling their story that the legacy of that day is a continuing one. Until
this writing, I hadn't realized that the lessons from my patients and capacity of my immediate family to "go on being" gave me the opportunity to
finally heal a relational trauma of my own. Though I had for the most part
overcome the very early childhood trauma created by my mother's repeated
seizure-induced falls, on September 11 I had to live through another great
fall. Because I already understood that seemingly invincible figures could
collapse as if suddenly dead but be revived to stand again, and that I could
help by maintaining a separate subjectivity, I thought I could help others
find that they, too, could recover from a frightening fall. But the deep engagement of finding empathy for my patients meant I also had to embody
their subjectivity. In doing so, I found the part of myself that needed the
comfort of togetherness—after all these years. Because of the recognition
of family, friends, and, yes, patients, this time I was not alone! While I may
have transcended my parents' limitations, I was merely muddling through
and was lucky to have the help of family, friends, and professionals whose
good sense scaffolded my own in those times of tremendous uncertainty. By
sharing my experience in an imaginary dialogue with you as my witness, I
have intended to stimulate a communal remembering of our triumphs of

spirit as well as of our tragic moments of mutual helplessness and sorrow. This is the work of mourning traumatic loss.

NOTES

Portions of this paper to appear in Pivnick (2011).

1. Throughout this period, I struggled to balance caring for my children's needs with my need to care for others' children. To keep the focus of this article clear, I have omitted most of my family's personal experiences, but the challenge of managing our disrupted existence was a continuing counterpoint to the events narrated here.

2. I received explicit permission to use the clinical material in extended case illustrations. Extensive changes were made to other clinical material in order to disguise identifying information.

3. Although this had become a rather unorthodox treatment, with all sorts of boundaries blurred, it seemed appropriate to the extent that each member of the family seemed to be carrying an aspect of what was a shared trauma. I continued to work with them in occasional pairs for several years until all were able to return to some sort of less hypervigilant and dissociated existence. I later read a paper by Adrienne Harris (2005) that illustrated a similar sort of treatment of a woman who had lost her husband in the World Trade Center attack and the young children she was trying to raise while grieving. She called this process "relational mourning" because of the fragmented and distributed self- and object representations that result from a disrupted system as well as from individual ruptures.

4. Perhaps it was a toxic mixture of longing, self-loathing, grief, helplessness, shame, and guilt that sundered Orpheus. He behaved as if dead while alive and was so fragmented that he couldn't protect himself from dying. That the Muses created the funerary rites for a proper burial suggested that burial without symbolization could not bring an end to a story of terrifying, violent death, because trauma inflicted by other human beings (as opposed to natural disaster) sundered trust, communication, and the fidelity to communal ideas. Without mourning, terrifying death can continue to pose a threat to the very foundation of our social world.

REFERENCES

Bernstein, J. W. 2000. "Making a Memorial Place: The Photography of Shimon Attie." *Psychoanalytic Dialogues* 10: 347–370.

Bion, W. R. 1959. "Attacks on Linking." In *Second Thoughts*. London: Heinemann, 1967.

Boulanger, G. 2007. *Wounded by Reality: Understanding and Treating Adult-Onset Trauma*. New York: Routledge.

Bowlby, J. 1973. *Attachment and Loss*, vol. 2: *Separation*. New York: Basic Books.

Bromberg, P. 1998. *Standing in the Spaces: Essays on Clinical Process, Trauma, and Dissociation*. New York: Analytic Press.

Bucci, W. 1997. "Symptoms and Symbols: A Multiple Code Theory of Somatization." *Psychoanalytic Inquiry* 17: 151–172.

Clifford, J. 1997. *Routes: Travel and Translation in the Late Twentieth Century*. Cambridge, Mass.: Harvard University Press.

Connerton, P. 1989. *How Societies Remember*. Cambridge: Cambridge University Press.

——. 1998. *The Art of Pilgrimage: The Seeker's Guide to Making Travel Sacred*. Berkeley, Calif.: Conari.

Felman, S., and D. Laub. 1991. *Testimony: Crises of Witnessing in Literature, Psychoanalysis, and History*. New York: Routledge.

Freedman, N., and S. Grand. 1985. "Shielding: An Associative Organizer." In *From Research to Clinical Practice*, ed. G. Stricker and R. Keisner. New York: Plenum.

Freud, S. 1920. *Beyond the Pleasure Principle*. In *The Standard Edition of the Complete Psychological Works of Sigmund Freud*, ed. J. Strachey, 18:69–144. London: Hogarth.

Gerson, S. 2009. "When the Third Is Dead: Memory, Mourning, and Witnessing in the Aftermath of the Holocaust." *International Journal of Psychoanalysis* 90: 1341–1357.

Harris, A. 2005. *Gender as Soft Assembly*. Hillsdale, N.J.: Analytic Press.

Hennes, T. 2009. "Exhibitions: From a Perspective of Encounter." *Curator: The Museum Journal* 53, no. 1: 21–33.

Howe, M. 1998. *What the Living Do: Poems*. New York: Norton.

Jung, C. G. 1960. *The Structure and Dynamics of the Psyche*. Vol. 8 of *Collected Works*. Oxford: Pantheon.

Klein, M. 1940. "Mourning and Its Relation to Manic-Depressive States." *International Journal of Psychoanalysis* 2: 125–153.

Langan, R. 2000. "Someplace in Mind." *International Forum of Psychoanalysis* 9: 69–75.

Margalit, A. 2002. *The Ethics of Memory*. Cambridge, Mass.: Harvard University Press.

Nelson, R. 2003. "Tourists, Terrorists, and Metaphysical Theater at Hagia Sophia." In *Monuments and Memory, Made and Unmade*, ed. R. Nelson and M. Olin. Chicago: University of Chicago Press.

Pivnick, B. A. 1990. "Symbolization and Its Discontents: Setting a Discharge Date During Inpatient Treatment." Paper presented at "Hunting Anomalies: Empirical Approaches to Short-Term Inpatient Psychotherapy" symposium conducted at the Twenty-first Annual Meeting of the Society for Psychotherapy Research, Wintergreen, Va., June 1990.

——. 2010a. "A Museum Visitor's Guide to the Universe." *Curator: The Museum Journal* 53, no. 3: 359–371.

——. 2010b. "Trauma in Translation: The Effect of Object Loss on Discourse, Reflective Functioning, and Symptomatic Behavior During Psychotherapy in Literature and Clinical Practice." Paper presented at "Trauma: Intersections Among Narrative, Neuroscience, and Psychoanalysis" plenary panel, "Reflective Functioning and Trauma Narrative" conference at George Washington University, March 5, 2010.

——. 2011. "Enacting Remembrance: Turning to Memorializing September 11th." *Journal of Religion and Health*. In press.

Rilke, R. M. 1985. *Sonnets to Orpheus*. Trans. Stephen Mitchell. New York: Simon & Schuster.

Shabad, P. 2000. "The Most Intimate of Creations: Symptoms as Memorials to One's Lonely Suffering." In *Symbolic Loss: The Ambiguity of Mourning and Memory at Century's End*, ed. P. Homans. Charlottesville: University of Virginia Press.

Silverman, P., S. Nickman, and W. Worden. 1992. "Detachment Revisited: The Child's Reconstruction of a Dead Parent." *American Journal of Orthopsychiatry* 62, no. 4: 494–503.

Tweed, T. A. 2006. *Crossings and Dwellings: A Theory of Religion*. Cambridge, Mass.: Harvard University Press.

Wolfenstein, M. 1969. "Loss, Rage, and Repetition." *Psychoanalytic Study of the Child* 24: 432–460.

CHAPTER 14

THE LOSS OF NORMAL

Ten Years as a U.S. Navy Physician Since 9/11

RUSSELL B. CARR

I AM not the same person my friends remember. Recently, I received an e-mail from an old medical school classmate who found me on Facebook. At first, pleased to hear from him, I replied. I looked at his family pictures, and he looked at mine. We seemed to be in the same place. Then he asked me during our e-mail conversation, "So I see you are still in the Navy. How do you like it?" When I read those words, I froze. I was transported to a place with mortars, dead young Americans, and triple amputees. I didn't know how to respond and felt a little nauseated. Like it? I find my work rewarding, but like it? How can I like it when I see eighteen-year-olds with their legs blown off? What can I like about bearing witness to the shattered emotional experience of so many Americans? I never responded to his e-mail question, or to him. I just lost touch, enacting with him my sense of disconnection with my past before 9/11.

How have I enjoyed anything since these wars began? Sometimes, I am not sure I have. I find myself looking at pictures of friends from before the towers fell. I see how their lives have unfolded. Sometimes we talk. They are part of the 99.5 percent of the American population that is not directly involved in the wars in Iraq or Afghanistan. Their lives are filled with the joys and stress of establishing themselves professionally, starting a family—the normal experiences of living life. I am doing some of these, too, but with deadened emotion. My sense of connection with others has faded. Instead, I feel numb most of the time now, not from specific traumas but from the pace and extent of it all. I find myself listening to music from the 1990s, longing for easier times. I long for the days of *Seinfeld*, when I could laugh along with a show about absolutely nothing, when all I had was the everyday stress of medical school. I didn't have to think through what to do if I were wounded by any of the mortars falling around me. I didn't have to try, like I do every day now in America, to leave at work the image of my patient in Iraq who committed suicide, leaving behind a note that simply said he didn't "see the light at the end of the tunnel anymore." I didn't respond to my friend's e-mail because I felt he couldn't understand all that, and I felt shame in the isolated traumatized state I entered when I read his innocent question. I also felt frustration. He, along with most people I know, hadn't left part of himself in a combat zone. Most people I know are not haunted by those who have died there or those who wish they had. They can live as if none of it were happening. They can be more interested in Charlie Sheen's antics than in the number of service members killed or wounded in Afghanistan today. They can live a normal life. My normalcy, and the sense of normalcy for thousands of American service members, is lost.

WHERE I WAS WHEN MY WORLD EXPERIENCE BEGAN TO SHATTER

When 9/11 occurred, I had been in the Navy a little over two years. I had completed an internship in psychiatry but decided I wanted to "go to the fleet," meaning I did not want to remain in graduate medical education. I had always wanted to become a psychiatrist, but this was a last chance to do something else first, to gain some life experience and have an adventure. I decided I wanted to work as a general medical officer (GMO) in the Navy for a while before I specialized further. In the summer of 2000, I was assigned to the navy ship USS *Seattle* as its only physician.

On the morning of 9/11, we were sitting in port in Norfolk, Virginia. I had just come up to my commanding officer's stateroom for a department head meeting, when he pointed to the television screen. As we watched, the second plane hit. There was no doubt for us then that this was no accident. My CO canceled the meeting, but several of the other department heads had already gathered there. I'll never forget my CO turning to us and saying, "Gentlemen, we are at war." As a crew we sprang into action, just as we would for the next ten years. We were given orders to get ready to go to sea immediately in order to refuel the USS *John F. Kennedy* as it headed up the

East Coast to New York. Over the next three days, we sat at the pier, ready to leave at a moment's notice. Actually, we never did go to sea. The situation became more stressful. There were many people crying, crew members from New York, trying to find out about relatives. We had little contact with anyone off the ship. Everyone wanted to help, but we felt powerless. Sitting there gave no distraction from the events or our feelings about them.

Shortly after 9/11, the ship's plans changed. The *Seattle* had been scheduled to deploy to the Persian Gulf in the spring as part of the routine deployments that Navy ships were doing throughout the 1990s to enforce the no-fly zone over Iraq. Instead, we were to deploy much sooner. Eventually, we left for the Persian Gulf in late January 2002, for what would be an eight-month deployment instead of the customary six. Leading up to the deployment, all of the preparations that usually would have occurred over a six-month timeframe had to be completed as soon as possible. This meant long hours for all the crew.

I had just gotten married in July 2001. I realized that since 9/11 I had not spoken with any friends who had been at my wedding. I just didn't have time. There was too much to do, too many important preparations to make. After the deployment, I did catch up with a few. Others I have still not contacted. That was the beginning of my separation from my friends outside of the military. I am sure they were affected by 9/11, but I imagine many of their lives eventually returned to a routine they had before the attacks. My life never did.

Overall, the deployment in 2002 was uneventful for me, particularly by post-Iraq-invasion standards for deployments. We were lucky as a crew. We remained very busy, but it had a sense of purpose and unity behind it. I remember the first night our ship was "on station" and directly supporting combat operations in Afghanistan. For us, that meant constantly providing fuel and bombs to the aircraft carrier and other ships in the area. That night, the admiral in command addressed the entire carrier battle group. It was a good speech, encouraging pride in our participation in history, in defending our country. I felt good. None of us on the ship, however, had to see the direct effects of that participation. We were never face to face with an enemy. There were fears of attacks on ships in the area, and we stayed on edge because of them. But we were lucky. We were able to come home without feeling the helplessness of facing one's own finitude or the shame of witnessing the human capacity for violence.

After our ship returned home, I was given the option to continue as a GMO for another tour. This time, I was at a "shore command," not at sea.

Fortunately, I did not have to deploy during that time. I was able to reconnect with my wife, and eventually we had our only child. My wife, also in the Navy at the time, chose to get out when our son was born. By then it was 2004, after the invasion of Iraq. She feared having to deploy and leave him behind. With a newborn, adventure no longer seemed as important to either of us as it once did. At that point, I decided to return to psychiatry training and ultimately to remain in the military. It offered me better pay and health care, some of the same reasons that many enlisted personnel remain in the military, particularly during the recent recession. I was also feeling that I had not fully participated in the war efforts, and I wanted to contribute more. Since my time on the *Seattle*, parts of my life had started to normalize. I was getting reconnected with some of my friends, and I thought that deployments or military life might not be so difficult after all. So in 2005, I entered psychiatry residency in the National Capital Consortium Psychiatry Residency Program, which is a military training program affiliated with the National Naval Medical Center (NNMC) at Bethesda, Maryland; Walter Reed Army Medical Center (WRAMC); and the Uniformed Services University of the Health Sciences (USUHS).

SEEING THE AFTERMATH OF COMBAT: 2005 TO 2008

I had my first direct exposure to the effects of combat during my three-year residency, which began in 2005. The numbers of casualties were increasing, especially from Iraq. I was witnessing the effects of our enemy's weapon of choice, the improvised explosive device (IED), on the bodies and minds of our service members. I was working mostly at Walter Reed, seeing soldiers with traumatic amputations and brain injuries. Many of these were tough to see. Eventually, I became accustomed to the sight of injured soldiers and Marines in wheelchairs and walking on prostheses. One day my wife had a medical appointment at Walter Reed and told me she felt sickened by what she saw there, whereas I was growing numb to what I was seeing in order to keep up with my busy pace and workload.

Many soldiers that I treated come to mind when I think about that time. Most had limbs blown off in blasts. Some had penetrating brain injuries with subsequent severe head deformities. Almost all had support from their families, parents, or spouses. But some did not. I remember one in particular with a severe pelvic injury from what is called an "explosive formed penetrator" or an EFP, a copper plate placed in some IEDs. It becomes molten and penetrates steel plates when detonated. They pierced many of our thick-armored vehicles, causing horrific injuries. For this young man, a large fragment from an EFP ripped through his pelvis, destroying his bladder and genitals. He had nightmares and severe pain. I met with him several times each week, for an extended period, on the inpatient consultation liaison service.

This soldier had a young fiancée who was at his bedside much of the time. Eventually, however, she grew weary of the strain of trying to be with him and ended their relationship. At this point, he felt utterly alone, frustrated with the slow process of healing and his future prospects. It seemed strange to me that his spirit seemed to lift when he got a chance to show people the metal that the surgeons pulled out of his pelvis. It was large, weighing at least five pounds. I watched him tell several people that "the surgeons said it was one of the biggest they ever pulled out of anyone." I think now that the temporary focus on surviving that piece of metal in his body served as an antidote to the extreme vulnerability he felt while recovering from its effects on him. Perhaps, as they gazed together at the metal fragment of a bomb, he was able to say to himself: "I may be in bad shape, but look what I survived." Perhaps, during those moments, he was able to escape the otherwise constant reminders of his finitude or human frailty. For me, it was also a concretization of the destruction and shattered state of his experience and therefore hard for me to look upon. During that time in the hospital, we never really spoke much about being eighteen and essentially castrated. It was too much for us to bear. I still wonder how he is coping with life now.

There has been research on the risk of developing PTSD in such severely injured, polytrauma patients. In 2006, Thomas Greiger and his colleagues found that patients who had pain or other problems from polytrauma a month after a combat-related injury were at significantly increased risk of developing PTSD. In the acute stages, right after the injury, we did not see as many people as one might expect with severe PTSD symptoms. I think some of this is not only the distraction of the injuries themselves but also the support they were getting from their families.

I have come to understand PTSD through the writings of Robert Stolorow (2007). According to him, the effects of trauma stem from the emotional experience of the traumatic event, not the event itself. Our emotions are highly dependent on being able to process them with those around us.

We have to put words to them in order to integrate them into our experiential landscape, which includes both our sense of our selves and of the world. Symptoms of PTSD develop when a person cannot find a relational home for dealing with their emotional experiences, whether these are being minimized or outright rejected by those around them, or whether it's just too much for anyone to bear. The effects of the trauma might overwhelm relationships. I think that for some with chronic physical injuries, processing the feelings about the original trauma and its long-lasting effects on them can be overwhelming. A traumatized emotional state then develops, consisting of a shattered experience of self and the world, producing the symptoms of PTSD.

I met many service members with shattered world experiences. For those who had no clear physical injuries, these experiences were even harder to bear. At times, their family and friends did not understand their feelings, either. This sense of not being "gotten," or understood, contributed to their intense isolation and shame. Many of them felt tremendous rage at their situations. Frequently, a first meeting with them would be a rocky experience. They might yell or be contemptuous. They did not assume the "sick role," we as therapists expect them to take. If a patient is requesting help, the therapist's job can feel much easier. Many service members I met were too ashamed of their need for mental health care to be cooperative patients. But as they calmed down and developed a sense of safety with me, they began to tell their horrific stories.

I heard many accounts of witnessing close friends being blown apart in IED blasts and what happened when they tried to respond. Sometimes, the response was to lash out at anyone around them, which then caused additional shame and guilt. Sometimes it was the horror of picking up the pieces of their friends, literally fighting off stray dogs from the body parts to do so. I will never forget one soldier who described his refusal to leave the scene where his best friend was blown apart until he was certain they had picked up all of his pieces. Another unforgettable soldier, a Marine, told me how he grabbed his wounded buddy to haul him to safety, only to find that the lower half of his friend's body was gone, his intestines dragging on the ground. I heard numerous other stories: service members who were afraid to sit with their backs to doors or windows, who choked their spouses during nightmares, who were trying to find some way to cope with their shattered world experience. Many were drinking themselves into oblivion. Others were attempting suicide more directly. I was learning from each of them.

I had not anticipated the level of shame my patients so often experienced. The Marine described above attempted suicide after another Marine, who had lost his leg, asked him why he was medically evacuated from Iraq. He had no apparent injury. Not being able to cope with combat left him and others like him with a feeling of falling short, of being extremely vulnerable and alone. Shame is very powerful and has a significant effect upon those who take pride in serving their country. I was just beginning to understand that, and I needed a way to fit shame into my conceptualization of the effects of trauma on the individual. It was not fitting easily into the intrapsychic model I was learning at the time, which focused on defenses and how the current experience of combat causes the traumatized individual to revisit earlier developmental trauma. I was not finding this in my patients, who were overwhelmed with trying to process an unendurable experience as an adult, feeling isolated and unable to find a relational home in which to bear their experiences. It left me searching for ways to connect further with my patients' experience and to help them reconnect with their present, post-combat world.

Of course, hearing these horrific stories and seeing the physical effects of combat was affecting me. Looking back, I was sharing in their traumatic experiences as I struggled to help them bear the trauma. I could imagine myself in the scenes they described, the feeling of trying to race against stray dogs to find every small piece of your friend. Such scenes were unbearable for me as well, and they began to alter my experience of the world as if I too had been traumatized. It was really not *as if* I had been traumatized: listening to these accounts and trying to bear the overwhelming experience with my patients *was* emotionally traumatizing. I found my view of war and violence being altered. Vicarious experiences of violence through television or movies were no longer tolerable. I did not just intellectually learn the effects of war. I was now experiencing war's emotional effects for myself.

At times, I felt overwhelmed with the level of pain and suffering I was witnessing. It was especially hard when children were involved, either as victims of violence in combat or as relatives of service members. I heard awful accounts of children being used as human shields or having IEDs strapped to them and being sent to the troops to ask for candy. I worked with traumatized, shattered soldiers who refused to see their own children out of shame. My son was only a few years old at the time. Listening to these patients, I became overwhelmed, thinking, "What if my son was caught in a combat situation? What if he were blown up? What must it be like for that child when his father refuses to see him after he returns from Iraq?" Sometimes, I would get distracted with these feelings and even get angry with patients because of how they treated their families and others. I tried to keep these feelings and thoughts to myself, at least on a conscious, explicit level. Looking back, I'm sure it created some distance between my patients and me. It is hard not to pull back at times from such overwhelming, traumatic stories and their aftermath. I was just beginning to recognize how much these service members needed to reconnect with someone who could bear their experiences, so I tried to remain as empathically attuned as I could.

As these encounters with patients multiplied, I needed an outlet, my own relational home. I first tried to talk about some of what I heard with my wife. A psychologist herself, she had discussed interesting patients with me in the past. But this was different. It was too traumatic. After the first few instances of describing these patients and their experiences, she told me to stop; she could not bear to hear any more. I felt the same sense of being disconnected as my patients. I was frustrated with her but also sympathetic. I also wished that I had not heard these stories or shared these experiences. I entered psychotherapy, which our residency provided as part of our training experience. It could help us process our feelings while also gaining an understanding of how patients feel when they enter therapy. While somewhat helpful, my assigned therapist, a civilian analyst affiliated with the training program, often took more of an educational approach to what we discussed in sessions. We did not dwell on my experiences with these patients, but I know now that what we discussed was co-determined. Just like my own patients, I was reluctant to address the shame of exploring these areas. I would have to admit that I was weak, a doctor who couldn't tolerate treating his patients.

In my third year of residency, I was given permission to start analytic training. I entered my training analysis through the Washington Psychoanalytic Institute. It was helpful finally to have a place to discuss my experience of hearing these traumatic stories. But, at the same time, I was finding other, probably less constructive ways to deal with the horror of what I was absorbing from my patients. I worked harder to distract myself with projects and study. My wife and family supported this form of self-protection, since they were trying to support my success. It also gave my wife and me other and less intense work-related issues to discuss.

It was probably no coincidence that I found a topic completely removed from trauma for my scholarly project in residency. I studied an uncommon side effect of valproic acid. I worked on it diligently in my spare time. It was a great distraction, right up my alley as an intellectual, unemotional pursuit. It was published in the *American Journal of Psychiatry* to much praise (Carr 2007). It all seemed a win-win, but beneath the surface I was beginning to enter a traumatized world, separate from the rest of my friends from medical school. Those friendships were already beginning to feel like they were from another lifetime, memories that were fading fast.

A PSYCHIATRIST IN IRAQ

After I completed residency in 2008, I was given orders to remain on the staff of the Naval Medical Center. With the growing number of casualties coming from Iraq and Afghanistan, the hospital needed more psychiatrists. I wanted to stay in order to continue analytic training. The senior mental health leadership saw me as a hard worker and agreed to keep me on. To their credit, they also felt that having analysts on staff would be beneficial to patient care and psychiatry resident training. But the Navy also needed psychiatrists to deploy to combat zones. I would be going to Iraq after I graduated. I could have waited six months, but I chose to leave right away. I was still pretty eager, even after the traumatic emotional experiences of residency.

As I got ready to deploy, it was hard to leave my family. I knew I would miss my son, and I felt guilty for not spending more time with him. One of the toughest things I have ever had to do was to make a good-bye video. This was recommended in our deployment materials, in case I was killed in Iraq. I said good-bye to them in the video and then hid it in a place I knew my wife would look if she had to get her financial affairs in order without me. It was gut-wrenching. I cried during and after it. I was starting to experience some of the pain my patients did as they leave home for combat.

I arrived in Iraq in August 2008. I was joining an Army Combat Stress Control (CSC) unit that was already there. The unit had orders to be there for fifteen months, but the psychiatrists rotated every six months. The heat was unbearable, especially in the heavy body armor we wore. Even with the training leading up to deployment, I did not fully acknowledge to myself that I was going to a combat zone until I was first exposed to the risks. While still traveling to the base where I would live for the next six months, I had some of my first encounters with insurgents. I had arrived at the larger base that held my CSC unit's headquarters, from where I would take a helicopter to the smaller base where I was stationed. Just prior to picking me up, along with some other personnel, the helicopter had transported several insurgents to a detention facility on that base. The insurgents were unloaded in front of us, in plastic wrist cuffs, and taken right past me as I stood waiting at the flight line to get on the helicopter. There was a delay while the helicopter was searched for any dangerous materials from the insurgents. We then got on board and headed for the remote base that would be my home. We left at 3:00 a.m., in the dark of night, to make the travel safer. If I wondered why we had to fly in the middle of the night, I would soon find out. The helo flew with no lights on, the pilots using only night-vision gear. As we flew fast over the city, I could see the blasts from rifle fire aimed at us. Yes, my CO from 2001 on the *Seattle* was right: We are at war. Now, I was experiencing that war firsthand, not just empathically through the accounts of others.

These next six months in Iraq were a stark contrast to my first deployment in 2002, which was at sea and not nearly as dangerous. All the same, my experience was much less intense than that of my predecessors and the soldiers who had been in Iraq a few years earlier. The insurgency was still present but overall in a much weaker state. But traumatic events did happen, and my exposure to accounts from traumatized service members continued. In Iraq, I was very busy as a clinician, seeing on average eight to ten patients per day, six days a week. As the only psychiatrist on our small staff, which also included a social worker, psychologist, and three techs, I got involved with the most difficult cases. I had final say if someone needed to be medically evacuated from our base for mental health reasons, mainly because all the paperwork required a physician's signature. So I frequently fielded consults from my colleagues on difficult patients, either for medication management, determination of duty status or need for medical evacuation, or simply help my colleagues understand the patient's experience.

I saw many service members who were suffering. The most common problems were sleep and marital concerns. There were some with more serious psychiatric diagnoses, including PTSD, major depressive disorder, and substance problems. Helping them during that deployment was some of the most rewarding work I have done. Many soldiers thanked me for being there and for helping them make it through the deployment. Their appreciation made the risk of being there worthwhile. They also helped me to understand better the experience of combat-related PTSD. I still struggled to treat it with psychodynamic-based therapy, and in my free time, I searched the analytic literature. One day, I discovered some of Robert Stolorow's writings on trauma and intersubjectivity theory. Right away, his ideas made sense to me, and I was able to use them effectively with my patients, adapting them to a short-term therapy model (Carr 2011). As I found a way through Stolorow's ideas to understand service members' experiences and help them reconnect with the present, my work with soldiers suffering from PTSD became rewarding. But this work was continuing to affect my experience of the world. The stress of the environment, from risks of traveling to other bases to the daily risks of mortar attacks, took its toll on me. I found myself changed in many ways. For example, I could no longer tolerate violent movies while in Iraq. One day, I was in a store looking at movies for sale and happened upon a horror movie. The cover was not very graphic, yet now I felt nauseated looking at it. I also experienced the same feeling when I watched violent scenes in *The Sopranos*, which previously had been one of my favorite shows. In those moments, I felt that these reactions were because of my work with traumatized patients, yet I continued on, remaining committed to this work. Looking back, there was a significant denial of the seriousness of the day-to-day danger I was experiencing. It was easier to focus on my work than on the extreme risk of being in Iraq. In many ways, I was still much safer than my patients. While I rarely traveled in convoys or left the base, many of them were "outside the wire" of the base every day.

Because of the stigma associated with mental health issues, many of my patients were difficult to engage in treatment. When they did engage, I was often able to help them, although their horrific experiences haunt me still. One senior leader was required by a medic to see me for a supposed sleep problem. I suspected that it was actually more serious, since the medic was adamant despite the soldier's high rank. After several minutes of heated discussion about the limits of confidentiality and numerous reassurances that our discussions would not affect his career, the soldier finally revealed why he was having trouble sleeping. One reason was physical pain. He had been in IED blasts in prior deployments, and he still had shrapnel embedded in his leg. But that was a minor source of his insomnia. More importantly, during his last deployment, he was in a crowded market when an IED exploded. After the blast, he saw a young girl, maybe four years old, lying on the ground. As he ran to help her, all he could think about were his own children. He lifted her up to carry her to the medic, but, when he looked down at her, he saw that shrapnel had ripped through her right eye and blown out the back of her skull. He could feel the inside of her head as he supported it. He recalled the girl's mother crying and pleading with him to help her, but there was nothing he could do. Though he could not understand her words, they shared an emotional experience about the horror of this young girl's death. Almost every night since then, he wakes from nightmares to find that girl standing by his bed. He cries himself to back to sleep. I can still see this experience in my mind and feel the same horror as if that child were killed in front of me.

As I listened to him recount this event, he began to sob. The sight of this heroic, tough soldier breaking down in my office overwhelmed me. He had borne the brunt of the war in Iraq for our country. With multiple deployments as an infantry soldier, he had progressed as a leader, bearing the experiences of war while guiding others. But it was becoming too much for him. As he shared this dark secret of his shattered experience, I felt like sobbing with him. Soon he calmed down and agreed to come back the following week, if missions permitted. He thanked me for listening. I hope I helped him at least start to bear his traumatic experience. I never saw him again.

At other times, tragedies occurred, leaving me feeling that I had failed to reach troubled soldiers. About three months into my deployment to Iraq, one of my patients committed suicide. It was devastating to his family, his unit, our mental health care team, and the medical providers on base who tried to resuscitate him (Carr 2011). I had already seen him three times for his depression. Then, one day after lunch, he shot himself in the chest. I experienced significant anxiety during the subsequent investigation of my care of him. The investigators found that my treatment of him met the standard of care. Nonetheless, I find it difficult to bear that I could not prevent his suicide. In the immediate aftermath, I had to process a multitude of emotions, not only about his suicide but also my experience of the investigation and the strain that it produced on the base. However, as the mental health care team for the base, we had to put our feelings aside for a while and treat the soldiers who themselves felt overwhelmed by it.

Our workload increased, which paradoxically suited my familiar mode of protection: in the face of stress, work harder. At the end of each long workday, late at night, I tried to process my experience of the events. For a week or so, I had nightmares. I talked with one of my peers on base, which helped. I felt a mix of guilt, shame, and anger at my patient and myself. I worried about whether I could have done something more, something that would have prevented his suicide. I feared I did not pay enough attention to the subtle signs he gave, or maybe I was too distracted when I saw him that last time, or too tired because the appointment was at the end of the day. I looked for what I might have missed and how I should have seen it coming. For a while, I second-guessed myself with patients. I medically evacuated several soldiers from our base to Germany because I could no longer tolerate the risk. I struggled to accept that, instead of my having done anything wrong, perhaps, as Gabbard (2000, 223) suggests, mental health issues can indeed be fatal.

I still think about that solider. Recently, I was cleaning out my desk at home and came across some papers from my time in Iraq. Among them was a flyer from the memorial service that we held for him on the base. Still saddened, I carry with me the memories of our sessions together and the effects of his suicide on all of us.

My patient's suicide added stress to my deployment. But the everyday environment was stressful for everyone there. Bases were mortared randomly. Everyone carried a weapon with them at all times out of fear of attacks on the base, including kidnappings. There were also risks from sniper fire. I traveled in convoys to see soldiers in even more remote bases, often passing large craters where IEDs had previously blown up vehicles.

While in Iraq, I lived in constant fear of dying. Two memories stand out. One is how I felt when an IED was detonated nearby. This happened often on the roads outside our base. They were unpredictable and occurred at indefinite intervals, making them all the more anxiety provoking. Overall, I was lucky. I was never closer than two hundred meters when one detonated. I often felt the blast before I heard it. They were only split seconds apart, but it was noticeable. I will never forget the physical sensation of being nearby an IED blast. They were terrifying in part because you could not help but know that, in that moment, someone had probably been mutilated or killed.

The second set of memories comes from my visits to a nearby base that was even more dangerous than ours, since it was more frequently attacked. That base experienced daily mortar attacks. I was there on Christmas Day when a mortar attack targeted the staff living area of the base hospital, killing several staff members. It was right next door to the mental health team offices. I had just been there less than an hour before. At the time, I tried not to think about how lucky I was to have left the base when I did. A few months later, on my way home from Iraq I had to travel through that very same base and remain there for nearly a week, waiting to get a flight to Kuwait, where I would turn in my gear and go home. Daily dust storms led to frequent flight cancelations. We were mortared several times a night. I remember waking up to the "incoming" sirens, wondering if it would be safer to run outside to a concrete embankment or to stay in place and risk a mortar landing on my sleeping quarters. It was difficult to endure the randomness with which death could come. With each mortar attack and flight cancellation, my anxiety reached a new height. After each attack, I could never calm down completely. I was always on edge. Finally, just as I was feeling like I could take no more, the dust storms settled, and I boarded a flight to Kuwait.

LIFE AFTER DEPLOYMENT

When I first arrived home, I was edgy and detached. I looked forward to seeing my wife and son again, but it was difficult to reengage fully. It is well known that, for service members and their families, there is a period of transition after their deployment. Several years earlier, returning from my first deployment, I had not experienced a difficult transition, but it had also been a less intense experience. This time, it took me a while to deescalate. While in Iraq, I had stayed in close touch with my family through Skype and e-mail, but it was not nearly the same as day-to-day interaction. One of my patients in Iraq had told me that he enjoyed the separation from home while on deployment: "You don't have to be emotionally available to anyone." Now I understood what he meant. At times, I felt overwhelmed reengaging with my family, then frustrated and ashamed at being overwhelmed. Gradually, I began to reintegrate and once again feel connected with my son and wife.

Upon my return, I faced a number of stressful commitments. In short order, I was scheduled to attend a conference where I was to receive an award from the American College of Psychiatrists. I also resumed analytic training but found my interest in the theory of intersubjectivity incompatible with my current institute. By the fall, I transferred to the Institute of Contemporary Psychotherapy and Psychoanalysis in Washington, D.C. I also resumed my training analysis, which had been interrupted for the deployment. That was no longer what I wanted either, and a year later I terminated treatment. At work, the Navy had hired civilian psychiatrists but now faced a shortage of active-duty psychiatrists to take leadership roles. I was asked to be in charge of inpatient psychiatry. I remained in that position for about a year, which allowed for some flexibility in my schedule. Between analytic training and my inpatient work, I was very busy.

Four months after returning home, I developed unusual medical problems. I permanently lost partial vision in my right eye. In addition, I needed to undergo a heart procedure. I also developed several other, more benign problems, all of which are nonspecific for autoimmune disorders. There is no evidence that any of these illnesses were because of my deployment to Iraq, but the timing raised my concern. At the very least, these medical problems were additional stressors for me. I was once again facing my own finitude, not knowing what was going to happen to me. Fortunately, I was able to continue working, yet for months I anxiously waited to see what illness would next befall me. I felt like I was falling apart. As usual, I responded by working harder—this time not so much to distract myself but out of fear that I would not accomplish what I hoped to before I died. In order to reflect on my experiences in Iraq, I began to write, aware of my growing sense of the indefiniteness of my mortality. I also wanted to focus on my son and enjoy the time I had with him.

As each day went by without a crisis, my sense of urgency slowly receded. At times, I still sense it—a sense that I am prematurely deteriorating. It adds to my feeling of being alone and alienated from my peers. I imagine that many people my age who have been in the military have to recognize early and come to terms with the fragility and indefiniteness of life.

Over the past year, I have moved through several leadership positions in mental health at the National Naval Medical Center. For about six months, I was in charge of our inpatient and outpatient programs dedicated to treating combat-related PTSD and traumatic brain injury. Because of a merger, my position was dissolved. Recently, I was named the chief of the outpatient behavioral health clinic. While giving me some control over my life, being a leader also provides some protection. Most of my time is spent in administrative matters now. I see fewer patients. Although it is difficult for me to admit, treating service members with severe PTSD throughout the day would probably be emotionally overwhelming. The shortage of active-duty military psychiatrists and the high causality rates from Afghanistan keep me and other providers at our hospital in a chronic state of stress. I rarely have time to reflect on how I feel about the events of the past few years, let alone the past ten years. But I notice more frequently how my experience of the world since 9/11 creeps into my awareness and makes its presence known.

TRAUMA AND ITS VICISSITUDES

Ten years of war has taken its toll on the military system and the people in it. It has taken a toll on me and shattered my sense of normalcy. Robert Stolorow's recent monograph *Trauma and Human Existence* (2007) describes aspects of the phenomenology of trauma, based on principles of intersubjective systems theory, on Martin Heidegger's *Being and Time*, and on Stolorow's own experiences of personal loss. According to Stolorow, a person who has endured a traumatic emotional experience must find a "relational home" in which the experience can be processed and borne in order to integrate it into the traumatized person's experience. Otherwise, the unendurable emotional state of unintegrated trauma shatters the person's pretrauma experience of the world.

The effect of trauma on an individual's emotional world can be profound. There is a loss of the sense of time, with the present often collapsing into the traumatic past. There is an overwhelming awareness of the randomness of death. It can come at any time. Traumatized people can no longer deny the fragility of life. They lose the day-to-day denial of human fragility that helps us engage in everyday activities that also carry risk, such as driving down the street. Because of these effects, the traumatized person feels separate from the "normals," whom he or she perceives as having never been traumatized. Instead, a sense of connection can develop among those who have been traumatized, which Stolorow refers to as "siblings in the same darkness." In the aftermath of trauma, such responses can vary depending upon how much the traumatized person is able to bear the emotional experience with others, put words to unendurable feelings, and process them.

The other day, I heard a Marine with multiple combat deployments comment that he has lived an entire lifetime between the ages of nineteen and twenty-five. I now understand that experience as well. It is an overwhelming sense that you have already seen and done too much. You cannot remember what happened before that time, and if you can remember, you cannot relate to your own prewar past. More and more, I feel disconnected from my past, before the War on Terror started. I remember what happened factually and can see images of the past, but I am losing my emotional connection to them. They seem like partially deteriorated memories that no longer interest me and bring me neither pleasure nor pain. When I meet friends from this distant time, I can no longer relate to them. They don't understand what I see, feel, and endure on an almost daily basis in my work with combat veterans.

As I reflect on the past ten years, I realize that, just like my patients, my chronic exposure to trauma has changed how I experience the world. While providing a relational home for others to bear their experiences, I am changed by the experience of relating to them. At times, I have trouble acknowledging and bearing my own traumatic emotional experiences, let alone admitting my feelings to other military psychiatrists. Military personnel rarely admit vulnerability to each other, and military psychiatrists are no better at dealing with shame. With staff shortages, we rarely have time to stop and process our experiences. My emotions now are focused around navigating one crisis after another: I look for and put out the next fire. When I can tolerate it, I try to save the next service member from despair and hopelessness and hope that the wars will end soon.

Many in the military share my sense of isolation from the rest of America. The journalist David Wood, in an online article entitled "In the Tenth Year of War, a Harder Army, a More Distant America" (2010), describes how military personnel who are coming home from Iraq and Afghanistan cannot reconnect with the peaceful worlds of most Americans. I was struck by how much the article resonated with my own experience as well as with what combat veterans and their families tell me. In the article, Wood describes how, with the large number of military personnel having served at least one combat tour since 2001, there is a growing "warrior class" in America. This sense of isolation from the "normals" (in this case, civilians) in America is something I also hear from service members that I treat for PTSD. Many feel isolated by the horror of having seen what humans, including themselves, are capable of doing to one another. Stolorow describes the loss of what he refers to as "absolutisms." Many in the military describe how they can never feel absolutely safe again. Their separateness and finitude never leave their minds, and they realize that most Americans don't live this way.

These isolating feelings affect their lives on a daily basis. Back here in America, most will not go into crowds, mainly because they cannot keep that essential watchful eye on everyone around them. Frequently, they can no longer relate to their families. While they are away from home for extended periods, their families adapt to life without them, while at the same time they miss them. It is hard to reintegrate with families that have adjusted to life without them. Feeling alienated makes reintegration difficult, if not impossible. Relationships become strained, and soon the service member begins to think about returning to combat, where he or she feels more attuned with the environment. They can only find their "siblings in the same darkness" back in a combat zone.

The traumatizing experiences affect family members as well. They might frequently feel that most of America is not as vigilant as they are about the casualties in Afghanistan and Iraq. In close-knit military communities, every family knows someone who is currently deployed. The list of recent combat deaths on the evening news could easily contain the name of a friend or a relative. Family members can also develop a sense of isolation from the rest of America and seek out community among themselves. I have spoken with several service members and their families who have struggled after being transferred to the Washington, D.C., area from a major military installation such as Camp Pendleton or Fort Bragg. They frequently say that they feel out of place here and even resentful toward their new neighbors who have no military affiliation. They are shocked that people go about their lives without paying much attention to the events in Iraq or Afghanistan. Of course, they cannot tolerate civilians' seeming indifference to the risks and sacrifices of deployed service members and their families. Often, military families eventually transfer back to a military installation, where they feel understood. They can no longer tolerate living among civilians, whom they perceive as "the normals."

The loss of normalcy—of being among "the normals"—saddens me. I long for the feelings I had before the last ten years, when the world was a safe place and where those I loved were safe. Even now, when I look at skyscrapers to admire their beauty, I imagine planes flying into them. I am still tied to those tragic moments on 9/11, and with a decade of war behind me, I now have many other devastating moments that remain with me. While I listen to my patients, I frequently find that my thoughts turn to my own traumatic moments in Iraq. Just a few days ago, as one of my patients described a battle in Afghanistan, I remembered hearing urban combat within a few hundred yards of our base in Iraq. When remembering these moments in a context such as therapy, there are elements of shame and isolation for me. I ask myself, "Why should I remember such moments now? I wasn't in that much danger, particularly compared to what my patient is describing." Even then, just as now, I feel there is no relational home for me to process these feelings, no sense of sharing them with others. That is why they have become emotionally traumatic for me. In my work, I am striving to provide for my patient what I did not find for myself: an understanding other. Perhaps the reemergence of my own traumatic wartime experiences in the context of therapy shows that the effects of moments of intense fear and vulnerability never really disappear. The best hope is to process them so that you spend most of your time with a more coherent sense of past, present, and future instead of simply a traumatic past.

I mourn the loss of a fully integrated sense of time, where part of me is not trapped with a traumatic past. I also feel frustration about my physical health now and wonder to what extent my current medical problems are linked to my deployments, whether through exposures in theater, excessive immunizations, or some other mechanism. Or was their emergence after my deployment to Iraq simply a coincidence? They have also violently and intrusively thrown my fragility and the indefiniteness of my existence before my eyes. I think, "These problems should not be happening to me. I'm young. I am supposed to live for years to come." I have been forced to realize what most of us deny: that not everyone lives to old age. Life can change and disappear at any moment. Over the past few years, as I have struggled to accept this fact of our existence, I have felt angry, isolated, and trapped in my current situation. I still struggle every day to process these traumatic emotional experiences from the past ten years and find myself trying to escape to an earlier time in my life when I could healthily ignore my own mortality. Unfortunately, I can no longer locate myself in that time of normalcy.

⬦ ⬦ ⬦ ⬦ ⬦

As my CO on the USS *Seattle* declared on 9/11 while the towers fell, my awareness that "we are at war" has never gone away. Over the past ten years, throughout the war in Iraq and now the intensified war effort in Afghanistan, it has only escalated. In fact, my sense of time during these past ten years has been altered. Time for me has partially collapsed: trauma becomes the major link between moments that don't seem as distant as they should. 9/11 does not seem to me to have happened almost ten years ago. I can't put 2001 on the end of that date. I can't place it in a year. I see no end for further traumatic experiences, neither for myself nor the rest of the American military, nor for any of us. As Woods (2010) noted, with the War on Terror, we have created a warrior class. For now, there is no sense that there will ever be an end or a surrender or that we will be able to look back on the War on Terror in the past tense, giving its participants, our service members, a chance to reflect and process the experiences with others. This war will not end with a treaty. There is a continued sense that the fight is not done, which makes finding a way to bear and process the emotional experience of it all the more difficult.

As I attempt to process and integrate my own experiences, I've had to realize that I'll never return to the times of *Seinfeld* and the normal lives my peers outside the military continue to enjoy. I will never have a normal sense of the phases in life, of settling into a home to raise a family in peace. I work hard not to convey to my son my sense of separation from the "normals." He is one of the reasons I feel I must process my experiences and find a renewed focus and meaning in my life as I come to terms with the past decade of war. I try every day to find a way in my current place, bearing the "thrownness" into my existence, as Heidegger (1927) describes, searching for a relational home. In times of despair, I wonder if this experience is what the terrorists of 9/11 hoped I would feel: a sense of isolation and vulnerability.

Yet, as I reflect on my military service, I feel a sense of pride. Every day, I make small steps toward processing these experiences from the last ten years. As the philosopher Levinas would say, I strive to find meaning in the face of the other (Orange 2010). I am learning how interconnected we all are and how much we depend on one another to bear traumatic emotional experiences. Recently, a soldier recovering from combat-related PTSD said to me that the road to healing is other-focused. At best, as we process and bear traumatic emotional experiences, we can, as Stolorow (2007) describes, develop an authentic resoluteness toward life and hopefully find new priorities and meaning in our lives. Gradually, as a leader I am finding a sense of meaning and purpose in my life through serving other health care providers. At times, I still wrestle with feelings of separateness and despair. Then, just as I imagine the rest of America does, I wish that I, too, could close my eyes to it all and feel as if it never happened—or at least feel a safe distance. Instead I feel trapped, but I don't want to remain there. I have met people who remain trapped in the past. I grew up with someone trapped in Vietnam, probably my first actual source of exposure to combat-related trauma. Now I struggle not to have the same life or to transmit it to my son. The importance of military service was ingrained in me from a young age. My service brings me pride, but it comes with a cost. Until one experiences at first hand the traumatic emotional experiences of combat, it is easy to ignore these potential costs.

Sometimes I tell myself that I stay in the Navy because of my health problems, the medical care I receive for them, and because of the possibility of retirement at twenty years of service. But these are rationalizations. I stay because of the responsibility I feel toward service members, for what they sacrifice for our freedom. And only recently have I begun to realize that I can find healing and purpose through recognizing our shared mortality. I find meaning and authentic resoluteness in helping them, and thus myself, to bear our mortality and humanness together. Frequently, when I am leaving work on Friday at the end of a long week, service members medically evacuated from Iraq or Afghanistan are arriving from Landstuhl, Germany. They arrive at Andrews Air Force Base and are then transported in a large mobile intensive care unit to the entrance of NNMC. I stop and watch their arrival. There is always a group of Marines waiting there to unload them and greet them, many themselves recovering from physical or emotional wounds. For me it is a sacred moment. It is what we are here for: to take care of the other, to look into the face of the other and say, "Yes, I too am mortal and will bear your fragility with you." Yes, I'll put the uniform back on tomorrow, to connect with them, to stand with them in the darkness, and to help us all.

NOTE

The views expressed in this article are those of the author and do not necessarily reflect the official policy or position of the Uniformed Services University School of Health Sciences, Department of the Navy, Department of Defense, nor U.S. government.

REFERENCES

Carr, R. B. 2011. "Combat and Human Existence: Toward an Intersubjective Approach to Combat-Related PTSD." *Psychoanalytic Psychology* 28: 471–496.

Carr, R. B., and K. Shrewsbury. 2007. "Hyperammonemia Due to Valproic Acid in the Psychiatric Setting." *American Journal of Psychiatry* 164: 1020–1027.

Gabbard, G. O. 2000. *Psychodynamic Psychiatry in Clinical Practice*. 3rd ed. Washington, D.C.: American Psychiatric Press.

Heidegger, M. 1927. *Being and Time*. New York: Harper & Row.

276 WHEN DISASTER STRIKES A COMMUNITY

Orange, D. 2010. *Thinking for Clinicians: Philosophical Resources for Contemporary Psychoanalysis and the Humanistic Psychotherapies.* New York: Routledge.

Stolorow, R. 2007. *Trauma and Human Existence: Autobiographical, Psychoanalytic, and Philosophical Reflections.* New York: Routledge.

Wood, D. 2010. "In the Tenth Year of War, a Harder Army, a More Distant America." *Politics Daily.* http://www.politicsdaily.com/2010/09/09/in-the-10th-year-of-war-a-harder-army-a-more-distant-america/.

CHAPTER 15

TIME

ROBERT WINER

TIME'S ARROW peers out at me from behind my awareness. It faces me full-frontal; it is aimed at my heart. I began writing about time during the year in which I turned sixty-five.

Too often, for our patients, and at times for ourselves, time petrifies. There are two reasons for this. One is existential, our anxiety about dying, the other neurotic, our fear of doing things differently. They wrap around each other. We wish for more life.

EXISTENCE

I live my life in calendar time, my future disappearing into my past. This is the time of the three-headed Greek god Chronos. And of his beautiful consort, Ananke, who represented inevitability, the force of time's arrow, and who marked the beginning of the heavens. Cosmologists say that time began when the singularity, so to speak, exploded—"time" has no meaning before that—and the history of our universe is the story of continually increasing disorder. An egg can break; a broken egg cannot unbreak: that is the increase of entropy that is time's arrow. We age, we turn to dust, our little lives are rounded with a sleep. Chronos, in this sense, is unbearable.

And so we yearn for timelessness, escape. Running through the history of human thought, we find the comforting idea that temporality and *chronos* are an illusion, that true reality is eternal. Religious beliefs of every sort, both Western and Eastern, offer some reassurance to anxiety about dying, whether through the promise of an afterlife, or reincarnation, or the conception of cyclic time. Ancient cultures like the Incan, Mayan, Hopi, Babylonian, Hindu, and Buddhist have a concept of a wheel of time, which regards time as cyclical and consisting of repeating ages.

And there is so much in my daily life that gracefully distracts me from the march of time. Nature revolves. Each dawn is a new beginning—and each evening an ending, but only momentarily so, for I know that another daybreak will follow. Tomorrow is the first day of the rest of my life. If today's sessions didn't go well, I remember that I'll have another chance tomorrow. I watch from my office window as one season yields to the next, and the seasons come full circle. With new leaves on the trees between us, the neighbor's house across the ravine disappears, only to resurface in the fall. Culture is shaped by repetition, whether commemorative, like Thanksgiving, or functional, like Election Day. Once again we gather here. There are, to be sure, individual differences. Some of us are more likely to seek out novelty, others familiarity—consider how you choose (or don't choose) vacations, how you select the television you watch and the websites you visit. But for all of us, in an overarching sense, so much of daily life is reiterative, obscuring time's passage. Today's newspaper will be followed by tomorrow's. This year's genocide will be followed by next year's. As soon as this paragraph ends, another paragraph will begin.

The feeling that living is repetitive can be simultaneously paralyzing and reassuring, although, as I have been pointing out, the alternative—the march of time toward the grave—is simply terrifying. Typically, when I've had occasion to say to a patient who is doggedly traveling the same old rut, "This is our only shot," there is a moment of recognition, and then the thought is pushed aside. Even so, time's linearity can't be entirely avoided. Birthdays are markers. In the early passage, there were physical things I could do each year that I couldn't do the year before, not that I thought about that much back then, but now that tide is reversed, and it's in my awareness. Becoming a parent and watching your children grow hoists you onto time's conveyor belt. In the movie *Best Friends*, Goldie Hawn is nervous about the idea of getting hitched to Burt Reynolds, and she tells a friend who happens to be sitting in a crib, holding her own baby, "I just keep thinking that life is in three stages—that you're born, you get married, and then you die." After a moment, her friend catches on: "Wait a minute, so you think that if you never get married, you'll never die?" Goldie muses: "Something like that."

The passage of time brings us up short. The August after the oldest child graduated college, he was setting out to find his fortune in sustainable community development in Oregon while the rest of the family was packing the van for summer vacation. He noticed that they'd loaded up more luggage for their trip than he was taking for the rest of his life. Over the next few months, with this awareness that his son was now an adult, the father felt drastically older. It wasn't a physical feeling, rather a shift of identity. More precisely, the father sensed that he was his own age, something he'd been hedging all his adult life. Time's arrow can catch us by surprise. As clinicians, we can pay attention to those moments—and to their avoidance.

I have the impression that with the exception of those who are actually dying, and often not even then, patients are quite chary about discussing their fears of death in treatment. I think that they can't bear that we are as scared about death as they are. From our patients' point of view, we may not be flawless—we may even be quite disturbed—but we are omnipotent, and that is part of our appeal. By associating with us, they unconsciously expect their own phantasies of indestructibility to be chaperoned. So instead we hear the battle sounds from foreign turf, all the panicking about the *chance* events that unexpectedly roil their lives, and their efforts to fit those events into a plausible narrative that makes psychological sense. If the story hangs together, if things happen for a reason, I can control my future. But for most of us, death will come in the middle, not when we're done. Allen Wheelis (1999) wrote, "We are unfinished business. No coming together of strands. The game is called because of darkness." I never have seen, and I never expect to see, a Hollywood movie in which the hero is busy vanquishing the enemy, and winning the heroine, when a block of cement, for no good reason, falls on his head. No one could stand to go.

Certainly anxiety about dying can represent a deflection of other concerns—fear of punishment for success or for failure, fear of merger or abandonment, fear of destructiveness or impotence, the list would be endless—and part of our work, of course, is to determine what lies beneath. To reduce anxiety about death simply to these issues is a seductive option—the conscious anxiety about death-as-death evaporates. For all these other anxieties, there are solutions: your success won't destroy your mother, if your partner leaves you'll pick yourself up, asserting yourself won't cut you off from the people who love you. But for death-as-death, we can't find relief through interpretation; it doesn't suffice to say that you won't feel *abandoned* because you won't *be*, and so we skitter away. Yet I think this anxiety is a powerful unconscious organizing force. Freud's concept of the death instinct situated death as a biological proposition rather than an existential one. This might also be thought of as an evasion.

So, what do we do? Acknowledging that our time is limited should encourage us to make the most of it. That's all we can do, and if we can resist despair, I think it's what's worth doing. As I write this, I am meeting with a couple I treated many years ago. They're my age, and suddenly he's dying from a terrible, acute neurological disease whose course is precipitous, ordinarily just a matter of months, no treatment of any use, a rapid dementia and motor collapse, death by suffocation. During the first couple of weeks, he was less upset about dying and more feeling grief that he was abandoning his wife, his children, his grandchild; he felt he was failing them. Within weeks, he became less clear. One day, he asked me what his prognosis was, and my sense of that moment was that he was saying that he couldn't understand what was happening to him, right then. But he had some better times. He found pleasure in watching his grandson play catch, in dining with friends. I told his wife that she should begin each day with the thought that he would be alive that day and that she could focus on trying to make that day worth living. She said that she'd actually been trying to do just that. That is, after all, all that any of us can do in the face of inevitable limitation: try to make the most of this day. It takes a certain kind of courage, and there is so much in us that works against that.

For the ancient Greeks, the alternative to *chronos*, chronological time, the time of our days, wasn't cyclic time; rather, it was *kairos*, the right time, the propitious moment. *Kairos* is the depth dimension of time, the instantaneous present in which one might seize the moment. *Chronos* is the passage of time; *kairos* is now. *Kairos* seems to me epitomized in Julius Caesar's reflection that "there is a tide in the affairs of men which, taken at the flood, leads on to fortune." It seems to me present in T. S. Eliot's writing (1952): "Not the intense moment / Isolated with no before and after / But a lifetime burning in every moment." And Michael Cunningham (1998, 225) captured a commonplace sense of *kairos* at the end of his novel *The Hours*:

> We live our lives, do whatever we do, and then we sleep—it's as simple and ordinary as that. A few jump out of windows or drown themselves or take pills; more die by accident; and most of us, the vast majority, are slowly devoured by some disease or, if we're very fortunate, by time itself.

There's just this for consolation: an hour here or there when our lives seem, against all odds and expectations, to burst open and give us everything we've ever imagined, though everyone but children (and perhaps even they) knows these hours will inevitably be followed by others, far darker and more difficult. Still, we cherish the city, the morning; we hope, more than anything, for more.

Roy Schafer (1970) linked the cyclic and linear psychoanalytic visions of reality to two of the literary theorist Northrop Frye's mythic forms, the comic and the tragic. The comic vision is founded on unqualified hopefulness, the fantasy of rebirth, the prospect of another chance. He writes: "The view of cyclic return implies that the past can be redone, if not undone. Thereby it implicitly denies the passage of time. It cancels out pastness. Its perspective is timeless. There can be and there is, again and again, what [Michael] Balint has termed a new beginning" (29).

By contrast, the tragic view is linear, expressing the idea that a choice once made is made forever, that the past can not be unmade, that "a truly cold mother, a savage or seductive father, a dead sibling . . . years of stunted growth and withdrawal, and so forth, cannot be wiped out by analysis" (38). Psychoanalysis positions itself between these two perspectives. Without a comic vision, it would be hopeless, pointless; without a tragic vision, interminable.

We can reframe this from a clinical viewpoint. In mania, we obliterate the past: everything that matters is imminent. When mania dissolves, we are left with its underside, Macbeth's despair:

> Tomorrow, and tomorrow, and tomorrow
> Creeps in this petty pace from day to day,
> To the last syllable of recorded time;
> And all our yesterdays have lighted fools
> The way to dusty death.

In depression, we are chained to the past, prisoners of what has befallen us. In the depressive position, in mourning, we try to transcend these polarities—try to be guided by the past and not controlled by it, try to live in the present, try to imagine a future that is not *only* determined by that which has gone before.

THE OBSTACLES TO LIVING OUR LIVES IN TIME

THE REFUSAL TO BEAR LOSS

Living a life in time is making the most of it, being open to all its possibilities. But when it comes to moving forward, we get in our own way because, in so many ways, we can't let go of the past. In fact, we're addicted to it.

So many of us are locked down in grievances that began in our childhoods, generally some form of either: Why did my parents (or, sometimes, my siblings) have to treat me that way? Or, why did *that* have to happen— *that* being the accident, the violation, the divorce, the financial failure. The dark side of a marriage, and the dark side of childrearing, generally have displaced versions of these childhood stories at their core, what Harold Boris (1994) called "old whines in new battles." Outside of awareness, we have a secret entitlement: we deserve to have these grievances redressed, by our parents (whether they're alive or not), more often by our current significant others. Some of us seek revenge; some of us just want the loss to be undone, so that we can be made whole. And entire lives can be fashioned on this basis, lives that are organized by the circumstances of childhood. In our phantasy of reversing time, we have become stuck in time. At the core of depression is this refusal to let go. While mourning acknowledges loss, it is the essence of depression that it denies loss. Letting go gets felt as capitulation, surrender, giving up your claim, and that's intolerable. (A life lived in time works its way through losses—the change of friendships, the loss of a teacher after a course ends, the loss of one version of oneself in favor of another.)

A woman a bit older than me spends her psychotherapy sessions complaining about how her mother bullied her when she was a child. She wants to do something about that, even now. And now it's the same with her husband and college-age daughter, both of whom she finds entirely intimidating. This woman still experiences herself as an angry, masochistic, wounded six-year-old. Her mother failed and then died last year, but she stayed away, justified by her continuing anger at her mother over childhood events. By clutching at her grievance and avoiding her mother's mortality, she was, among other things, turning her gaze away from time's arrow.

I'm of the opinion that, at the emotional level, the heart of the analytic process is mourning. Every choice means a loss of other possibilities; being unable to bear the loss of murdered alternative selves keeps us paralyzed.

The very *shape* of analysis can facilitate mourning. Patients usually enter analysis with the private hope of being reborn, a new beginning, a world of possibilities. I think that this is even true of those who enter analysis with what appears to be profound skepticism about their prospects; it may be more true of them, which is why they are running so hard for cover. There are things in the nature of analysis that encourage such phantasies. For the patient, analysis is a brand new kind of relatedness in which he can say whatever he wants, the analyst will be reliably present and available and nonjudgmental, he can take as long as he needs, anything seems possible, it appears recurrent and timeless. Transference, by its very nature, makes our primal relationships sempiternal. In what might be considered the bait and switch of a competent analysis, life actually becomes life sized. While part of that will come from being clearer about what one is up to as one gets to know oneself better, it's also just inevitable in the process that one comes to discover that there will be no miracles. In a useful analysis, the phantasy that the analyst can rebuild the world wears away not in a shocking moment of discovery, like in *The Wizard of Oz*, but more through ordinary attrition. Analysis manifests itself as the cure for great expectations. Revenge, served hot or cold, won't be found. Hanging in effigy is endless and unsatisfying. Some things happen for no good reason and others for deep and complicated reasons, and getting our minds around that isn't exactly pleasant or satisfying, but becoming reconciled to the truth, as best we can understand it, is what's possible. And we go from there. That's a brief sketch of how the nature of analysis can enable mourning. If it goes well, the future opens up a bit; it's not just more of the same. When it doesn't go well in spite of an analyst's competent efforts, it may be that, setting the particulars aside, the patient is simply unwilling to let go of his claims, although it will never be framed that way.

The process of mourning involves developing a new relationship to the events of one's past—new, I would say *additional*, meanings to what took place. I want to describe how treatment facilitates this. Freud used the term *nachträglichkeit* (*après-coup*) to acknowledge that every remembering is a new construction, as the traces of the memory are reorganized in the context of present experience. We now know that a memory is not located at a specific site in the brain—rather, its shards will be scattered in lots of places, all over the brain. The act of having a memory is the bringing together of a lot of those fragments, and we will never do that the same way twice, even moments apart. In addition, when we assemble a memory, we will be including related fragments that come from our present experience, including why we're remembering that memory. That's how the brain works. This is foundational in the process of analysis, as past experience is given new meaning. But the new meanings are driven, in part, by the circumstance that they are emerging, specifically, in the context of the analytic relationship, with everything that entails. When words are spoken in an analysis, not simply thought, they are experienced, reframed, in the context of the analytic relationship, with all the meanings the relationship carries. I'm sure this is hard to get unless you've actually had the experience of thinking about something quite personal in analysis, in the privacy of the couch, and then actually saying it and noticing how different that feels. The thought has entered the conversation with your therapist, and it becomes a new thought, changing the past you carry within as your living history (Loewald 1972). Your own history is always being made. By the same token, there are things we will never relate, not only because they are embarrassing but also because we can't bear their being touched by another; we clutch them to our breasts, they're too much to let go of. None among us bears all losses. (For a further discussion of the relationship between mourning and existing in time, see Bell 2006.)

THE SECURITY OF REPETITION

So we stay embedded in the past, because we aren't disposed to quit a claim. But in another sense, we can't do otherwise. As though we lack imagination, we keep restaging the same old melodrama. We have lots of explanations for our stubborn holding on. We repeat because libido is sticky and we can't let go of our objects. We repeat because we refuse to let go of our incestuous longings, in all the displaced ways those desires are manifest. We repeat because the struggle is sequestered in our unconscious minds, out of the reach of our more adaptive egos. And we repeat in the hope that this time the story will have a different ending. We repeat with the insistence that these events are not of our creation, that they are being done to us, that it's just our bad luck that once again we've found a friend, a lover, a boss, an analyst who is just like the swindler from our childhood. We repeat when we are locked up with partners and analysts we chose who, in important ways, are in fact just like our troubling parents. In our repetitions we are entirely lost in time: yesterday, today, and tomorrow are indistinguishable.

And there's another way of understanding our repetitions, which I find quite compelling: The ways in which we all negotiate the world are, from our point of view, *the very best we can do*. From very early on, we put ourselves together in the ways that will minimize anxiety. Avoiding dysphoric affects becomes more important than seeking pleasure. At the center of this is managing our relationships in the world of others, and what works becomes habitual. However ineffective our lifestyles and choices may seem to others, we really believe that any alternative would be worse. As therapists, sitting with patients whose lives seem abysmally self-defeating, we find it hard to get our minds around this fundamental truth. I've written (1994) about a young woman who was her mother's miserable rotten child (those being her mother's words). That was how she knew connection, and she and her mother tortured each other. In time, she would torture me and experience me as torturing her. As the glacier melted a bit, there were moments of intimacy between us, and then she felt to me like a stranger in a strange land, lost in the wilderness. And then she'd get a fight going and she'd feel safely connected again. What is endangering will be particular for each person— for one it may be the sharp cut of anxiety, for another humiliating shame, for a third caustic blame. The quest for connection or pleasure will always take a back seat to the avoidance of pain. These ways of living become bred in the bone.

What further nail these solutions in place are the secondary satisfactions that become available—moral masochism, covert sadism, secret voyeurism. Overall, the possibilities for hidden pleasure are protean, and they offer compensation for the price of the sacrifice.

We become addicted both to our well-trod paths and to our perverse satisfactions. I am not using the word "addiction" casually here. If the transference neurosis is the roadmap and the repetition compulsion offers the security of staying on the highway, what would persuade one to wander in uncharted wildness? The question shifts from "Why don't patients change?" to "Why in the world would they?" And I believe that it is as difficult to get a patient to relinquish his secondary gains—which are all the more poignantly defended precisely because primary gains aren't allowed—as it is to get an addict to give up drugs or alcohol or food or gambling.

In a sense, psychoanalysis is like a twelve-step program in this regard: we offer the patient a form of connection that's an alternative to the one they're locked in to. We have to make ourselves worth investing in, and we do that by working very hard to be in touch with them where it counts. And we offer them, implicitly, a new relationship, draped over the old one, something to tide them over through the torture of withdrawal, something to help them bear the anxiety (the shame, the guilt) they've spent their lives avoiding. As analysts, we move from being the mother of timelessness to becoming the father of separation, father time, in all the ways you can imagine that.

REFERENCES

Bell, D. 2006. "Existence in Time: Development or Catastrophe." *Psychoanalytic Quarterly* 75: 783–805.

Boris, H. 1994. "About Time." *Contemporary Psychoanalysis* 30: 301–322.

Cunningham, M. 1998. *The Hours*. New York: Farrar, Straus and Giroux.

Eliot, T. S. 1952. "East Coker." In "Four Quartets," in *The Complete Poems and Plays*. New York: Harcourt Brace.

Loewald, H. W. 1972. "The Experience of Time." *Psychoanalytic Study of the Child* 27: 401–410.

Schafer, R. 1970. "The Psychoanalytic Version of Reality." *International Journal of Psychoanalysis* 51: 279–297.

Wheelis, A. 1999. *The Listener: A Psychoanalyst Examines His Life*. New York: Norton.

Winer, R. 1994. *Close Encounters: A Relational View of the Therapeutic Process*. Northvale, N.J.: Aronson.

CONCLUSION

But now I see what I am climbing towards: Acceptance, its name is in lights....
I finally reach it. But something is wrong. Grief is a circular staircase.

—Linda Pastan

TRUTH BE told, we all have disquieting memories that linger in the shadows of our work. As we have seen in the preceding chapters, those who come through the doors of our consulting room inevitably leave their traces on our psyche. We bear witness to their pain, and we cannot remain untouched. We bear witness, too, to those events that shatter the world, whether in a private, interior realm or on a greater, more global scale—events that affect our patients and ourselves equally. After our patients are long gone, we miss the work we had been engaged in with them and the sense of ourselves in the room with them. Ultimately, we are left with our own unfolding narratives of our work and of ourselves.

Loss is a necessary and, indeed, an inevitable aspect of life. It propels us forward. Whether for patients or therapists, there is no solution to grief; it is unavoidable. Mostly, as therapists, we like to think there's something we can do, but in the end everyone must mourn in their own way. There's nothing to be done but to bear it along with our patients. In this way, we are no different from our patients: we do the best we can.

Yet, in our profession, we all face a particular kind of conundrum, which is how to immerse ourselves fully in the work while keeping ourselves apart at the same time, mindful of the process, the frame, the constructs, all of those things that set the therapy apart from any other relationship. Like our patients, we feel we are changed when something therapeutic happens, but we are reluctant to own up to our own investments and gratifications. Similarly, while we try to understand as fully as we can the contours of our patients' grief, it can be difficult for us to recognize or, at times, acknowledge, our own fallibility and limitations.

Regrettably, our profession lacks the rituals for bearing witness to the multitude of losses we experience. As we have read in these pages, there are many reasons why we inhibit ourselves from speaking openly about our losses. We cannot help but worry about the disapproval of others—have we gone too far, immersed ourselves too intensely, allowed ourselves to care too much? Have we forgotten to take account of our history and of the ghosts that linger in the shadows, allowing them to seep too deeply into the treatment? How involved in our patients' lives have we become, and how dependent are we on them? And have we been taken unawares by those traumatic world events that affect our work in amorphous yet far-reaching ways?

We work with patients to help them understand and process a myriad of losses and traumas. We help them put words to their experiences, appreciating their wish to have their losses known and recognized. Similarly, as therapists, we, too, yearn to give a name and a voice to our own losses. This book provides a venue to articulate and explore these issues and to examine the many ways that therapists encounter loss in their work.

Many authors whose chapters appear in this book remarked on the profound effect that writing about the bereaved therapist had for them. For some, it was an opportunity to revisit and rework painful experiences of loss that significantly changed the course of their personal and professional lives. Others understood for the first time the full effect that these losses had on them. All express the notion that grief is never completed. Rather, it is a dynamic process that ebbs and flows. At times, grief is in the foreground and obscures feelings of hopefulness or the ability to go on; at other times, it recedes to the background and only occasionally casts its shadow as a reminder of what once was.

We hope these chapters have begun to pave the way for a much-needed dialogue about the effect of our losses, from individual and private traumas to far-reaching, global ones. We afford a view of grief as a process that unfolds, changes, and deepens throughout the course of one's life rather than one that progresses through universal stages, reaching an ultimate goal. A

clear endpoint to grief is unattainable. Throughout this process of mourning, the bereaved is faced with a multiplicity of psychological and developmental tasks, both conscious and unconscious: to work through conflict
and ambivalence and to repair and restore one's sense of self following a
destabilizing experience. Ultimately, over time, we weave together a new
self-narrative that incorporates both the loss and subsequent reinvestment
in a permanently changed world, one in which the lost one is absent. From
the vantage point of this middle-distance, we are able to find our way to a
new inner landscape, one that holds both the traces of what was lost and the
reshaped contours of what the "now" has become.

We are profoundly grateful to our contributors, who have shared their
stories openly and candidly in the pages of this book, and engaged us with
them as they examined the effects of loss on their personal and professional
selves. We were deeply moved by their stories and their remembrances. They
have provided us with a window into the unique nature of the therapist's
bereavement and the particular obstacles that stand in the way of exploring
it. Most importantly, these authors illustrated how our own losses are ever
present and form an integral part of who we are, and who we become, with
our patients.

THE FIVE STAGES OF GRIEF

The night I lost you
someone pointed me towards
the Five Stages of Grief.
Go that way, they said,
it's easy, like learning to climb
stairs after amputation.
And so I climbed.
Denial was first.
I sat down at breakfast
carefully setting the table
for two. I passed you the toast—
you sat there. I passed
you the paper—you hid
behind it.
Anger seemed more familiar.
I burned the toast, snatched
the paper and read the headlines myself.
But they mentioned your departure
and so I moved on to
Bargaining. What could I exchange
for you? The silence
after storms? My typing fingers?
Before I could decide, Depression
came puffing up, a poor relation
its suitcase tied together

with string. In the suitcase
were bandages for the eyes
and bottles of sleep. I slid
all the way down the stairs
feeling nothing.
And all the time Hope
flashed on and off
in defective neon.
Hope was a signpost pointing
straight in the air.
Hope was my uncle's middle name,
he died of it.
After a year I am still climbing,
though my feet slip
on your stone face.
The treeline
has long since disappeared;
green is a color
I have forgotten.
But now I see what I am climbing
towards: Acceptance
written in capital letters,
a special headline:
Acceptance.
Its name is in lights.
I struggle on,
waving and shouting.
Below, my whole life spreads its surf,
all the landscape I've ever known
of dreamed of. Below
a fish jumps: the pulse
in your neck.
Acceptance. I finally
reach it.
But something is wrong.
Grief is a circular staircase.
I have lost you.

—Linda Pastan (in *Carnival Evening: New and Selected Poems, 1968–1998*)

INDEX

therapist illness, 156; impact on
therapist work, 143–44, 153,
154; literature on, 143; patient
unawareness of, 178; during
residency training, 138–42, 144–52;
selfobjects and, 154; support during,
154, 206; therapist aloneness during,
140, 141, 146; therapist emotions
about, 141–42, 150–51; therapist
identity and, 206, 210; therapist-
patient relationship and, 207;
therapist work continuance under,
199, 201, 207, 211; war impact on
therapist with, 269
therapist illness, impact on patient,
139–41, 143–44, 146, 153, 206; clinical
vignette, 149–52; countertransference
and, 134, 137, 150–52, 203–5;
ethical lapses in, 178; growth in,
199; literature on, 203; overview,
133–35, 137–38, 178, 199–200,
210; problematic, 187–92, 209;
therapist disclosure and, 201–2,
204–5, 207, 210; therapist lapse in,
150–51; therapist-patient dyad in, 135;
therapist-patient relationship and,
142; therapist vulnerability in, 202;
transference and, 137, 150–52,
203–5; unique nature of, 202–3.
See also dying therapist, impact
on patient
therapist illness, impact on supervisor,
141, 142, 144, 150–53; failures in,
155; overview, 138, 155–56; personal
involvement in, 145–49, 152, 155;
psychological rewards of, 145,
147, 155
therapist impairment, impact on patient:
institution and communal response
to therapist impairment and,
183–92; overview, 134–35, 184–86;
problematic, 187–92; therapist old
age impact, 134–35. *See also* therapist
illness, impact on patient

therapist loss: of colleagues, 164,
192–96; middle-distance and, 29–30;
overview, 15–16, 287–89; patients and,
29; process compared to common
rituals of loss, 3–4; of self and
therapist loss of patient, 50–51, 53–56,
64, 66; self-as-therapist loss and,
2–3, 16
therapist loss, of analytic community:
overview, 182–84; therapist identity
and, 134, 182, 195. *See also* therapist
loss, of hospital
therapist loss, of hospital: Chestnut
Lodge, 158–59, 164–76, 176n1,
176nn7–8; overview, 134, 158–60,
175–76; replacing, 174–76; Searles
correspondence about, 134, 158, 159,
165–73; therapist identity and, 134. *See
also* Chestnut Lodge; therapist loss,
of analytic community
therapist loss, of institution: overview,
134, 158–60, 175–76, 182–84; as
professional home, 134, 171. *See also*
therapist loss, of hospital
therapist loss, of patient: helplessness in,
2, 70, 71; loss of joy in, 16; missing
patient in, 53, 287; overview, 2; self-
as-therapist loss and, 2–3; therapist
aloneness and, 53–55; therapist loss
of self and, 50–51, 53–56, 64, 66;
therapist self expectations about,
52. *See also* therapist loss, over
termination
therapist loss, of patient to death, 200.
See also therapist loss, of patient to
suicide
therapist loss, of patient to suicide:
countertransference and, 127; denial
in, 127–28; early in therapist's career,
118–20, 125; helplessness in, 128, 131;
narratives around, 131; overview,
71, 118, 131; support systems for,
120; therapist analysis of, 121–22;
therapist emotions about, 119, 120,

CPSIA information can be obtained at www.ICGtesting.com
Printed in the USA
LVOW04s0855070915

453119LV00009B/37/P